UNDERSTANDING COMMON STOCKS

Revised Edition

This book will show you:

★ Why common stocks are one of the two great
fortune-builders

★ How to begin investing in common stocks

★ How to read stock price quotations

★ What to look for in brokers and mutual funds

★ How to share in the growth of American
business

THE NO NONSENSE LIBRARY

NO NONSENSE FINANCIAL GUIDES

How to Finance Your Child's College Education
How to Use Credit and Credit Cards, Revised Edition
Understanding Tax-Exempt Bonds, Revised Edition
Understanding Money Market Funds, Revised Edition
Understanding Mutual Funds, Revised Edition
Understanding IRA's, Revised Edition
Understanding Treasury Bills and Other U.S. Government Securities, Revised Edition
Understanding Common Stocks, Revised Edition
Understanding the Stock Market, Revised Edition
Understanding Stock Options and Futures Markets, Revised Edition
How to Choose a Discount Stockbroker, Revised Edition
How to Make Personal Financial Planning Work for You, Revised Edition
How to Plan and Invest for Your Retirement, Revised Edition
The New Tax Law and What It Means to You

NO NONSENSE REAL ESTATE GUIDES

Understanding Condominiums and Co-ops, Revised Edition
Understanding Buying and Selling a House, Revised Edition
Understanding Mortgages and Home Equity Loans, Revised Edition
Refinancing Your Mortgage, Revised Edition

NO NONSENSE LEGAL GUIDES

Understanding Estate Planning and Wills, Revised Edition
How to Choose a Lawyer

NO NONSENSE CAREER GUIDES

How to Use Your Time Wisely
Managing People

NO NONSENSE SUCCESS GUIDES

NO NONSENSE HEALTH GUIDES

NO NONSENSE COOKING GUIDES

NO NONSENSE WINE GUIDES

NO NONSENSE PARENTING GUIDES

NO NONSENSE FINANCIAL GUIDE®

UNDERSTANDING COMMON STOCKS

Revised Edition

Arnold Corrigan
& Phyllis C. Kaufman

LONGMEADOW PRESS

Understanding Common Stocks, Revised Edition

© 1984, 1987 by Arnold Corrigan and Phyllis C. Kaufman. All rights reserved.

ISBN: 0-681-40237-7

Production services: W. S. Konecky Associates
Text and cover design: Adrian Taylor

Printed in the United States of America

0 9 8 7 6 5 4 3 2 1

TO

Paul

CONTENTS

1 · COMMON STOCKS AS A FORTUNE BUILDER

This book is about fortune building. It's not a fairy tale set in a mythical kingdom; it's about real opportunities, available today, for making your money grow. This book is about investing in common stocks.

Probably the two greatest fortune builders in America have been ownership of all types of business corporations, and ownership of real estate. Investing in real estate is often difficult except in large dollar amounts. But each of us knows of individuals who, with little capital, started and built up a business successfully and prospered—sometimes prospered greatly. While most of us may not intend to become business owners ourselves, we recognize that owning and building a business can be a way to economic well-being.

There is a way to become a business owner indirectly and, moreover, to share in the growth and prosperity of the leading corporations in the United States. This way is by investing in common stocks. Through common stock investments, an individual with relatively little to invest can still become a part owner of growing corporations and gain many of the benefits that a business owner enjoys.

Since the opportunity exists for every person with savings to invest in America's leading corporations, one would think that investing in common stocks would be universally popular. But that isn't so. Investing in common stocks has been popular at times but unpopular at others. People have sometimes expected too much too soon from their investments, and waves of overenthusiasm have given way to waves of disappointment. One of the purposes of this book is to put common stock investments in perspective, and to explain what they can and cannot do for you over the long run.

We stress that this book is written from a long-term point of view. When you invest in a business, you shouldn't expect instant returns. Your concentration should be on the long run—looking ahead to a period when today's efforts result in greater value, greater earnings, and a greater payout of these earnings to the owners in the form of dividends. You should also expect temporary periods when the business may not do well, and you should be prepared to ride these out patiently if the business is basically good and well-planned.

There have been times in the past when the American economy seemed unshakably prosperous and when the idea of investing in the growth of American business seemed natural and likely to turn out well. But since around the late 1960s, people have not been that confident. There have been doubts about the economy. Inflation has been a serious problem. The growth of productivity seems at times to have slowed.

Nevertheless, the United States is the one country in which everyone in the world wants to invest. Foreigners take a more balanced view of our problems. They recognize the stability of our political system and the overall strength of our economy. Money comes flooding into the U.S. for investment from every continent.

These remarks about the economy are not a digression. In a country where the economy is stagnant or the problems insoluble, or where political difficulties outweigh the economic possibilities, investing in business ownership may be a questionable idea. In a sick economy, even the best companies may be a poor investment. You want to be sure that the long-term odds are favorable.

All this doesn't necessarily mean that common stocks are for you. But it means that for Americans, common stocks and common stock investment—investment in the ownership of major corporations—continue to have great possibilities. It's worth thinking about and learning about. This book will tell you some of the things you need to know.

2 · A BRIEF HISTORY

To understand the stock market and common stock investments today, a little history is needed.

We said that common stock investing has gone through waves of overenthusiasm and disappointment. The period of the greatest overenthusiasm was the boom of the 1920s. Speculation in common stocks during that period was unprecedented. There was no effective government regulation. People could buy stocks by putting up only 10 percent of the price and borrowing the other 90 percent ("buying on margin"—see Chapter 16). The opportunities for getting rich quickly and easily seemed endless. Prices of many stocks went up out of all relation to economic realities.

The end came in late 1929. Within a few months, stock prices had tumbled, on the average, by almost 50 percent. The downtrend continued for three years. The stock market collapse coincided with the onset of the Great Depression. Throughout the 1930s, both the economy and the stock market managed only a feeble recovery.

In the first years after World War II, people continually expected a new depression and a new stock market collapse. The general atmosphere was one of skepticism. However, as no depression materialized, and as the postwar economic boom began to gather momentum, the stock market entered a golden period—a tremendous rise which stretched from 1949 to 1972 and carried the Dow Jones Industrial Average from a low of 160 in 1949 to a high of over 1,000.

The stock market rise seemed to be based on a solid foundation of economic growth, as American industry recovered from the war and then met the tremendous unsatisfied needs that had developed not only during the war, but also during the preceding depression. However, a long upward move in the stock market tends to develop its own exaggerations and illusions, and the boom of the 1950s and

1960s ended in a classic binge of overoptimism and speculation. As the 1949–1972 rise reached its later stages, old fallacies were revived that carried more than a touch of the 1920s:

1. Experts decided that the price increases would go on forever, and found various rationales to support this view. Instead of buying stocks because of the real values of the companies, people bought stocks simply on the blind expectation that they would continue to rise in price.
2. Stocks of companies that had shown exceptional growth, such as Xerox, IBM, and Polaroid, were the heroes of the boom. Some experts proclaimed that such "growth" stocks could be bought safely at any price, because the growth of the companies would validate the price paid.
3. New speculative techniques became popular, and speculation in new companies and new stocks was rampant.

The reckoning came in 1973–74 with the deepest market decline of the postwar period, made worse after the Arab oil embargo in late 1973 curtailed oil supplies and touched off a historic explosion of crude oil prices. By late 1974, the Dow Jones Industrial Average and other market averages were down almost 50 percent from their peaks. Many individual stocks were down even more sharply.

The market recovered briskly in 1975 and the succeeding years. But many of the stocks that had been favorites in the boom of the 1960s and 1970s continued to lag, and many investors seemed unable to recover their optimism after the shocks of 1973–74. Although a number of investment managers did well by concentrating on newer companies and newer industries, the sluggishness of the old favorites made it hard for many people to believe that the stock market was really back in good health. And so many investors were standing on the sidelines when the market began a move in 1982 which was to develop as one of the broadest and strongest upturns in history.

At the market low in 1982, the Dow Jones Industrial Average, which is still the most popular measure of the market (see Chapter 15), was below 800. By mid-1987, after rising in several strong stages, the Dow was above 2,500—more than triple the 1982 low.

As the market scaled these record heights, the experts were deeply divided as to whether, as some thought, the momentum of the market would carry it further up, to levels of 3,000 or 3,500 on the Dow—or whether stock prices were ripe for a major decline, perhaps even on the scale of 1973–74.

The investment opportunities in common stocks are tremendous. But in a market capable of such wide price swings, you need all the perspective and understanding you can get. Overpessimism can be as dangerous as over-optimism. This book will tell you the whys and hows of common stock investing.

3 · COMMON STOCKS AS AN INFLATION FIGHTER

Common stocks have two major advantages over other investments.

First, as discussed above, ownership of common stocks gives a U.S. investor a way of participating in the growth of virtually every major corporation in what is probably still the strongest and most flourishing economy in the world.

Second, common stocks help you *protect yourself against inflation.*

About Inflation

There are some doubts as to whether the U.S. economy is growing as fast as it did in the early postwar years. But there's no doubt at all about inflation. It's gotten worse.

Inflation was at a low rate during most of the 1950s and early 1960s. Productive capacity was rising rapidly both in the U.S. and in the rest of the world. The supply of goods was rising fast enough so that upward pressure on prices was moderate.

Somewhere in the late 1960s, inflation began to be a perceptible problem. The blame for that is usually put on the Vietnam War, when the U.S. tried to have both guns and butter without raising taxes, and federal budget deficits began to mount. But there may also have been more basic factors at work. The postwar boom had gone on for about twenty years. Some strains were beginning to develop. Many of the best factory sites were already taken. Many cities had expanded rapidly and lacked adequate support facilities. People had begun to recognize that rapid economic growth was polluting and endangering the environment, and a movement was beginning under which large amounts of money and resources would be devoted to cleaning up and preserving the nation's natural heritage for the future. In short, growth was no longer cheap.

In the 1970s, inflation received the most violent boost of all, this time from oil prices. Beginning in 1973–74, the OPEC cartel (Organization of Petroleum Exporting Countries) raised the world price of crude oil from roughly $3 per barrel to a peak of over $40 per barrel in 1981. Oil is the basic fuel of almost all economies. As prices of oil products skyrocketed, inflation soared and economic growth slowed throughout the world.

After 1981, oil prices leveled off (and even dipped) and the shock of the price increases appeared finally to have been absorbed. But it remains true that economic growth is no longer cheap.

Supply and Demand

Prices depend on the relationship between supply and demand. When demand grows faster than supply, prices go up. Because growth is no longer cheap, supplies can't be expanded as easily as they used to be. So the trends we have been discussing may not have made inflation inevitable, but they have certainly made the world more vulnerable to it.

Borrowing

There's another related problem. As growth becomes more expensive, people tend to borrow more. Businesses find that they can't pay for expansion out of earnings, so they borrow. Governments find that tax receipts don't keep up with the cost of necessary programs, so they borrow more. Individuals find greater difficulty saving enough for a home or a car, so they borrow more and pay less of the cost out of savings.

In the U.S., the growth of borrowing and debt has reached staggering proportions, and this accentuates the inflation problem. Unfortunately, the process acquires a momentum of its own. In the case of the U.S. government, we have found that the trend toward larger budget deficits is extremely hard to reverse once it has begun. In the private economy, all sorts of consumer industries are built around convincing people to borrow heavily, buy now, and repay later. Finally, inflation itself becomes a reason for borrowing more. If you will be able to repay loans five or ten or twenty years later with cheaper dollars, why not borrow now? Many businesses have intentionally increased their debt on just this rationale.

Why all this history and explanation? To emphasize that inflation is not a fleeting phenomenon, but a reality tied to many underlying economic trends. It's not impossible to control inflation, and in fact the inflation rate was brought down from peaks of over 12 percent in 1979 and 1980 to around 4 percent in the 1982–86 period. But most economists agree that it will be very difficult to bring inflation down for any long period to the 2 percent to 3 percent annual rate we enjoyed in the 1950s and early 1960s.

Obviously, you have to inflation-proof your own financial planning.

Common Stocks and Inflation

That's where common stocks come in. Over the long run, money invested in common stocks has grown, on the average, well ahead of the rate of inflation. This fact may surprise many people, since inflation is often viewed as a danger to the stock market. While it's true that the short-run impact of inflation on stock prices is often negative, the long-run trend is well established—stock prices really do adjust to inflation.

There's a good solid reason for this. Common stocks represent the ownership of corporations. These corporations may own factories, land, forests, oil reserves or railroads. Or the corporation's "assets"—its property or resources—may be in the form of services, patents, or accumulated technical skills. These corporate assets make up much of the accumulated wealth of the country. As inflation continues and prices rise, the value of these assets rises accordingly, and the corporation's owners—its stockholders—indirectly own greater dollar wealth than they did before.

The market prices of common stocks don't always reflect such changes in underlying asset valuation immediately, and the stock market as a whole certainly does not track the inflation rate closely, but forges ahead in some years and falls behind in others. Still, over the long run, stock prices inevitably reflect the real worth of their companies.

One of the factors that does tend to have an immediate effect on stock prices is corporate earnings. In the 1970s, inflation took many corporations by surprise, and bottom-line earnings often suffered temporarily as a result. But U.S. corporations now generally adjust for inflation in their financial planning, and, in the future, corporate earnings may grow more closely in line with the inflation rate.

Of course, you can never be sure that past experience will be repeated in the future. But in the forty-year period from 1947 through 1986, money invested in common stocks grew at an average annual rate of *better than 11 percent**. During that entire period, the rate of inflation averaged a little over 4 percent. This means that money invested in common stocks over that period, with all dividends reinvested, grew at an average rate more than 7 percent ahead of the rate of inflation. Even if we choose to be extremely conservative, and exclude the sharp market gains of 1985–86, we can state that *investments in common stocks, on the average, have given investors growth averaging 6 percent ahead of the rate of inflation.*

You may feel that in these days of high returns, 6 percent isn't a very high number. But 6 percent *better than inflation*—or 6 percent *real growth,* as an economist might say—is a different matter. Over the whole period,

*Based on the Standard & Poor's 500 Stock Index, adjusted for reinvestment of all dividends. The figures are adapted from *Stocks, Bonds, Bills, and Inflation: 1987 Yearbook* (Chicago: Ibbotson Associates, Inc.; 1987).

1947–1986, investments in the average savings account (with all interest or dividends reinvested) grew at only around 5 percent annually, or about one percent ahead of the rate of inflation—that is, with very little *real* growth in purchasing power at all. Investments in U.S. Treasury bills (the shortest-term debt obligations of the U.S. government) did about the same. Investments in U.S. Treasury *bonds* (the government's longer-term debt) did no better—the bonds paid higher interest rates than the bills, but they declined severely in price over most of the period, and in terms of "total return" they fell a shade behind the bills. None of these investments came close to equaling common stocks for growth over the long term.

Let's briefly examine what a 6 percent real growth rate means. Here's what $1,000 invested at 6 percent grows to as the years go by:

		Growth at 6%
Start		$ 1,000
After	1 year	1,060
	5 years	1,338
	10 years	1,791
	20 years	3,207
	30 years	5,743
	40 years	10,286

Note that we are talking about growth *above* the rate of inflation—growth in *real purchasing power*. In the table above, $1,000 invested now grows to purchasing power of $3,207 after 20 years—a *real* triple. If you didn't think that 6 percent would grow so fast, this is a good introduction to what has been called the "miracle of compound interest." (In this age of skepticism, compound interest may well be as close to a miracle as you are likely to get.)

We hasten to emphasize that none of these figures proves what return will be achieved from common stock investments in the future, even though the results have prevailed for a long period in the past. Remember also that we are talking about *long-term averages*. The year-to-year fluctuations in common stock prices can at times be deeply disappointing, at least temporarily. And if common stocks are badly chosen, they may perform much more poorly than the averages, a point that will come up often in this book.

Common stocks are not the only way to protect against inflation. You can buy real estate, but real estate often is not practical for the average investor. You can buy gold, or jewels, or antiques—experience shows that there are many kinds of "collectibles" that tend to rise in value with inflation. But when inflation dies down, these investments are frequently disappointing.

Common stocks have the exceptional advantage of not *depending* on inflation for investment success. In common stocks, the *primary* purpose is to invest in successful businesses, which can do well with or without inflation. The protection against inflation comes as something of a bonus—very valuable, but not the main show. If inflation turns out to be less than forecast, you don't have to run for cover.

4 · THE PROBLEMS WITH COMMON STOCKS: RISKS AND UNCERTAINTIES

In the previous chapter, we described the possibilities of common stocks in glowing terms. Well-chosen common stocks represent investments in growing businesses. Over the long run, they also protect against inflation. Over most of the postwar period they have made money grow, on the average, more than 6 percent ahead of the rate of inflation, a rate that is high enough to compound quite dramatically. What more could one ask? And why doesn't everyone put all their long-term savings in common stocks?

The answer can be summed up in two words: *risks* and *uncertainties*.

Investing always involves a trade-off between risk and reward. The higher the reward you aim for, the greater the risks and uncertainties are likely to be. In common stocks, a glance at the table on page 10 will show that you are aiming for very substantial rewards indeed. Your money can double or triple in terms of real purchasing power over the course of several years. But you can also lose money (that's the risk), or perhaps earn less than if you had left the money quite safely in the bank (another version of the risk). Even if the investment eventually does for you all that you had hoped, you will see the value of your investment fluctuate, sometimes sharply, from day to day and from year to year, and, as a business owner, you can never be quite sure just what the next day or the next year will bring. (That's the uncertainty.)

Common stock prices are by no means the riskiest of all investments. Compared with the fluctuations in gold prices, for example, the swings in common stock prices seem relatively moderate. But in personal investing, some people find almost any degree of uncertainty deeply uncomfortable. Such people want safety and certainty. They may be perfectly willing to put aside thoughts of rapid growth for their long-term investment dollars in order to achieve peace of mind.

For the person who prefers to sacrifice growth possibilities in favor of complete safety, there are perfectly reasonable investments available. Money market funds came into existence in the 1970s to give the average saver/ investor the same favorable market rates of interest previously available only to those who had large amounts of money to invest. Banks now also offer the average investor competitive interest rates and a wide variety of savings options.

Here also, history can't prove what will happen in the future. But it strongly suggests that if a person puts money in a bank or money market fund and lets the interest accumulate, over the long run the value of the investment will probably keep up with inflation, and perhaps do a little bit better. (See the No Nonsense Financial Guide, *Understanding Money Market Funds.*)

Toward the end of this book, we will have some advice for the person who sees the great potential of common stock investments but who finds the safety question deeply worrisome. Meanwhile, just what are the risks and uncertainties in stocks?

We can't repeat too often that as a common stock investor, you become part owner of a business. Businesses are subject to changes in sales, costs, and earnings. The changes may be frequent and sometimes unsettling. Moreover, the common stocks in which you are likely to invest are stocks of major corporations, and these stocks are traded in vast marketplaces where prices are set freely from day to day, and in fact from minute to minute, by supply and demand. Ultimately, the strongest influence on the price of a stock is likely to be the company's earnings. But over any given period, stock prices will fluctuate widely in response to news about the company itself, changes in industry conditions, and changes in broad economic and political factors—business activity, interest rates, inflation, etc. Prices also move in response to investor psychology and changes in opinion, marked often by wide swings from optimism to pessimism and back again.

Sometimes the fluctuations are deeply unsettling. Common stock prices have tended to move in major waves averaging approximately four years from peak to peak. Look at the chart of long-run stock prices below. The long-term upward trend is clear, but the owners of common stocks had to ride out particularly deep declines in 1962, 1970, and 1973–74. These fluctuations were not easy to live through; in 1973–74, the worst decline of the postwar period (aggravated by the Arab oil embargo and skyrocketing oil prices), the stock market averages dropped nearly 50 percent below their former peaks.

And, as you can see from the chart, the Standard & Poor's 500 index did not recover to its previous peak until 1980. The person who had the bad fortune or bad judgment to buy a package of stocks at the top of the 1972 boom may well have seen the prices of those stocks average below his/her buying point for seven or eight years. Even taking into account the yearly dividends received on those stocks, the investor was probably behind for five years or so. The person who is setting his or her sights 10, 15 or 20 years down the road can afford to ride out such fluctuations in favor of greater long-term growth; but common stocks are obviously not a dependable investment for the short run.

We have been talking about risks and uncertainties in the general stock market, but remember again that one is usually buying particular stocks. This means that there is also a risk of selection—you can choose stocks of companies that turn out to be more successful, or companies that turn out to be less successful. Every stock market enthusiast can tell you how rich you would have become if you were one of the early buyers of General Motors, or IBM, or Xerox. But what about all those competitors of General Motors who disappeared? In the 1920s you might easily have decided to buy, not General Motors, but Stutz or

STOCK PRICES 1946-87

Standard & Poor's
500 Stock Index
(1941-43 = 10)

Studebaker. Picking the great growth stocks of history is easy by hindsight, but it's never easy at the time.

People sometimes talk as if dealing with all these risks were a matter of pure luck or speculation. Often we will hear someone talk about "taking a flyer in the market," as if buying stocks were no different from betting on a horse race. That simply isn't true. In the vast majority of cases, judgments about common stocks can be made on a completely rational basis.

True, the element of luck does sometimes enter in. Even with the most careful thought and planning, some future events and developments aren't predictable. One oil company with perfectly good geologists may drill in a new area and find a large oil field; another company with equally good geologists may drill in another area and find nothing. For reasons like these, some common stocks may be less predictable than others. But in this book we take the position that common stock investments can be handled logically and intelligently, and that with careful planning the average investor can keep the risks and uncertainties within limits that she or he can live with successfully—and, in the long run, happily.

5 · WHAT ARE COMMON STOCKS?

We have already said that common stocks represent shares of ownership in a business. Before we go on to further discussion of common stocks as an investment, a little more explanation of what a common stock is will probably be useful.

Forming a Corporation

Small businesses are often owned by an individual, or by a partnership consisting of two or more people. As a business grows, it may become desirable for the owner(s) to form a *corporation.* Ownership in a corporation is represented by shares of stock. A corporation is a separate legal entity, responsible for its own debts. The individual owners, called stockholders, are not liable for corporate obligations. This concept, known as *limited liability,* has made possible the growth of the giant corporations, with thousands of owners who have put up money to buy stock, but who know that they can't be hauled into court to put up more money if the corporation fails. Their liability is limited to the amount they paid for their shares.

In a small corporation, the stock may be held by only one or two people. Then there may be a need for more capital—that is, more money to run the business. A small restaurant may be successful and decide to expand. A chain of two or three computer software stores may be successful and decide to open more outlets. These needs may be met by selling additional stock to family members, employees, friends, and neighbors.

Going Public

If the business is very successful, it may decide to "go public"—that is, to sell additional shares of stock to the general public. Going public has two advantages:

First, it gives the corporation an opportunity to raise more capital than it ever could by going to friends, neighbors, etc. Second, it creates a *public market* for the company's stock.

The process of going public is very complex. The company must work with one or more investment firms (termed, in this function, "underwriters") that actually manage the offering of the stock to the public. If the offering is a large one, it must be registered with the U.S. Securities and Exchange Commission ("SEC"). Interested stock purchasers must be given a "prospectus," a legal document giving full information about the company, its finances and its prospects. Arrangements must be made so that the members of the public who buy shares will subsequently be able to "trade" their shares—that is, to buy or sell them—freely. This means either "listing" the shares on a securities exchange (the New York Stock Exchange is the best known, but it is only for relatively large corporations) or arranging for certain securities dealers to "make a market" in the shares by standing ready to buy or sell from or to the public.

Corporate Structure

The structure of a corporation is basically simple. The stockholders, who own the company, exercise control by electing a board of directors. Typically this is done annually, with each share of stock having one vote. The function of the board of directors is to set basic policy and supervise management. The board elects a president and other officers to run the company from day to day, and the board then meets at regular intervals to review management actions.

As a stockholder (owner) of a corporation, you have certain basic rights in proportion to the number of shares you own. You have the right to vote for the election of directors. If the company earns money and the directors decide to pay out part of these earnings to shareholders as *dividends*, you have a right to receive your proportionate share. And if the corporation is sold or liquidates, you have a right to your proportionate shares of the proceeds.

What evidence do you have that you are a stockholder? Traditionally, when you buy shares of stock, you receive a *stock certificate* stating that you own a given number of shares of the corporation. For convenience, you may leave this certificate on deposit with the broker through whom you bought the stock. However, certificates are old-fashioned, and the securities industry is moving away from them and toward a system of computer entries and confirmations, which works perfectly well.

Stocks vs. Bonds

An important point: We have been talking about common stocks and stockholders. What about bonds and bondholders? Since stocks and bonds are often referred to together, it is worth distinguishing clearly between them before we go further.

We have explained that common stock represents ownership in a corporation. As a stockholder, you have owner's rights, but you are not entitled to any particular return, and you have no right to demand that the corporation buy back your stock. If you want to sell your shares, you must sell them in the open market to someone else who wants to buy them.

A bond is completely different. A bond is evidence not of ownership, but of a *loan* to a company (or to a government, or to some other organization). It is a debt obligation. When you buy a corporate bond, you have bought a portion of a loan to a corporation. Your rights are those of a *lender*. You are entitled to interest payments at a specified rate, and to repayment of the full face amount of the bond at a specified date. Whether the company is more or less successful hardly matters to you, as long as it earns enough to meet your interest payments and to repay your bond when it is due. The only possible growth of your money is through the fixed interest payments you receive

19

(usually semi-annually), but your risks are obviously far less than those of stockholders.

The investment industry is endlessly creative, and there are bonds that carry certain ownership features. In particular, there are *convertible* bonds that are convertible into common stock at the option of the holder. But for most practical purposes you can think of the distinction between common stocks and bonds in very simple terms: owner *vs.* lender.

6 · HOW STOCKS ARE TRADED

We have already introduced the subject of how stocks are traded—i.e., bought and sold. Now for a few more pointers.

First, remember that we are only talking about *publicly traded* stocks. Stocks of private companies can be bought and sold in private transactions. That isn't what concerns us here.

The Stock Exchanges

The stocks of most of the largest corporations in the U.S. are listed on the New York Stock Exchange (NYSE). While they are also traded elsewhere, the NYSE is the major trading place for IBM, Exxon and other major oil companies, General Motors, Ford and Chrysler, Du Pont and other major chemicals, Sears, A.T.&T. and its spin-offs, and about 1500 other corporations. The stocks of many other companies, somewhat smaller on average, are listed on the American Stock Exchange and on such regional exchanges as the Pacific Stock Exchange. Thousands of additional "unlisted" stocks are traded effectively, not on any exchange, but in the "over-the-counter" market, a network of hundreds of securities dealers linked together by telephones and highly automated price quotation and reporting systems.

The volume of trading in these marketplaces is staggering. The daily figures vary considerably, but on a typical day in 1986, trading averaged around 140 million shares on the NYSE, more than 10 million on the American, more than 20 million on the regional exchanges, and more than 100 million over-the-counter. The dollar volume was roughly in the $7 to $8 billion range—sometimes more. All this trading is reported during the day on electronic screens (still referred to, by tradition, as the "ticker," or the "tape"), tabulated by computer, and summarized for the

21

next day's newspapers. (For more information, see the No Nonsense Financial Guide, *Understanding the Stock Market.*)

Markets and Liquidity

As an investor, you don't need to know all the specifics of how this trading is accomplished. What is important to you is the tremendous depth and activity of the markets. On a given day, you can usually dispose of large quantities of any recognized stock with only a small effect on its trading price. Your stock investments are *liquid.* That is, you can always convert your investment into cash at whatever the market price happens to be—unlike real estate, for example, where it may take a long time to find a willing buyer for a particular piece of property. That doesn't mean that you can be sure of getting your entire cost back when you want to sell—prices may fluctuate widely, as we have been stressing. But for most investors, the great *liquidity* of common stocks, compared with many other long-term investments, is a prime advantage.

There are exceptions. An investor who buys a large percentage of the stock of a small company that is not actively traded, may have trouble in attempting to dispose of the stock quickly. Sometimes, when the stock market is falling rapidly or deeply depressed, there may be a shortage of buyers even for better-known stocks. But the amount of stock that any average investor normally buys can almost always be disposed of quickly and easily.

Brokers and Dealers

The securities markets are tightly regulated. To buy or sell a security in any of these marketplaces, you must act through a registered broker or dealer. These firms are closely regulated and monitored by the SEC. They must show that they have adequate working capital, and they must abide by strict rules in handling customer transactions. This is to prevent fraud and manipulation, and to ensure that the broker-dealers don't profit unfairly at the expense of their customers.

To execute a trade (i.e., to buy or sell a stock) on a particular exchange (such as the NYSE), a broker must be a member of that particular exchange, or must act through another broker who is a member. In the over-the-counter market, there is no membership structure, but dealers trade basically only with other dealers who are members of the National Association of Securities Dealers (NASD), and the NASD sets rules and standards to govern trading and the behavior of its members.

Do brokerage firms ever fail financially? It happens rarely, but it happens. To protect the customers, the firms are required to belong to the Securities Investor Protection Corp. ("SIPC"), which insures the securities you have on deposit up to $500,000 in case the firm should fail (including insurance on any cash balance up to $100,000). Although SIPC dates only from 1970, it has become one of the cornerstones in the whole structure of regulation and investor protection.

The combination of tight regulation and high professional standards makes the securities markets unique in their operations. A dealer in Philadelphia can pick up the phone and call a dealer in Seattle and buy several hundred thousand dollars' worth of stock in thirty seconds or so. Neither has ever seen the other face to face; they may never have done business with each other before. All that each really knows is that the other is a member of the NASD, bound to abide by its strict rules. The phone call has accomplished what would have taken a firm of lawyers a week to put into written contractual form. Yet each dealer knows that the trade will be honored, the securities delivered and paid for, no matter which way prices move subsequently, and no matter how much one of them may regret having made the trade. Does a dealer ever default on a trade? Yes, once in a long while. But you can be sure that it won't happen twice. In the securities business, reputations are precious, and a person's word is truly as good as his or her bond.

7 · INVESTING FOR YOUR FUTURE

We now return specifically to you, and your investment objectives. We have talked about the potential of common stocks and the risks involved. In considering common stocks for your own investment planning, the question you must ask yourself—and the answer has to be a personal one—is, "Am I willing to take some risks and to suffer some uncertainties in the hope of making my money grow faster?"

Before you answer that question, think carefully about your future financial needs, and give some thought to the risks involved in *not* making your money grow. Consider the problems everyone faces today.

People are living longer. That's a healthy fact, but it's also a problem. It means that having enough money for your retirement is more difficult than it used to be.

Social Security can't do the whole job, and was never intended to. When the Social Security system was introduced in the 1930s under the New Deal, it was seen as a foundation on which individuals would build for their retirement. Now, with more people living for many years beyond the normal retirement age, the resources of the Social Security system have been spread thinner, and it's probable that benefits in the future will give you even less of a foundation, relatively speaking, than in the past. You can't rely on Social Security, by itself, to give you anything approaching a comfortable retirement.

It's very likely that you are also covered by some type of private or government pension plan. But here too, consider the problems and whether the plan can really—by itself, or in combination with Social Security—give you the degree of comfort in the future that you expect and desire.

It's also very likely that you have an IRA (Individual Retirement Account). But in most cases, an IRA also won't be able to do the job alone.

Even if your pension benefits and your IRA look sizable, consider whether they will adjust adequately to inflation as the years go by. Inflation makes your planning much more difficult, but it has to be taken into account if you want your financial efforts to be meaningful. Of course, it isn't only retirement that requires more savings effort on your part. The cost of all the major things you save for has gone up sharply in recent years. Young people saving to buy a home find that the price of housing has risen sharply, and that higher interest rates have made home mortgages much more burdensome. Education costs, particularly the cost of sending a child to college, have skyrocketed at the same time that government aid for students has been curtailed. The cost of medical care has soared. Without substantial savings, all of these are almost impossible for the average person to afford. You may pay more for an automobile today than you would have paid for a house in 1950.

How can you build for the future well enough to meet all these needs? If you have been accustomed to putting savings aside regularly in a bank or a money market fund, one way to have more in the future is simply to put more aside now. But for most people, squeezing more savings out of current income is extremely difficult.

The other way is to make your savings grow faster (including the savings you have in an IRA and/or any other retirement plan). As we showed in the first chapters of this book, common stocks offer an opportunity to make your money grow faster than bank accounts or other fixed-income investments. And over the long run, they also offer you a way to protect against inflation.

We have put considerable stress on the risks and uncertainties involved in being a business owner—and in owning common stocks. We think that you must be forewarned. But in the rest of this book, we will be discussing the practical ways in which *you* can become a common stock investor, and we will pay particular attention to ways of managing the risks and keeping them down to a level that you are likely to find acceptable.

We will also pay attention to the problems you face if the money you have to invest is limited. Some investment approaches are relatively expensive for the small investor. But there are practical ways to start out as a common stock investor even on a very modest scale. (See Chapter 10).

Take another look at the table on page 10. Think what that extra 6 percent could do for you. It's worth a little thought and planning on your part, and a little initiative too.

8 · GROWTH AND INCOME: A CLARIFICATION

Up until now, we have talked about using common stocks to make your money *grow*. The emphasis has been on long-term *growth*.

From the above, you might reasonably conclude that common stocks are useful only for long-term growth of your money, and that if you want current spendable income you should look to other types of investments. In fact, many people make exactly that assumption. It's customary to talk of a distinction between "growth" and "income" investments, and it's natural to assume that there's a reasonably clear line between one and the other.

From an accountant's point of view, the distinction between growth and income is quite clear. If you own a stock that grows in value by 10 percent a year and pays you 4 percent a year in dividends, the 10 percent is growth in value (until you sell the stock, the accountant will call it "unrealized appreciation") and the 4 percent is income. If after five years you sell the stock for a 61 percent profit (10 percent compounded for five years), the distinction between growth and income is still clear. (The growth has now taken the form of *realized* appreciation.)

But from the viewpoint of your investment strategy, the distinction is less clear. For example, bank accounts are traditionally thought of as pure *income* investments, because the number of dollars deposited in the account stays fixed and earns regular interest. You can spend the interest if you wish, or you may choose to leave the interest in the account to make your money *grow*. So, your bank account may act as either an income or a growth investment, or both.

Inflation makes the whole situation more complicated. Because of inflation, your dollars are worth less in terms of real purchasing power every year. In the example of a bank or money market fund, you might choose to let your income (interest or dividends) accumulate in the account simply to keep the *real* value of the account from shrinking because of inflation.

Yet there is a distinction between traditional "growth" and "income" investments, and the terms do have significance for your own investment decisions. Let's talk about two choices that you have to make in planning your investments.

Degree of Risk

The first choice involves the degree of risk you are willing to take. This is a subject which we introduced in Chapter 4. What generally distinguishes the so-called income investments is that they are *lower-risk.* The value of your original investment holds completely constant (as in a bank) or fluctuates only moderately, while a relatively predictable amount of income (interest or dividends) is added to the account every year. The investment is lower-risk because its rewards are more predictable.

In a "growth" investment, the results are less predictable and the risks are greater. The rise in value you hope for may take place much more slowly than you expected, or may not take place at all. If the investment is unsuccessful, its value may decline rather than grow. In choosing between "income" and "growth" investments as they are traditionally defined, you are primarily making a choice of *degree of risk.*

Spending Income or Spending Growth

The second choice has to do with your need for money to spend. Do you depend on your investments to provide you with spending money? Some people do, some don't. It's obvious that the more money you withdraw from the account each year to spend, the less the buildup of your money will be. If you are trying to protect your financial future in an inflationary world, the best policy is to spend only what you absolutely need and to let as much as you can accumulate. But some retired people, for example, must have spendable income from their investments, even at the cost of doing without growth in value.

Traditionally, people who need spendable income tend to choose conservative "income" type investments, where a relatively predictable amount will be added to the account each year. But it doesn't have to be that way. We saw above that a person might pick an "income" investment as a way of making his or her money grow slowly but steadily. The opposite works too: a person who wants spendable income can concentrate on higher-risk "growth" investments while withdrawing spending money from the account on a regular basis. In effect, the investor is *spending part of the growth* as he or she goes along.

Raising Your "Total Return"

Now for a word about the concept of "total return." Recognizing that "growth" and "income" don't always mean what they seem, in recent years many professional managers have begun to talk primarily in terms of "total return," that is, the combined growth and income recorded by an investment. Looking at it slightly differently, total return is the growth rate achieved by an investment when all income from the investment is reinvested.

And this brings us back to common stocks. The key point to be made about common stocks is that they have given investors a higher *total return*, over the long term, than most other forms of investment. You can benefit from this whether or not you need spendable income from your investments; the real question is what degree of risk you want to take.

Let's imagine a time when the inflation rate is averaging 7 percent a year and when bank money market accounts and money market funds are paying, say, 8 percent. Under these conditions a well-managed common stock account or common stock mutual fund (well enough managed to do somewhat better than the averages) might quite possibly achieve an *average* total return of 15 percent or so—though we hasten to add that this is an average, and that the yearly figures would probably vary greatly. The common stock investor might be able to withdraw 9 percent a year (more than the return from a money fund) and still see his or her money grow at around 6 percent (15 percent minus 9 percent equals 6 percent). Look at the table on page 10 and see what this 6 percent growth might be worth over a period of years. It's worth thinking about.

So even if you regard yourself as an income investor, don't rule out common stocks. Consider the risks involved, but also consider the possible rewards.

9 · RELYING ON PROFESSIONALS: BROKERS AND ADVISERS

Knowing which common stocks to buy, when to buy them, and when to sell is as difficult as any other skilled profession. It can also be pleasurable and exciting, and you may want to try to learn to do it yourself. But in the beginning, at least, you are likely to want to rely on the advice of a professional.

There are a few different ways of doing this. Since there is no such thing as a free lunch, you obviously will pay for the advice. If the advice is good, it will be worth paying for. But in some cases the payment will be clearer than in others.

Think back to Chapter 6, where we discussed how securities are traded. To buy stocks, you need to deal through a broker. You can't wander onto the floor of the New York Stock Exchange and buy ten shares of General Motors yourself. In any stock transaction, a brokerage firm is executing your order. Strictly speaking, execution of orders is what a broker does. But over the years, brokers have also taken on the function of giving *advice*, and in a typical broker-customer relationship, you may be paying more for *advice* than you are for *brokerage*, even though the charge for advice may simply be built into the commission rates you pay when you buy or sell securities.

Two Kinds of Brokers

In other cases, the charges may be separated more clearly. A little history may be useful. Until 1975, commission rates charged by all brokers on the major exchanges were fixed according to a uniform schedule, and brokerage firms competed primarily in terms of the quality of their advice and service. In 1975, fixed rates were abolished, and firms became free to set their own rates. The rates charged to institutions on large transactions came down quickly, but most of the old "full service" brokerage firms kept the rates charged to individuals close to the old levels and continued to provide generous amounts of advice and research.

Recently, a new group of "discount brokers" has evolved. They provide brokerage service (execution of orders) and very little else, and their commission rates are generally less than half of those charged by full service brokers. They are useful if you simply want to give orders to buy and sell certain stocks (or other securities). Their function is *not* to give you advice. In 1983, banks were given permission to enter the brokerage field, and many have either set up their own brokerage units or have entered into working arrangements with established discount brokers as a way of offering additional services to their customers. (For more information, see the No Nonsense Financial Guide, *How to Choose a Discount Stockbroker.*)

Investment Advisers

Before saying more about full-service brokers, let's note that there are firms called *investment advisers* whose function is *only* to give investment advice, and who charge for the advice—usually on the basis of the size of the account being advised or managed. Bank trust departments do a very large business functioning, in effect, as investment advisers. There are also many independent advisory firms—you may have heard the names of some of the large ones, such as Loomis-Sayles, T. Rowe Price, and Scudder, Stevens & Clark.

Most of these advisers don't find it economical to serve the average person. The minimum account size they accept may be $100,000, or $500,000, or even higher. Still, by understanding how they function, you can better understand some of your other alternatives.

The adviser can work for you on a "nondiscretionary" or a "discretionary" basis. In a "nondiscretionary" arrangement, the adviser consults with the client and advises about each decision, but the client actually makes the decision. It is probably now more common for the adviser to have "discretion," that is, to be given the authority to act on behalf of the client. This arrangement makes more sense if the adviser is doing a professional job and if the client is inexperienced. To put it in plain terms, if you are using an adviser, the best course probably is to follow his or her advice, watch the results, and fire the adviser if the results aren't good.

(Note that if you are using an adviser who is only an adviser, you still need a broker actually to execute transactions. But the advisory firm will usually be glad to take care of the brokerage arrangements if you so desire.)

You and Your Broker

Now back to those full-service brokers. You probably know the names of some of the largest ones—Merrill Lynch, Prudential-Bache, Shearson Lehman/American Express, Sears Dean Witter, and so on. (Note that we are not in any way suggesting that the larger firms are necessarily better than the smaller ones.)

As an average customer of a full-service firm, you deal with an individual account executive or "registered representative" (so called because he or she is *registered* with the stock exchanges and the NASD). The "registered rep" or "RR"—whom we will refer to simply as "your broker"—draws on the volume of research and recommendations from the firm's research department.

Sometimes this works well for the client; sometimes it doesn't. The firm's research and recommendations may be good or not so good. The individual broker may be more or less experienced, and may or may not have a talent for telling the good from the bad, and for adapting the firm's ideas to the needs of individual clients.

There's usually no simple way to tell how well a

brokerage firm, or an individual broker, has done for clients in the past unless you know someone who has had excellent experience with a particular broker. By all means talk to that broker and see if he or she might be right for you. If you walk into a brokerage firm off the street and have a broker assigned to you, be careful. If you have doubts about the broker, or if your first experiences aren't satisfactory, don't hesitate to talk to the firm manager or branch manager about making a switch. See if the conversation gives you a clue as to whether you need merely a different individual broker, or perhaps a completely different firm.

You must also remember that most individual brokers are in a position that involves a potential conflict of interest. For better or worse, the average broker is paid as a salesperson—whose compensation depends primarily on the amount of brokerage commissions generated from buy or sell orders. The more orders a broker executes, the more money he or she makes. The broker may also be under pressure to recommend certain investment products or packages where both the broker and the firm make higher-than-average commissions. Under these pressures, it's not always easy for a broker to give impartial advice.

How do you avoid having the broker's needs come ahead of yours? First, most brokers are honest and want to do a good job for their clients. Second, most brokers recognize that the greatest success comes to those who have helped their clients invest profitably and who have built up a loyal following. Third, in a well-managed common stock account, there will be reasonably frequent transactions in response to changes in business conditions, research developments, and market prices; so a broker who is doing his or her job the way it should be done will be well enough compensated in the normal course of things without "reaching" for extra commissions.

You shouldn't brood about the conflict-of-interest problem, but you should keep it in mind. One protection may be to deal with a very successful broker who has no particular need to make extra commissions off *you*. But human nature is hard to predict, and it may not be the most successful broker who proves most reliable in putting *your* interests first.

Brokers as Advisers

Some brokerage firms think of themselves primarily as advisers rather than brokers, and many have registered with the SEC in both forms so that they have the right to charge separately for investment advice. Your brokerage firm may specifically offer you the choice of an *advisory* account in which you pay a fee related to the size of the account, and the commission rates you pay are below those paid by a nonadvisory client. If you feel that the firm gives good advice and management services, and if your account is large enough to qualify, this arrangement is worth considering. Since the firm is earning an advisory fee from you, it can be less concerned with the amount of commissions you are paying on transactions. The arrangement is straightforward, and should you obtain better advice, it will more than compensate for the advisory fee.

The advisory account will probably involve giving *discretion* to the firm to buy and sell for you (at their *discretion*). In this case you need to exercise some extra care, since professionals can make mistakes in any case, and in the case of a broker-adviser there is the extra temptation, conscious or not, to lean toward an approach that generates higher commissions.

But there can be advantages in having your investments managed for you on a discretionary basis. Many people are accustomed to an arrangement where a broker calls the client to make each decision on a purchase or sale. If the broker is acting primarily as a salesperson for his or her firm, you obviously need to exercise your own judgment. But if a broker or adviser is really acting in good faith as an *adviser*, remember that the adviser can do a better job for you by spending more time on research and decision making, and less time on the phone with clients.

Ask Before You Leap

Whatever kind of arrangement you are entering into with any kind of broker or adviser, don't begin until you have had a full interview and have asked every question you can think of about the firm's experience and procedures, the individual broker's experience, and the ability of both of them together to meet your needs, preferences, and objectives. Don't hesitate to ask hard questions about commission rates; and if you don't get clear answers, go elsewhere.

Keep in mind that brokers and advisers are strictly regulated by the SEC—both the firms and the individuals. Ultimately, every broker knows that if a customer is treated unfairly, the customer can complain to the SEC— or to the NASD or the various stock exchanges, all of which are considered self-regulatory organizations. It's unlikely that you will ever have to go through such a complaint process. But the fact that there's a policeman on the corner has certainly helped to keep order on the street.

10 · RELYING ON PROFESSIONALS: COMMON STOCK MUTUAL FUNDS

There's another way of having complete professional supervision for your common stock investments. It's a way that may be more convenient and practical for many, and that probably reduces risk. That way is by buying *common stock mutual funds*.

A mutual fund is a way of pooling the money of many investors so that it can be managed efficiently and economically as a single large unit. The best-known type of mutual fund is perhaps the money market fund, where the pool is invested for complete safety only in the shortest-term income-producing investments. But the mutual fund industry was originally built around common stock funds, which put all of the advantages of common stocks into a package tailored for the average investor. As of early 1987, various types of common stock funds were handling about $200 billion of investors' money.

Mutual funds bring common stock investing within the reach of even the smallest investor, for whom the costs involved in a brokerage account are likely to be out of proportion to the amount invested. At the same time, the funds are also favored by many wealthy individuals and large institutions.

Advantages of Mutual Funds

Mutual funds have several advantages. The first is *professional management.* Decisions as to which stocks to buy, when to buy, and when to sell are made for you by professional managers. The size of the pool makes it possible to pay for the highest quality management, and many of the individuals and organizations that manage mutual funds have acquired reputations as being among the finest managers in the profession. Several of the best funds were started by investment advisory organizations as a way of bringing their services to the average investor.

Another of the advantages of a mutual fund is *diversification*. Because of the size of the fund, the managers can easily *diversify* its investments, which means that they can reduce risk by spreading the total dollars in the pool over many different stocks representing many different companies and industries.

The funds also give you *convenience*. First, it's easy to put money in and take it out. The funds technically are "open-end" investment companies, so called because they stand ready to sell additional new shares to investors at any time or to buy back ("redeem") shares sold previously. You can invest in some mutual funds with as little as $250, and your investment participates fully in any growth in value of the fund and in any dividends paid out. You can arrange to have dividends reinvested automatically, and there are other arrangements to make the investment process easy. If the fund is part of a larger fund group, you can usually arrange to switch by telephone among the funds in the group—sometimes for a small charge, sometimes for no charge at all. And most funds have toll-free "800" numbers for added convenience and for quick answers to your questions. (For a full discussion of mutual funds, read the No Nonsense Financial Guide, *Understanding Mutual Funds*.)

Types of Common Stock Funds

Some common stock funds take more risk and some take less, and there is a wide range of funds available to meet the needs of different investors. When you see funds "classified by objective," the classifications are really according to risk, though the word "risk" doesn't appear in the headings. "Aggressive growth" or "maximum capital gain" funds are those that take the greatest risks in pursuit of maximum growth. "Growth" or "long-term growth" funds may be a shade lower on the risk scale. "Growth-income"

funds are generally considered middle-of-the-road. There
are also common stock "income" funds, which in fact try
for some growth as well as income, but stay on the conservative side by investing mainly in established companies
that pay sizable dividends to their owners. These also are
termed "equity income" funds, and the best of them have
achieved excellent growth records.

Load vs. No-load

There are "load" mutual funds and "no-load" funds. A
"load" fund is generally bought through a broker or salesperson who helps you with your selection and charges a
commission ("load")—usually from 4.5 percent to 8.5 percent of the total amount you invest. This means that as
little as 91.5 percent of the money you invest is actually
applied to buy shares in the pool. In contrast, you choose a
no-load fund yourself without the help of a broker or
salesperson, but 100 percent of your investment dollars go
into the pool for your account.

Which are better—load or no-load funds? That really
depends on how much time and effort you want to devote
to fund selection and supervision of your investment.
Some people have neither the time, inclination nor apti-
tude to devote to the task—for them, a load fund may be
the answer. The load may be well justified by long-term
results if your broker or salesperson helps you invest in a
fund that performs outstandingly well.

How to Pick a No-load Fund

If you have decided in favor of no-load funds and intend to
make your own selections, just how do you pick the fund
or funds that are best for you? The more you intend to
concentrate on growth and accept the risks that go with it,
the more important it is that you entrust your money only
to high-quality, tested managements.

There are several publications that compile figures on
mutual fund performance for periods as long as ten or

even twenty years. One that is found in many libraries is the *Wiesenberger Investment Companies* annual handbook. The Wiesenberger yearbook is the bible of the fund industry, with extensive descriptions of funds, all sorts of other data, and plentiful performance statistics. You may also have access to the *Lipper Mutual Fund Performance Analysis,* an extensive service subscribed to primarily by professionals. It is issued weekly, with special quarterly issues showing longer-term performance. On the newsstands, *Money* magazine has frequent mutual fund articles and quarterly performance surveys; *Barron's* weekly has quarterly mutual fund issues in mid-February, May, August and November; and *Forbes* magazine runs an excellent annual mutual fund survey issue in August or September. (For additional sources, see the No Nonsense Financial Guide, *Understanding Mutual Funds.*)

These sources (especially Wiesenberger) will also give you descriptions of the funds and their investment policies and objectives. When you have selected several funds that look promising to you, call each fund (most have toll-free "800" numbers) to get the fund's prospectus and recent financial reports. The prospectus is the legal document describing a mutual fund's policies for prospective investors. It may be dry reading, but the prospectus and the reports together should give you a picture of what the fund is trying to do and how well it has succeeded over the latest ten years.

In studying the records of the funds, and in requesting material, don't necessarily restrict yourself to a single "risk" group. The best investment managers sometimes operate in ways that aren't easily classified. As mentioned above, you will find certain "income" funds that have excellent growth records. You will find some "growth" funds that have held up relatively well in bad markets. Sometimes the classifications are at least partly arbitrary. What counts is the fund's record.

Obviously, you will want to pick one or more funds that have performed well relative to other funds in the same risk group. But don't simply pick the fund that happens to have performed best in the previous year; concentrate on the record over five or ten years. A fund that has made its shareholders' money grow favorably in total over a ten-year period, covering both up and down periods in the stock market, can be considered well tested. It's also worth looking at the year-to-year record within the whole period to see how *consistent* management has been.

You will note that the range of performance over most periods among the different funds is quite wide. Don't be surprised. As we have stressed, managing investments is a difficult art. Fund managers are generally experienced professionals, but their records have nevertheless ranged from remarkably good to mediocre and, in a few cases, quite poor. Pick carefully.

Your biggest problem in selection will probably be that there are several very fine funds in every risk group, and you obviously can't invest in all of them. Once you have narrowed your choice to a small group of funds with superior records matching your objectives, how to pick one over the others may be a puzzle. If two funds have similar performance records, and if there's nothing in their policies to make you prefer one over the other, then it's virtually impossible to forecast which of the two will do better for you in the future. A perfectly reasonable course is to pick one or two of these funds arbitrarily; stay with them for a year or so; compare them again with the competition; continue with them if they've done well, and switch to others if they haven't. Since you are dealing with no-load funds, there's no cost in getting out and no cost in getting in.

Spending as You Go

In Chapter 8, we discussed what to do if you need spendable cash from your common stock investments, and we suggested that you consider investing for growth and spending part of the growth as you go along.

Mutual funds fit into that type of approach particularly well. You can invest money and take it out in relatively small amounts and with great flexibility. If you invest in common stocks directly, the commissions on small transactions will be relatively large. With no-load funds, that isn't a problem.

If you want to take money out on a regular periodic schedule, the funds make it simple. You set up an "automatic withdrawal plan" under which you instruct the fund to send you a specific amount monthly or quarterly, and the fund redeems just enough shares each time to provide the necessary cash. The rest of your money continues to work for you without interruption. Since mutual funds allow you to purchase fractional shares, your purchase or redemption is adjustable down to the last penny. If it's convenience and flexibility you want, the mutual funds will do their best to oblige.

A list of selected larger no-load fund groups follows:

SELECTED LARGER NO-LOAD MUTUAL FUND GROUPS

Name of Group or Manager	Toll-free Telephone Number
Dreyfus Funds**	800-645-6561
Fidelity Group*	800-544-6666
Financial Programs	800-525-8085
Neuberger & Berman Management	800-367-0770
T. Rowe Price Funds	800-638-5660
Scudder Funds	800-225-2470
SteinRoe & Farnham Funds	800-621-0320
Twentieth Century Funds*	800-345-2021
USAA Investment Management	800-531-8181
Value Line Group	800-223-0818
Vanguard Group	800-662-7447

*Group also includes one or more low-load funds.
**Group also includes load and low-load funds.

Other Pooling Arrangements

Mutual funds are not the only way of gaining the advantage of pooling arrangements. Some companies offer savings plans in which you can have your money invested in a common stock program. And it is estimated that as many as 400,000 investors may belong to *investment clubs*, whose members generally invest regular amounts and plan and manage their investments as a unit. (For more information, write the National Association of Investment Clubs, 1515 East Eleven Mile Road, Royal Oak, MI. 48067.)

11 · PICKING STOCKS YOURSELF

Years ago, it was common for an individual investor to choose which stocks to buy, perhaps with a moderate amount of help from his or her broker.

Today, that approach is harder to justify. Stock prices change rapidly on research information that flashes through the professional community but that comes to you, the amateur, only later. Individual companies are researched by thousands of professional "security analysts" working for brokerage firms, advisory firms, pension funds, mutual funds, and other institutions. The chances of finding a "neglected" stock have diminished. Because of federal budget deficits, high interest rates, and inflation, the economy itself has become more difficult to predict.

But investing remains more of an art than a science. Some of the professionals produce only mediocre-to-poor results, while some amateurs have turned out to be remarkably capable investors. If you are intent on learning more about the principles of common stock investing, by all means go ahead.

Even if you intend to leave the decisions to professionals, some knowledge will help. Unless you have an understanding of what's involved in selecting and managing stocks, it may be hard for you to judge what your professional is doing.

If you do progress to the point of making more of your own investment decisions, you'll probably find that selecting and managing common stock investments is exciting. You might even call it *fun*. Investment research involves looking at the whole world, often from a fresh and different viewpoint. Your thinking must be:

- *alert* to news and new developments,
- *flexible* enough to change rapidly when conditions change,

- and *thoughtful* enough to consider all information seriously without jumping to conclusions.

Of course, we can't make you a professional investment manager overnight. But let's look briefly at some of the factors to consider as you learn more about your common stock investments.

12 · WHAT ANALYSTS LOOK FOR

There are many qualities that may make a company, and its stock, a good investment. A "security analyst" is a professional trained to study individual companies and securities and to make judgments about their quality and investment value.

While you can't hope to compete on equal terms with the professionals, you *can* begin to think more systematically about the important factors you should look for in common stock investments.

Stock prices fluctuate endlessly. As we have pointed out, prices move in response to changes in the economy, changes in general investor psychology, and news about a particular company, such as the company's latest sales or earnings results. Often price movements are exaggerated on the upside by enthusiasm or on the downside by fear. Common sense tells us that the real underlying value of a company usually doesn't change as often or as violently as the price of its stock. So there are times when the price of a company's stock is relatively higher, compared with the underlying values, and times when the price is relatively lower. For varying reasons, prices may move far out of line with what business experts might regard as real company values.

Note that the "real underlying value" of a company can't be measured precisely and involves diverse elements of judgment. But a security analyst tries to make these judgments, and looks for opportunities to buy stocks for less than their real values, or at least for less than the value the analyst forecasts a company will be worth a few years down the road.

The Price-Earnings Ratio

Perhaps the most important single concept, if you want to understand what security analysts are talking about, is the *price-earnings ratio* of a stock—also known as the price-earnings multiple, the P/E ratio, the P/E multiple, or sometimes simply the "multiple."

The price-earnings ratio is the ratio of the *price per share* of a company's stock to the *earnings per share* behind the stock.

This is the first time we have talked about "earnings per share." It's an easy concept. Let's imagine the Bigelow Toy Company, which in its latest year sold large quantities of toys and ended up with $8,000,000 of net profits, or earnings. The company has a simple financial structure, and there are two million shares of stock "issued and outstanding"—that is, in the hands of shareholders. You calculate the earnings per share by simple division:

$$\frac{\$8,000,000}{2,000,000 \text{ shares}} = \$4.00 \text{ earnings per share}$$

In other words, Bigelow earned $4.00 for each share of its common stock. That doesn't mean that the $4.00 will be paid out to the shareholders. At least part of the $4.00 will normally be plowed back into the business, to build toward higher earnings in the future. However, *part* of the $4.00 might be paid out to shareholders as a dividend (see below). In either case, if you were a Bigelow shareholder, the $4.00 would be working for you—either as additional cash invested in the business, or as cash paid out to you. So for a Bigelow shareholder, the $4.00 is the simplest measure of the year's results.

Having found the earnings per share, you then calculate the price-earnings ratio by another piece of simple division. Let's say that the stock of Bigelow is currently selling in the market at $36 per share:

$$\frac{\$36.00 \text{ (price per share)}}{\$4.00 \text{ (earnings per share)}} = 9.0 \text{ price-earnings ratio}$$

Investors are currently willing to buy Bigelow stock at a price equivalent to nine times last year's earnings on the stock. This ratio, or multiple, tells you more about how investors view a company than any other statistic. Investors will pay a higher multiple for a company whose earnings are expected to grow rapidly in the future—the multiple may be high in relation to current earnings, but may be only average in relation to expected future earnings. If a company's future looks uninteresting, the multiple will be low.

Multiples also change with the broad waves of enthusiasm and caution that characterize the stock market. Look at the chart below, which shows the *average* price-earnings multiple on the stocks in the **S&P 500 Stock Index**. In periods of enthusiasm and speculation, such as 1964–72, the average multiple was generally well above 15. In the late 1970s, it was well below 10. In 1986, with the market soaring, the average multiple was above 16. Whatever the *average* multiple is, the multiples on individual stocks will range widely above and below it.

So multiples are *relative*. But that's what you need. The price-earnings ratio will tell you whether a given stock is cheap or expensive *relative* to other stocks in the same industry and to the market as a whole. And using the chart, you can even get some idea of whether the whole market is cheap or expensive relative to past history.

Because the whole subject is so important, perhaps we should make sure that there's no doubt about the basic mathematics. If the market price of a stock goes up without any change in earnings, the price-earnings ratio goes up too; if other things remain equal, the stock has become relatively more expensive. If the market price goes down, the reverse is true. If the *earnings* per share go up without any change in price, the ratio goes *down*, and—always assuming other things equal—the stock has become relatively cheaper.

In the case of Bigelow, we calculated a price-earnings ratio based on last year's earnings per share. That's a common procedure, but you should note that analysts often

PRICE-EARNINGS RATIOS 1946-87

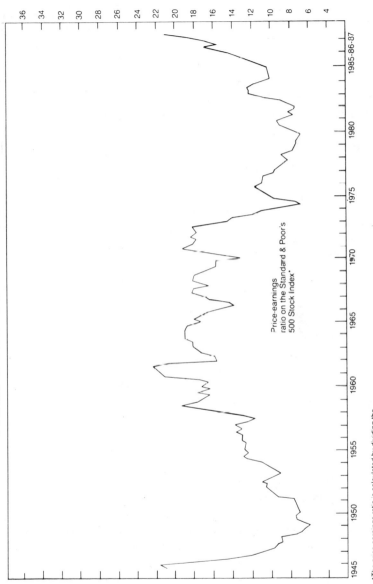

Price-earnings
ratio on the Standard & Poor's
500 Stock Index*

* The price-earnings ratio is calculated by dividing the
price index at the end of each calendar quarter by earnings
for the previous 12 months

calculate the ratio based on *estimated* earnings per share for the current year, or for some future year. If the analyst is estimating growth in earnings, this makes the multiple look lower and the stock look cheaper. That's legitimate, as long as you understand that the calculation is based on *estimates* (which could turn out right or wrong), and as long as comparisons among different companies are made on an equal basis.

Shopping for Values

Now that you know something about price-earnings ratios, we can talk further about the steps involved in selecting common stocks. Each company and each stock must be looked at individually. But many stock opportunities fall into certain broad categories, and while the categories aren't precise, it may be helpful to list a few of them.

(1) Perhaps the simplest opportunity an analyst might look for is one where a company's earnings are growing at a faster-than-average rate for its industry (or so the analyst believes), but the stock is still selling at a price-earnings multiple no higher than the average for that industry. For lack of a better phrase, we will call this a *moderate-growth* stock. Comparing the multiples based on present earnings is easy; the trick is in really being able to forecast which companies will show better-than-average growth as time goes by.

(2) The familiar term "growth stock" covers so wide a territory that we hesitate to use it. But we might define a *high-growth* stock as the stock of a company which is *recognized* as growing much faster than average, and where the stock, as a result, sells at a higher-than-average price-earnings multiple. These stocks are more speculative. The premium that you pay can range from small to outrageous. In buying these stocks, you are competing with a large number of professionals who make these their specialty. The potential rewards are high, but the stocks can drop in price at incredible rates when earnings don't grow as expected. Remember that only a small minority of com-

panies really succeed in making earnings grow rapidly over any long period.

(3) There are *cyclical* stocks—stocks of companies that may not show any strong long-term growth trend, but where the stocks fluctuate in line with the business cycle (prosperity-recession-prosperity, etc.) or with some other recognizable pattern. Obviously, you can make money if you buy these near the bottom of a price cycle and sell near the top. But timing the cycles isn't easy; and sometimes, when you think that a stock is near the bottom of a cycle, it may instead be in the middle of a long-term decline. Be careful.

(4) *Special situations* are cases where some special corporate development—a merger, change of control, reorganization, sale of property, etc.—seems likely to raise the value of a stock. This type of investment often has the advantage of being less affected by general stock market fluctuations than the types discussed above. But if the expected development doesn't occur, the market price of the stock is likely to suffer. Know the facts.

(5) *Slow-growth* stocks: we can't resist including these, which many people don't regard as a separate category at all. If you are a conservative investor, there's nothing wrong with buying the stock of a company that may grow only as fast as the whole economy—perhaps 3 percent or 4 percent annually, over the long term—but where the growth is steady and reasonably assured, and where the company pays out acceptable dividends as it goes along (which you can spend or reinvest, as you prefer). Unlike a bond, such a stock should give you some long-run protection against inflation. In today's fast-changing economy, it's not easy to find companies where you can be assured of steady growth. Before it was broken up in 1984, AT&T used to be thought of as the prime example of such a stock; some of the regional telephone companies will probably continue to give investors the same attraction in the future. Retail stores and other consumer-oriented companies are often looked upon as candidates for this kind of investment. Banks and electric utilities used to be consid-

ered fine "slow but steady" investments, but both groups have developed special problems that have tarnished their image.

Some Other Indicators

So far we have talked mainly about *corporate earnings* as the measure of value of a company and its stock. There are many other factors to consider. Let us briefly mention a few of the most important:

Dividends: When a company is growing rapidly, it usually has to plow most of its earnings back into the business. As the company grows and matures, it can afford then to pay out part of its earnings to its owners, the shareholders. These payments are *dividends.* Where dividends are sizable, they should have a stabilizing effect on the stock price. (Examples: Exxon, General Telephone, etc.) But remember that a large dividend is usually a sign of slower growth.

More on earnings: An analyst looks not only at the company's current earnings, but at the earnings *history*—the long-term trend. The same is true for dividends, and also for the company's sales or revenues.

Book value: The book value of a stock relates to the value of the company as an accountant sees it. You start with one of the company's critical financial statements, its balance sheet (always found in the company's Annual Report—see Chapter 13). You add up the values of the company's "assets"—what it owns—which may include plants, land, inventories, cash, etc. From this total you subtract the company's "liabilities"—what it owes to others—primarily short- and long-term debts. The balance remaining after this subtraction is the company's "net worth"—that part of a company's value which actually belongs to the owners. If there is only one class of stock, you merely divide by the number of shares outstanding to get the "book value per share"—the net worth behind each share, as stated on the balance sheet.

Asset value: Asset value is often used as a synonym for

book value. But it sometimes has a different meaning. Book values can be misleading. On a company's balance sheet, its properties are usually valued in relation to their *original cost.* The company might have bought land many years ago for $1 million which now has a market value of $10 million; on the balance sheet, it would probably still be shown at $1 million. In such cases, a good security analyst makes adjustments to book value to arrive at what he or she thinks is the true "asset value" or "appraised value" of the company and of the stock. You will often see these estimates in research reports on oil companies and on other companies owning large natural resources. These values are particularly important if the company is about to be sold or liquidated, but in any case they are likely to give some clue as to the long-run possibilities of a stock.

Other balance sheet items: The balance sheet tells a great deal about a company. In particular, it tells you about a company's debts, and whether the company's long-term debt is heavy compared to the value of the common stock. It shows whether the company has enough cash to operate comfortably. It tells whether there is more than one class of common stock, and whether there is any *preferred* stock that may have a claim on dividends (and on the company's assets) ahead of the common stock.

Technical factors: All the above items—earnings, dividends, book value, etc.—have to do with the real value of the company that underlies the stock. But analysts also look at "technical" factors which involve only the *market behavior of the stock* and of the stock market as a whole. Basically, this involves an attempt to forecast where the price of a stock is going by looking at where it has been. A whole school of "chartists" use as their primary raw material not the financial statements of the corporations, but innumerable charts showing the past patterns of individual stock prices and of the market as a whole. Whether you can make investment decisions based merely on "technical" factors, as some chartists maintain, is a matter of debate. But it's true that a picture can be worth a thousand words, and that you can understand the background of a company and a stock much better with a chart than without it.

Where You Stand

At this point, how much do you know about security analysis? In truth, not very much. But you may be able to talk more intelligently with your broker or adviser; and if you are a mutual fund shareholder, you may have a better understanding of what the fund management is telling you in its reports.

Hopefully, you will have been stimulated to read more and learn more. We've stressed the difficulty of competing with the professionals. But there are all sorts of smaller companies that the professionals don't study carefully, and some larger companies that they neglect as well.

The professionals now have access to computer services that put the business and earnings trends of thousands of companies at their fingertips. But all those computer printouts are based on past trends. They don't tell when the unexpected may happen, or when a trend may change. In security analysis, nothing has yet replaced independent, original thought.

13 · SOURCES OF INFORMATION

If you want to study the art of investing, the supply of available information is overwhelming. With critical decisions to be made every day regarding billions of dollars, investment managers spend vast amounts for the best information available, and a whole industry has developed to supply research data and opinions on every conceivable type of investment.

For general books on the subject, try your local library or bookstore. You might also write to the New York Stock Exchange, Publications Department (11 Wall Street, New York, NY 10005), and ask for a price list of their publications for individual investors.

We pointed out earlier that it may be worth paying higher commissions to a full-service broker (as compared with a discount broker) in return for investment advice. A full-service broker will also provide all sorts of research material. He or she should be able to offer you the studies of individual companies and industries prepared by the firm's research department and also statistical and research material compiled by the industry's two leading statistical and news sources, Moody's and Standard & Poor's.

Moody's and Standard & Poor's both publish encyclopedia-like manuals that include histories and descriptions of thousands of companies, and reams of statistics. There are daily or weekly updates to keep the information completely current. If you want a quick picture of a company, both services publish individual pages on all major companies providing condensed information. These not only offer a surprising amount of data, but also give a clue as to what the experts regard as the most important facts—the two pages (front and back) function like a short course in security analysis essentials. If you don't have access to these through a broker, try your library. (If you can get access to a local business school library, all the better.)

For information on individual companies, one of the best sources is the company itself. If you don't have easy access to a company's report through a library or broker, find the company address in the library and write to the office of the secretary. Ask for the latest annual and quarterly reports to stockholders. Almost all companies will oblige.

Don't neglect the information to be found on the newsstands. *Forbes* magazine (twice monthly) makes good reading, and *Barron's* weekly is another good source of articles. *Money* magazine carries many articles on investments, and you will also find interesting articles in business magazines that are less oriented toward investments, such as *Business Week* and *Fortune*.

There's one source we haven't mentioned. What about those "hot tip" investment ideas that almost all of us have gotten at some time from friends and relatives? If you think that your friends or relatives are a step ahead of the professionals, perhaps you should take their advice. It's always possible that you know someone who is knowledgeable about a particular industry or a particular company. But investment selection generally involves great care and hard work. There's little room for miracles.

14 · HOW TO READ THE NEWSPAPER QUOTATIONS

One valuable source of information that wasn't mentioned in the last chapter is the daily newspaper tables of stock prices and related data. These tables provide complete reports on the previous day's trading on the New York Stock Exchange and other leading exchanges. They can also give you a surprising amount of extra information.

Some newspapers provide more extensive tables, some less. Since the *Wall Street Journal* (WSJ) is available nationwide, it may provide the most convenient examples. You'll find a prominent page headed "New York Stock Exchange Composite Transactions." This table covers the day's trading for all stocks listed on the NYSE. "Composite" means that it also includes trades in those same stocks on other exchanges (Pacific, Philadelphia, etc.) where the stocks may be "dually listed." The entries look like this:

52 Weeks High	Low	Stock	Div.	Yld %	P-E Ratio	Sales 100s	High	Low	Close	Net Chg.
104¼	52⅜	EKodk	2.52	2.5	26	8878	100½	98⅝	100⅜	+1⅜
39¼	28¾	PSvNM	2.92	10.2	10	1690	29⅜	d28¼	28½	− ⅞
84¼	58¾	ScottP	1.36	1.6	16	998	83⅞	83	83½	...

You may find the abbreviated names puzzling at first, but you will get used to them. The three above are Eastman Kodak, Public Service Co. of New Mexico (a utility), and Scott Paper. The lines are excerpted from the *Wall Street Journal* of September 1, 1987, and the trading reported is that of August 31, 1987, the previous day.

First, let's look at the columns that actually report on trading. Near the center of the table you will see a column headed "Sales 100s." Stock trading generally takes place in units of 100 shares and is tabulated that way; the figures mean, for example, that 887,800 shares of Eastman Kodak traded on August 31. The next three columns show the highest price for the day, the lowest, and the last or "closing" price. The "Net Chg." (net change) column to the far right shows how the closing price differed from the previous day's close.

Prices are traditionally calibrated in eighths of a dollar. In case you aren't familiar with the equivalents, they are:

$$⅛ = \$.125$$
$$¼ = \$.25$$
$$⅜ = \$.375$$
$$½ = \$.50$$
$$⅝ = \$.625$$
$$¾ = \$.75$$
$$⅞ = \$.875$$

Kodak traded on August 31 at a high of $100.50 per share and a low of $98.625; it closed at $100.375, a gain of $1.375 from the day before. Public Service of New Mexico lost on the day, while Scott Paper was unchanged. Public Service of New Mexico traded at a low of $28.25 and earned a "d" notation because this was a new low for the past 12 months (a new high would have earned a "u").

The two columns to the far left show the high and low prices recorded in the latest 52 weeks (not including the latest day, in this case August 31). It is worth noting that on August 31, Public Service of New Mexico was at the bottom of its "price range" for the last year, while the other two stocks were nearer their tops (individual stock price charts would show these trends in detail).

The other three columns give you data of use in making judgments about the stocks. Just to the right of the name, the "Div." (dividend) column shows the current annual dividend rate on the stock or, if there's no clear rate, then usually the actual dividend total for the latest 12 months. The dividend rates shown here are $2.52 annually for Kodak, $2.92 for Public Service of New Mexico, and $1.36 for Scott. (Most companies pay dividends quarterly: it's actually $0.63 quarterly for Kodak, etc.) The "Yld.%"

column relates the dividend to the latest stock price. In the case of Scott, $1.36 (annual dividend) / $83.50 (stock price) = 1.6 percent, which represents the current yield on the stock.

And finally, we have our old friend, the P/E Ratio (see Chapter 12). These are based on the earnings reported for the latest 12 months, rounded to the nearest whole number. In the table, it's 26 for Kodak, 10 for Public Service of New Mexico, and 16 for Scott. Here's another lesson in security analysis: Kodak was selling at a relatively high ratio to earnings because it commands a premium as a leading high-technology company. The multiple for Scott was moderate, while Public Service of New Mexico sold at a relatively low multiple by 1987 standards, denoting a stock at least temporarily out of favor.

What else will you find in the financial tables? Too many statistics to list all of them, but we'll mention a few.

Somewhere near the main NYSE table, you'll find small tables showing the 15 stocks that traded the greatest number of shares for the day (the "most active" list), and the stocks that showed the greatest percentage price gains and declines.

You'll find a large table of "American Stock Exchange Composite Transactions," which does for stocks listed on the AMEX just what the NYSE-Composite Transactions table does for NYSE-listed issues. There are smaller tables covering the Pacific Stock Exchange and other regional and Canadian exchanges.

There are large tables showing trading in the over-the-counter markets. For the major over-the-counter stocks, actual sales are reported and tabulated just as for stocks on the NYSE and AMEX. For less active over-the-counter stocks, the paper may only list "bid" and "asked" prices. The "bid" price is the price that dealers were willing to pay to *buy* the given stock at the close of trading on that day; the "asked" price is the price at which they were willing to *sell.* Unlike actual trading results, the bid and asked prices sometimes turn out to be only approximations when you actually go to buy and sell.

A table that may be very important to you is that showing mutual fund prices. Here "NAV" stands for net asset value, or the underlying value of each share as calculated at the close of the day. The NAV is determined by totaling the market values of the fund's securities (stocks and bonds), subtracting any liabilities (such as fees and other expenses owed by the fund), and dividing the balance by the number of shares outstanding. The result is the "net asset value per share" (NAV). The NAV is also the price at which most funds would have *redeemed* (bought back) shares on that day from investors who wished to sell. "Offering price" is the price at which shares could have been *bought* by investors on that day. For a no-load fund, the offering price is the same as NAV; for a load fund, it's NAV plus a commission. (For more on mutual fund pricing, see the No Nonsense Financial Guide, *Understanding Mutual Funds.*)

There are other tables that don't have to do with common stocks, strictly speaking. There are tables listing prices of bonds, options, commodities, etc. No matter how unfamiliar any of these tables may seem to you, you can be sure of one thing: somewhere out there are hundreds of traders for whom that table is the news of the day.

15 · STOCK MARKET AVERAGES

We haven't yet mentioned the most famous figures in the newspaper. We mean the stock market averages.

Everyone has probably heard the question, "How's the market?" and the answer, "Up five dollars," or "Down a dollar." With 1500 common stocks listed on the NYSE, there has to be some easy way to express the price trend of the day. Market averages, or indexes, are a way of summarizing that information.

Despite all competition, the popularity crown still goes to an average that has some of the qualities of an antique—the Dow Jones Industrial Average, an average of thirty prominent stocks dating back to the 1890s. This average is named for Charles Dow—one of the earliest stock market theorists, and a founder of Dow Jones & Company, a leading financial news service and publisher of the *Wall Street Journal.*

In the days before computers, an average of thirty stocks was perhaps as much as anyone could calculate on a practical basis at intervals throughout the day. Now, the Standard & Poor's 500 Stock Index (500 leading stocks) and the New York Stock Exchange Composite Index (all stocks on the NYSE) provide a much more accurate picture of the total market. But old habits die slowly, and when someone calls out, "How's the market?" and someone else answers, "Up five dollars," or "up five"—it's still the Dow Jones Industrial Average (the "Dow" for short) that they're talking about.

The importance of daily changes in the averages will be clearer if you view them in percentage terms. When the market is not changing rapidly, the normal daily change is less than half of 1 percent. A change of half of 1 percent is still moderate; 1 percent is large but not extraordinary; 2

What % Changes Would Have Meant in Points

	Value 6-30-87	¼%	½%	1%	2%
Dow Jones Industrial Average	2418.53	6.05	12.09	24.19	48.37
Standard & Poor's "500"	304.00	0.76	1.52	3.04	6.08
NYSE Composite Index	171.07	0.43	0.86	1.71	3.42

percent is dramatic. The table above shows the values of the leading averages on June 30, 1987, and how changes of these magnitudes would have looked in points.

As you study the financial pages, you'll note that there are also indexes of utility stocks, transportation stocks, and others. They all have their uses; but for your general understanding of the market, they're far less important.

What's important is that when someone asks, "How's the market?"—now you know how to answer.

16 · MORE TECHNICAL POINTERS

In the last few chapters we have given you information on many technical points. Here, in no particular order, are some other things you may want to know.

Placing orders: When you place an order with a broker to buy or sell a stock, you have certain choices. You can buy or sell "at the market," which means at the best price the broker can get for you at that time. Or you can place a "limit" order, under which you buy only if the price dips to a specified level, or sell only if it rises to a specified level. If you place a limit order, it can be for that day only or else "open" or "good till cancelled," which means that the order stays on the books until it is executed or until you cancel it.

Cash and margin: You can buy securities for cash, which means that you pay in full, or on margin, which means that the brokerage firm lends you a certain percentage of the price—up to 50 percent, as the limits set by the Federal Reserve stood in 1987. By borrowing 50 percent, the margin arrangement lets you buy twice as many shares of a stock with a given amount of cash. This means that you can make twice as much or lose twice as much. Since you pay interest on the money borrowed, you have to expect enough profit to offset the borrowing cost. On any type of purchase, your money is due at the brokerage firm five business days after the "trade date."

Odd lots: We stated earlier that stocks normally trade in units of 100 shares. These are called "round lots." There are also arrangements that let you buy "odd lots" of 1 to 99 shares. In some cases you may pay a premium of one-eighth point over the current round-lot price, and in any case you should remember that commissions are likely to take a higher percentage on small transactions.

Long and short: You are "long" a security when you own it. "Selling short" means that you borrow a security and sell it, in the hope that you can later buy it back more cheaply and repay the loan. It's a way of betting that a price will go down, and it's for very experienced investors only.

Options and Futures: An *option* is a piece of paper that gives you the right to buy or sell a given security at a specified price for a specified period of time. A *call* is an option to buy, a *put* is an option to sell. In simplest form, these are a high-risk way to speculate on the expectation that the price of a stock will go up or down. The most popular options are now those on the various stock market indexes ("index options"), which make it easy to speculate on the direction of the whole market rather than on individual stocks. *Financial futures* offer another way of speculating on future price trends. Futures based on the stock market indexes ("index futures") are now traded in tremendous volume. Other types of financial futures include futures on foreign currencies, and "interest rate futures," which are based mainly on the prices of U.S. Treasury securities, and which let you speculate on the future direction of interest rates. Generally, options and futures are highly speculative instruments which are intended for use mainly by professionals and other expert investors. However, many trading and investment techniques used by the experts now involve the use of options and futures, and some of these techniques are designed to reduce risks rather than for speculation. (For more information on options and futures, see the No Nonsense Financial Guide, *Understanding Stock Options and Futures Markets.*)

Rights and warrants: When a company itself issues an option to buy its stock (or other securities), different terms are used. A *right* gives you the option of buying a stock or other security at a specified price for a relatively short period (as when a company is marketing additional shares to raise capital). A *warrant* gives you a similar option for a longer period, sometimes without limit. If you don't wish to use ("exercise") a right or warrant, you can usually sell it to someone else.

Convertible securities: a convertible bond (or convertible debenture) is a corporate bond that can be converted into the company's stock under certain terms. A convertible preferred stock carries a similar "conversion privilege." These securities are intended to provide the advantages of common stock ownership with more protection against possible risks.

Stock splits: To put it simply, stock splits mean very little, and people care less about them than they used to. Assume that a company has ten million shares of stock outstanding, selling at around $100 per share, and it thinks that the stock might have better trading markets at the more modest price of $50 per share. The company splits the stock 2-for-1. Now there are twenty million shares outstanding, each old share has been transformed into two new shares, and the stock is trading around 50. Earnings per share have automatically been cut in half, and the price-earnings ratio remains the same. No one is really any better or worse off. But the split is usually taken as a signal from management that the company is doing well, and the price of the stock may rise from 50 to 52 or 55 out of market enthusiasm. In addition, the stock split may be accompanied by a dividend increase—instead of the dividend rate per share being cut by 50 percent, the board of directors may set it higher.

Bulls and Bears: A *bull* is an investor who expects the market (or a particular stock) to go up; a *bear* is one who expects it to go down. The phrases originated long ago and probably refer to the way each animal fights. A bull lowers its head and tosses its enemy up in the air, while a bear rakes downward on its foe with its claws. A *bull market* is one that is going up, and a *bear market* is one that is going down. This book is generally *bullish* on common stocks, just as a well-known brokerage firm proclaims itself to be *bullish* on America.

17 · COMMON STOCKS AND TAXES

The Tax Reform Act of 1986 eliminated some of the tax breaks that previously favored common stock investors. But there is still a tax advantage when you invest in common stocks for the long term. This chapter will very briefly describe the taxes you pay as a common stock investor.

Taxes on Dividends

When a corporation pays dividends to its shareholders out of earnings, those dividends are generally taxable as ordinary income, at full rates. The 1986 law did away with an "exclusion" that previously made the first $100 of dividends (or $200 for marrieds filing jointly) completely free from tax. But the law also reduced income tax rates across the board, so that most investors now pay lower rates of federal income tax on their dividends than they did before. For the person who invests primarily for income, the lower tax rates are generally a boon. (For more information on the Tax Reform Act of 1986, see the No Nonsense Financial Guide, *The New Tax Law and What It Means to You.*)

Taxes on Capital Gains

However, the 1986 law was far less kind to capital gains. In a sweeping change, the law completely eliminated the traditional favored treatment of long-term capital gains. Beginning with the 1988 tax year, long-term capital gains are taxed at exactly the same rates as other types of income.

A capital gain (or loss) is the profit (or loss) you make when you sell a security or other asset above or below your cost. Prior to 1988, investors had to be concerned about the difference between *long-term* gains or losses (on assets owned for longer than six months) and *short-term* gains or losses (on assets owned for six months or less). Now, from an investor's standpoint, the distinctions between long-term capital gains, short-term capital gains, and dividend income have lost much of their importance.

The Remaining Tax Advantage

There is still one significant tax advantage for the investor who buys and holds common stocks for long-term growth. It's this: When a stock you own goes up in value, you pay no tax on the increase until you sell the stock. That may sound obvious, but remember the comparison with a savings account, where even if you plow back the interest and let it accumulate, you must pay income tax on the interest every year. A stock that you have held for a number of years may have increased in value several times, and may be paying dividends several times as high as when you bought it—there's still no tax on the increase in value until you sell, although you do pay ordinary income tax each year on the dividends.

A true "growth" company is likely to pay out relatively small dividends, and to plow back most of its earnings into the expansion of the company. So a stock of this type, if you are successful in finding it, becomes a sort of built-in tax shelter, giving you a buildup of value with relatively little tax to pay until the time that you sell.

How important can this advantage be? Assume that you put $1,000 into a savings account or other fixed-income investment paying 10 percent annually, with taxes payable every year on the interest. And assume that at the same time you invest $1,000 in a growth stock that pays no dividends but that gains 10 percent in value every year. If you sold the stock at the end of the period and paid tax on the capital gain, here's how your money would have grown in each case after payment of taxes, assuming that you were in either the 28 percent or 33 percent federal tax bracket:

	Value of Investment			
	28% bracket		33% bracket	
Years	Fixed Income	Common Stock	Fixed Income	Common Stock
1	$1,072	$1,072	$1,067	$1,067
5	1,416	1,440	1,383	1,409
10	2,004	2,147	1,913	2,068
15	2,837	3,288	2,645	3,129
20	4,017	5,124	3,658	4,837

The differences may not be monumental, but they are big enough to be worth thinking about.

18 · WHEN TO BEGIN

Let's say that you have decided to become a common stock investor. Does it matter when you begin?

Remember, common stock prices tend to move in broad cycles. Sometimes the cycles seem to average about four years in length, but you can't be sure how any particular cycle will behave. Obviously, if you could pick one point at which to invest in common stocks (or common stock mutual funds), it would be best to invest when prices are at a low point rather than a high point in the cycle.

Unfortunately, predicting market movements is difficult even for professionals. Only rarely are the price fluctuations so extreme that you can be sure you are near a bottom or a top. We can't give you any magic passwords in this area.

Handling Price Fluctuations

However, we can warn you against certain common mistakes. Many amateur investors react to the usual fluctuations of the stock market in exactly the wrong way. They tend to buy stocks toward the end of a long rise, when people have begun to get overenthusiastic; and they panic and sell near the end of a decline, just when the market is close to turning up.

There are a few things you can do to guard against this. First, recognize that market movements are never certain, and distrust the person who tells you that the market is "bound to go up" or "bound to go down."

Second, try not to be caught up by market fads and crowd psychology. When prices have gone up sharply and everyone you know has become enthusiastic, be cautious. When prices have dropped sharply and everyone assures you that they will drop further, try to collect your courage enough to do some buying.

Third, consider spacing out your purchases on a regular schedule. Don't do your buying all at once. If you can invest a certain amount, for example, every three months over a period of years, you will probably do some buying when prices are high and some when prices are low, and you will end up with a reasonable cost average. Moreover, if you develop the habit of making regular purchases and stick to it over the years, you will have achieved the kind of long-run savings program that almost everyone intends to follow but which few people actually achieve.

19 · MANAGING YOUR PORTFOLIO

In Chapter 12 we talked about some of the factors security analysts consider in researching a company and recommending its stock. Security analysis tells you how to evaluate an individual security. *Portfolio management* is a related art that tells you how to manage the whole *collection* of securities you own (your *portfolio*) in such a way as to reduce risks and improve your total results.

Portfolio management addresses the risk problem. No matter how carefully you research and select any single stock, you are subject to the unexpected. So you need *diversification.* You should own enough stocks so that if one of them drops sharply in price, the change in value of your total portfolio won't be a disaster. If you can't afford to buy at least six or eight different stocks, you should consider investing through mutual funds, at least until your portfolio has grown. (Note also that if you invest less than $2,000 or so per stock, the commission costs will be very high in percentage terms.)

Diversification takes some thought. Remember that you are trying to spread your risks. Eight different stocks, all in the same industry, won't do the trick. Make sure that your choice includes some real variety.

Managing your portfolio means that you need to *review* your stocks regularly. Business conditions change, market conditions change, and prices change. The most common failing of investors is to hold investments long after the original reason for buying them has weakened or disappeared. When you review, the question you should ask about every security is: Would you buy it today, at today's price? If not, you should probably consider selling the security and replacing it with one that looks like better value today.

Your review will be helped if you set a specific *price objective* for each stock that you buy. Write it down. The market won't follow your forecasts, but comparing the market price regularly with your objective will help you see whether the investment is really developing as you expected. If not, think carefully about whether you may have made a mistake.

Don't be afraid to *take losses*—to sell a stock for less than you paid for it. Accept the fact that you, like all investors, will sometimes make mistakes. If a stock goes down by more than 5 percent after you buy it, think doubly hard whether your original reasoning was correct, and whether you are still comfortable owning the stock. The successful long-term investor is the one who catches his or her mistakes early and keeps the losses small. If you have diversified your stocks as we suggest, a small loss in one or two of them won't be devastating.

You should also not be afraid to *take profits* when your investment judgment tells you that a stock should be sold. Some people hesitate to sell a stock and pay tax on the profit. Beware of anything that makes you hold a stock when you're no longer convinced that it's a good investment at the current price.

Keep clear enough records so that you can *compare your performance* with the market averages at the end of the year. If your money has grown less (or shrunk more) than the averages call for, go carefully. If this happens for two years in a row, perhaps you should be investing through a mutual fund instead. In any case, invest carefully and moderately until you (or your broker) establish a track record that justifies taking greater risks.

20 · COMMON STOCKS FOR YOUR IRA OR KEOGH

There's a way for your common stock investments to grow even faster than ordinarily possible. In an IRA (Individual Retirement Account) or Keogh plan (self-employed retirement plan), your retirement dollars *earn and compound tax-free* until withdrawn. There are no taxes to pay as you go along. To be technical, the taxes aren't eliminated—they're *deferred.* But over many years, this deferral can be tremendously helpful in making your money grow.

An additional attraction is the tax deduction you may get on amounts contributed to your plan. Contributions to a Keogh plan are fully tax-deductible. Contributions to an IRA, as explained below, may or may not be tax-deductible, depending on your circumstances.

IRAs have become immensely popular with the American taxpayer, and for good reason. Prior to 1982, IRAs were only for persons who were not covered under any other retirement plan. Beginning in 1982, IRAs were opened to everyone who works for a living, whether covered by another retirement plan or not. The IRA became, in effect, a *tax shelter for everyone.* The law permitted anyone with *earned income* to deposit up to $2,000 a year (or up to the amount of earned income, whichever is less) into a tax-sheltered IRA and to take an income tax deduction for the amount set aside.

IRAs and the New Tax Law

The Tax Reform Act of 1986 preserved the basic structure of IRAs, but put restrictions on the tax deduction. Now, if you do *not* participate in any other retirement plan, you can still take the full tax deduction for your IRA contribution, whatever your income level. However, if you participate in any employer's retirement plan, or if you have your own Keogh plan, the situation changes: You can still put up to $2,000 in an IRA, but you can only take the tax deduction if your income is below certain specified levels.

Whether your IRA contribution is tax-deductible or not, there's no change in the rule that the money in an IRA *earns and compounds tax-free* until withdrawn. Over a period of 15 or 20 years or more, this tax-deferred accumulation can do more to build up your money than the original tax deduction. (For more information on IRAs, see the No Nonsense Financial Guide, *Understanding IRAs.*)

Keogh and IRA Opportunities

The rules regarding *self-employed retirement plans* were changed beginning in 1984 to allow substantially larger contributions. These plans have become more complicated, and should be discussed with your accountant or tax adviser. We won't go into the contribution limits in detail, but if you are self-employed or have extra income from self-employment, these plans generally permit you to contribute up to 20 percent of this income and take a tax deduction for the contribution. (For more information, see the No Nonsense Financial Guide, *How to Plan and Invest for Your Retirement.*)

What is important here is that common stocks can be an excellent investment for an IRA, Keogh, or retirement plan of any type. A retirement plan is a long-term investment program into which common stocks, or common stock mutual funds, fit almost perfectly. Over the long term, with no taxes to pay as you go along, the buildup of your money can be dramatic if your investments are well chosen.

Most mutual funds and brokerage firms have IRA plans which are simple to use and which meet all legal requirements. Most also offer Keogh plans. The choices available are very wide.

The fees charged by mutual funds for these plans are generally very low. The fees charged by brokerage firms are higher, and may seem disproportionate when you are starting your IRA or Keogh and it is still small. But a brokerage firm plan does permit your own choice of securities, if that is what you want. It's perfectly practical to start your plan with a common stock mutual fund and to switch to a brokerage firm after a few years, as the plan becomes larger.

In most investment programs, taxes take a big bite out of your total growth rate. Over many years, the results of *tax-free* growth can be impressive and even spectacular. Take the opportunity when you can.

21 · CONCLUSION

We have tried to give you two sides of a very important picture. We've talked considerably about the *risks* involved in buying and owning common stocks. An experienced investor wants to know the risk in any investment before starting out.

But look again at the chart on page 15. Risks are not the main story. The main story is the long-term *growth* that has been achieved by common stock investments over the years.

We've pointed out that common stocks let you participate in the growth and prosperity of corporations that form the backbone of the U.S. economy, and that many great (and small) American fortunes have been built through owning shares in these corporations.

Has the U.S. economy grown old and tired, as some people seem to think? Not according to the facts. In mid-1987 the economy was providing jobs for over 112 million people, compared with less than 100 million as recently as 1980. Some old industries have gone into declines, but new ones have sprung up to take their place. The U.S. still remains an envied model for the Western world.

Your Personal Equation

Common stocks let you participate in the growth of the world's leading economy. They are an investment that will grow and protect you against inflation. They have the potential of giving you a brighter financial future.

At this point it's up to you. We don't think you should miss this potential. We have shown you that there are ways of investing in common stocks to keep the risks moderate in relation to the possible rewards. With a little care and prudence, you can build an investment program for yourself aimed at greater long-term growth for your money.

Many factors may have kept you from previously investing in common stocks. You may have been told that common stocks were "too risky"—or you may have been told not to buy common stocks because we were in a recession, or because of inflation, or because of a dozen other economic problems. These problems are real. But somehow, despite the problems, the economy continues to grow, and well-managed corporations continue to expand and prosper.

You may have always kept your money in banks or money market funds, and the change to common stocks may seem like a large leap. But it doesn't have to be. Particularly with common stock mutual funds, you can start out with a small amount—$500 or even less—and gradually add to it as you go along. In all probability, the experience will give you confidence to do more. You can set your own pace.

Where should you look for security and safety? For today's needs, your money is safest in a bank or money market fund. But over the long run, your greatest security may come from investing in the growth of the American economy. Thousands of investors have found it that way in the past.

Consider common stocks. They could be the best investment for your future.

GLOSSARY

Adviser See Investment Adviser.

Asked Price (or *Asking Price*) The price at which a dealer offers to sell a security.

Automatic Reinvestment A plan by which income dividends and/or capital gains distributions are automatically applied to buy additional shares of a mutual fund or other security.

Balance Sheet The financial statement showing a company's assets, liabilities, and "net worth" (the net equity of its owners).

Bear See Chapter 16.

Bid Price The price at which a dealer offers to buy a security.

Bond A long-term debt security issued by a government or corporation promising repayment of a given amount by a given date, plus interest.

Book Value See Chapter 12.

Broker-Dealer See Brokerage Firm.

Brokerage Firm A term including several types of firms in the securities business that usually do business with the public.

Bull See Chapter 16.

Call An option to buy. See Chapter 16.

Capital Wealth invested or available for investment.

Capital Gain, Capital Loss The profit (loss) from sale of a security or other asset at a price above (below) its cost.

Common Stock A security representing a share of ownership in a corporation.

Common Stock Fund A mutual fund investing primarily in common stocks.

Convertible Bond See Chapter 5.

Corporate Bond A bond issued by a corporation. See Bond.

Corporation A legal entity whose owners, called stockholders or shareholders, enjoy limited liability.

Dealer A person or firm in the business of buying and selling securities. Specifically, a dealer acts as principal rather than agent, buying and selling for his/her own account (unlike a broker, who acts as agent for a client).

Debenture A type of corporate bond.

Diversification The practice of spreading investments over several different securities to reduce risk.

Dividend A share of earnings paid to a shareholder by a corporation.

Dividend Reinvestment See Automatic Reinvestment.

Individual Retirement Account (IRA) See Chapter 20.

Investment Adviser An individual or organization in the business of giving investment advice. Investment advisers must be registered with the SEC.

Investment Company A company in which many investors pool their money for investment. Mutual funds are the most popular type.

Liquid Investment An investment that can be converted easily into cash.

Listed Refers to a security listed for trading on an exchange.

Load The sales charge or commission charged on purchase of some mutual funds.

Money Market Fund A mutual fund that aims at maximum safety, liquidity, and (usually) a constant price for its shares. Its assets are invested to earn current market interest rates on the safest, short-term, highly liquid investments.

Municipal Bond A bond issued by a state or local government. The interest is usually exempt from federal income tax.

Mutual Fund An open-end investment company that pools the investments of many investors to provide them with professional management, diversification, and other advantages.

NASD The National Association of Securities Dealers, Inc. A broad industry organization, one of whose functions is to regulate over-the-counter trading.

Net Asset Value In a mutual fund, the market value of the securities and other assets underlying each share of the fund.

New Issues New securities offered to the public by corporations or governmental agencies to raise money (as distinct from sales of previously issued securities by their present owners).

No-Load Fund A mutual fund that sells its shares at net asset value, without any commission.

Open-End Investment Company A mutual fund. Technically called "open-end" because the fund stands ready to sell new shares to investors or to buy back shares submitted for redemption.

Portfolio The total list of investment securities owned by an individual or institution.

Portfolio Manager An individual who makes decisions regarding buying, selling, or holding securities for an investment organization.

Price-Earnings Ratio (or Price-Earnings Multiple) See Chapter 12.

Principal The capital or main body of an investment, as distinguished from the income earned on it.

Prospectus The official document describing a security being offered to the public and offering the security for sale. (Every mutual fund must have an annually updated prospectus.)

Put An option to sell. See Chapter 16.

Redemption The procedure by which a mutual fund buys back shares from shareholders on demand.

SEC The U.S. Securities and Exchange Commission. The federal agency charged with regulating the securities markets and the investment industry.

Security General term meaning stocks, bonds and other investment instruments.

Security Analyst See Chapter 12.

Stock A security representing an ownership interest in a corporation.

Stock Certificate See Chapter 5.

Tape The electronic screen or other device on which stock exchange transactions are shown in sequence as they occur (replacing the old-fashioned "stock ticker" which printed transactions on a paper tape).

Total Return   See Chapter 8.

Trade   (Verb) To buy or sell a security. (Noun) The purchase or sale.

Underwriter   An investment firm taking the responsibility of offering new securities to the public.

Unlisted   Refers to a security not listed on any exchange and therefore traded over-the-counter.

Warrant   See Chapter 16.

Yield   The return on an investment. In securities, the dividends or interest received, usually expressed as an annual percentage of either the current market value or the cost of the investment.

INDEX

ABOUT THE AUTHORS

ARNOLD CORRIGAN, noted financial expert, is the author of *How Your IRA Can Make You a Millionaire* and is a frequent guest on financial talk shows. A senior officer of a large New York investment advisory firm, he holds Bachelor's and Master's degrees in economics from Harvard and has written for *Barron's* and other financial publications.

PHYLLIS C. KAUFMAN, the originator of the *No Nonsense Guides*, is a Philadelphia attorney and theatrical producer. A graduate of Brandeis University, she was an editor of the law review at Temple University School of Law. She is listed in *Who's Who in American Law*, *Who's Who of American Women*, *Who's Who in Finance and Industry*, and *Foremost Women of the Twentieth Century*.

Prologue

I cannot remember the first time I heard his voice. It started quietly, a soft whisper in the back of my mind with an ominous message:

Avoid the step on the landing, or you will have an awful day.

You need to hold your breath for five seconds when you see unlucky number seven. Otherwise, bad luck will follow.

Then it started to bug me at school.

You need to write the letter so it is EXACTLY touching the lines in the notebook, or there will be trouble. There now, do it again. It must be EXACTLY touching the lines like so . . .

It followed me when I went to Taekwondo practice.

Every time you do a spinning kick on the left side, rotate around on the right side to balance things out.

Over time, the commands increased in menace and insistence.

If you step on any of the cracks on the floorboards between your room and the kitchen, something terrible will happen.

Do not eat foods with marks on them—they are POISONED!

Even bedtime did not offer an escape.

If you let Mom and Dad go downstairs at bedtime, when you wake up the whole world will turn into a rock of evil. Everything will be gone, and you will be the ONLY. SOLITARY. PERSON. LEFT. IN. EXISTENCE.

I call the voice "the Dictator," because I know it is not my voice, but an unwanted intruder in my head. An invisible bully. We learned in social studies that a dictator is an *authoritarian*, someone who wants to control others to make them do their will. Someone with unlimited governing power. That is what this is, an unwanted invader who has convinced me if I do not bow to his will, something horrible will happen to me, or my family.

Chapter 1

A CANCELLED PARTY

"Is it cancelled for real?" I ask. Normally, most kids would get upset if their birthday party was called off. I am secretly relieved.

"I'm so sorry, Louie." The corners of Mom's mouth turn down. I can tell she is disappointed for me. She has already planned the party, sent the invites, and organized all the goody bags lined up on the living room windowsill.

In the background, I can hear the soft tones of the radio. The newsreader announces there are over 47 million confirmed COVID cases around the world, and I understand.

I would rather not take my chances.

I watch Mom gather my books into my backpack. School is still on despite what they call a "global pandemic." This means everyone is experiencing this

new virus at the same time. Because it's so new, and because doctors don't have a cure yet, we have to try to avoid catching it.

This makes me nervous.

More nervous than usual.

I double check that at least two of my favourite masks, (the ones with the shark teeth stretched across the mouth), are in my school bag. I glance over my shoulder and reach under my bed, pulling out the rubber gloves I have secretly stashed. I chuck those in as well.

In the shadows beneath the couch, I spot the Dictator quivering.

He winks.

I check my bag again just to make sure my masks are still there.

"I'll message the moms to cancel. I *promise* the second these measures are lifted we will reschedule your party." Ten years and double digits, Mom insists, is a reason to celebrate. She rubs her hand reassuringly around my back and kisses me on the head. As I adjust my mask and head out the door, she reminds me to let my friends know the party is off this weekend.

I check my bag again to make sure my spare masks and gloves are still there, and then head outside into the poisoned air.

Chapter 2

AN UNEXPECTED MATH QUIZ

"OK, class," exclaims Mrs. Andrews, "you have five minutes to complete this test. Please keep your paper turned over until I tell you to start. Three, two, one, begin!"

I hate pop math quizzes. The timed ones are even worse. Normally, I get this kind of math; however, the Dictator has lately become especially distracting during tests. I have to keep re-reading the instructions to make sure I have understood things just right. This slows me down.

As I pick up my pencil, my heart is pounding and my palms are sweaty. I race to answer the first question and the pencil slips from my hand onto the floor. I lean over to pick it up and notice a piece of

old gum stuck to the bottom of the chair leg. It is so disgusting and germy. I wish I could reach into my backpack and put on my rubber gloves. Mrs. Andrews doesn't let me wear them in class, as we have to use hand sanitizer all the time anyway.

I start to feel filthy all over, like a stampede of invisible germs is running from the gum onto my arms. When I sit up, I vigorously rub my arms again and again to try to erase the infectious feeling. My best friend Sammy looks over and raises his eyebrows as he watches me. I shrug and quickly bow my head over my test.

"One minute down, class."

Forcing myself to put the gum out of my mind, I write my first answer in its box. I know it is the right answer, but something keeps telling me I need to rewrite it so the number is perfectly lined-up in the middle. I erase and rewrite my answer until it feels just right.

This happens four times.

The next question has loads of the number sevens in it. I groan. The unlucky number! Every time I see a seven, I have to hold my breath for five seconds. I stare at the second hand on the clock above my teacher's desk. Thirty-five seconds later, I feel like I'm going to burst and exhale loudly. Mrs. Andrews looks up sharply. I can tell she is getting cross.

"Three minutes left, class."

Three minutes left and I've only answered two questions! I start to panic. Furiously I tackle the next problem. I know the answer, but the Dictator is unrelenting and I have to re-read the question several times just to be sure. By the time I fill in the box, Mrs. Andrews calls time.

"Pencils down, class."

I feel a lump in my throat. Only three out of ten questions answered. I've failed my test without even getting the chance to complete it! I know the answers, but a malignant force stops me from writing them down on time.

I'm so scared Mom and Dad will find out.

You are going to be in so much trouble.

If you have ever lived through a terrible experience—like a hurricane, or a car crash, or the death of a family member—you will understand how scary the Dictator can be. Mom and Dad can't hear him, but I can—every hour of every day.

If I do not do exactly what he asks, the most terrible, horrible, awful thing in the world will happen. Imagine waking up and finding your world is gone. No Mom or Dad, no home, no pets, no friends. Just a grey, lifeless rock of evil.

This is what I worry about every day.

Chapter 3

KNIGHT OF THE BROKEN TABLE

As soon as I come home from school, I try to slip past Dad's home office unnoticed. Muting his teleconference, Dad calls out, "How was your day, Louie?"

"Fine!" I shout back, escaping to my room.

After holding back the need to perform some of my more vigorous compulsions at school, (after all, I don't want my friends to think I'm weird), this is my safe space to let everything out. Breathing in deeply, I carefully peel off my mask and gloves. Next, I fling my arms around in circles. Six times one way, then six times the opposite way, being particularly careful to avoid a seventh rotation.

I start to feel better.

Looking around my room, I notice my fortress is looking a little tilted. Like most of my friends, I like building blanket forts. I have a giant one in my room made out of a duvet cover patterned with stars. *My* fort, however, is a little different: I have garrisoned my room to keep me safe. I think of this as my war room. Here I am away from the virus and other things that worry me. Here the Dictator is less demanding. Here is where I can make my combat plans to take on the day.

My fort blanket stretches over my headboard and spans halfway across the room. It covers the back of my reading chair and my round bedside table. I have pinned the blanket's end in place with a large pile of books balanced on the table, next to a pilfered tin of biscuits. Beside my bed are my favorite weapons: my knight's mask, my wooden sword, and my moulded breastplate. (I admit these were once been part of an old Hallowe'en costume, but they serve me well now).

Resting on my reading chair is my favorite book: *The Illustrated Tales of King Arthur.* My armour looks just like the ones in the pictures of the knights in the book. When I wear it, I feel a little braver.

When Arthur was a boy, a great wizard named Merlin placed an enchanted sword in a stone declaring, "Whoever pulls the sword from this stone will be the rightful king of all Britain."

Imagine being an ordinary boy one day and then an all-powerful king the next! I love how fearless

Arthur and his warrior knights are. They go on epic adventures and always defeat their enemies. Arthur wasn't just brave, he was clever too. He made sure his knights did not fight one another by having them sit at a round table so no one could consider himself more important than the others. I haven't finished all the tales, but so far there is no evil in the world that can overcome Arthur!

Clutching my book, I put on my knight's helmet. It covers my entire head. I lower my visor, which leaves only slits open for my eyes. Next, I adjust my breastplate around my chest and grasp the hilt of my sword. With my armour in place, I start to relax.

Suddenly, I hear scratching at my door. Baily is asking to come into my room. He helps me to calm down by letting me stroke his velvety ears and rub his belly.

Baily is anxious like me. He had a hard start at life as a puppy abandoned in a garbage dump. We rescued him when he was a few months old, and because we can't have any friends over due to the virus, he's my best buddy these days.

I love reading stories to Baily. He is a first-rate listener. He especially loves hearing about King Arthur and his Knights of the Round Table. As I start to read, he places his head on my knee and wags his tail at the best bits—usually when King Arthur wins in battle.

I wish I could be like King Arthur. He commanded dragons and knights and was not afraid of any force of evil. Maybe I could fight the Dictator like King Arthur, I ponder. If the Dictator is a figment of my imagination, maybe I can use my imagination to destroy him!

Inspired by this idea, I stand up and unsheathe my sword. At first I feel a little silly, but then I have fun slashing at the Dictator.

"Now I have you in my power!" I shout as I jump onto my bed for the upper hand.

Jabbing with my sword, I launch a flying side kick off the bed, followed by another sword strike.

"Hah! Take that! I will *never* yield!" I bellow as I swoop through the air.

This is the precise moment when things go spectacularly wrong.

Because my helmet's visor blocks most of my vision, I can only see a small slit of the room in front of me, and nothing on either side of my face.

As I jump off my bed and swing my sword at the same time, I catch the blinds covering my window. I land and furiously pull back to launch another attack and my sword catches the slats of the blinds again, yanking the wooden curtain rod off the wall and causing it to crash onto the floor.

Frightened by the commotion, Baily leaps up from his basket. Spinning around to avoid the rod,

I accidentally trip over him. As I fall unseeing to my oblivion, my arms flail and I slam into my bookshelf, knocking over my vast collection of building block castles. I hear them collapse in an explosion of tiny bricks. As I pull myself up to stand, my bare foot rams onto one of the blocks. Shrieking in pain and bouncing up and down on the other foot, I accidentally step on Baily's paw. I hear him yelp as he sprints out of the room.

Wildly grasping to remove my helmet so I can finally see, I blindly hop around my room and crash into my bedside table. It collapses in a heap, catapulting old biscuits, my fort blanket, the pile of books, and a large glass of water onto the carpet.

When I finally fling my helmet off in frustration, it strikes the wall next to my bed and rolls miserably onto a pile of wrecked castles and soggy biscuits.

My breathing is ragged as I survey the catastrophe before me. The blanket fortress lies in a heap beneath the broken curtain rod. There are two holes in the wall where the rod's screws had supported the blinds. Building blocks and cookie crumbs are scattered everywhere on the carpet. Water seeps into the tumbled pile of books.

I screw my eyes shut.

Mom and Dad will be furious, I think.

You are going to be in so much TROUBLE, hisses the Dictator.

Chapter 4

FIFTY PUSH-UPS

People have stopped banging pots in their doorways at 7:00 p.m. to thank the healthcare workers battling the virus. The clamour was my signal that Mom would be home soon. Looking down at my watch, I hurriedly clean up my room before Mom arrives home from her shift at the hospital.

Tucking away my knight's costume under my bed with the rest of my treasures, I put on another warrior's uniform. This one is real: my Taekwondo *dobok*. After the first lockdown, the virus put a stop to in-person Taekwondo classes, but I continued online. Though virtual classes were not as much fun because I'm practicing in the basement without my friends, there was no way Mom and Dad were going to let me take a break, like some kids in my class.

Because Mom has been practicing Taekwondo for a long time, she is always going on about "indomitable spirit," "self-control," and "finishing what you've started." I can't tell you how many times she has cheerily repeated her favorite mantra, "You'll miss 100 percent of the shots you don't take, Louie."

Sometimes it drives me crazy.

Another reason I can't pause is because I'm a brown belt, one belt away from the ultimate prize: the coveted black belt. I've been training since I was four. I know from my coaches what a huge achievement this is because so much time, energy, and practice is involved. Secretly, I can't help but wonder if getting my black belt means I will no longer be under the Dictator's power. Like maybe this belt holds some mystic force to help me be a little less anxious.

As one of the youngest class members to get this far, I'm excited and nervous. If we didn't have the pandemic, I would have already been tested. My test is now only one month away and I need to *focus*.

Focus and self-control are two creeds of our practice, but the Dictator does his best to disrupt me.

This week, the academy announced it was going to re-open for in-person classes, so long as we stayed within our taped-off square in the *dojang* and wore our masks. I'm excited to go back because I hope to see some of my friends, and because we all have to wear masks, which is fine by me. Also, the counting

is in Korean, so I don't have to hear the unlucky number seven. For some reason, the Dictator is OK with the Korean seven.

"OK, class!" Master Yung, our instructor, cries out.

"*Chariyot!*"

Fifteen sets of hands slap the sides of their legs as we come to attention in perfect unison. This is the moment we have to stand perfectly still with our hands at our sides and our feet together. No shifting, no twitching, no wiggling—no movement at all is allowed at this moment.

Normally, I'm pretty good at this, but tonight something doesn't feel right.

You must adjust your mask now. Poisoned air is getting inside.

I try not to listen but start to feel a little panicked.

"*Kyung-nae* . . ."

Fifteen students bow low together before Master Yung. Distracted, my head bobs a few seconds behind.

"*Shee-jak!*"

Our master calls on us to begin our warm-up drills. I quickly turn my back and adjust my mask until if feels right. The class has already begun its series of drills by the time I turn around, so I know I need to hurry to catch up.

After we have finished our jumping jacks, push-ups, and sit ups, it is time to demonstrate our kicking combinations in our designated safety spot. One of

my favourites is the tornado kick, where you spin all the way around before jumping up and kicking your target.

We begin and I get lost in the moment as I execute ten tornado kicks to the right. Holding my breath for the seventh kick, I finish before the others. I catch my breath, feeling a little dizzy from all the spinning. To balance things out I start rotating counter-clockwise.

I *kihap* as loudly as I can through my mask, "Hiya!"

I picture myself striking the Dictator's head. "Yah!"

Another blow in my mind. "Hah!"

"Yah!"

Round and round I go, *kihap*-ing so enthusiastically I don't notice the rest of the class has stopped and I have rotated outside of my taped box towards the mirrors at the front of the class.

As my instructor approaches, I accidentally kick over the stationary target, which lands heavily on Master Yung's foot. There is a sharp curse in Korean, which snaps me out of my reverie.

The class is completely silent. Fifteen wide sets of eyes peer at me over their masks.

Master looks disapprovingly, standing with his arms crossed and his right eyebrow arched.

"Are you quite done, Louie?"

Embarrassed, I freeze and quickly remember to bow.

"Yes *sir*!"

"Remember, self-control is a hallmark of a true martial artist, Louie."

"Yes *sir*!"

"Fifty push-ups!" He points to the mats at the back of the class.

"*Yes sir!*"

I bow and head to the end of the mats. I'm not too upset. At least the other students have stopped staring and no one has asked me to remove my gloves, so I don't have to touch the mats with my hands. We have to do 100 push-ups for the black belt test anyway.

At least this counts towards test practice.

Chapter 5

A BIRTHDAY SURPRISE

I wake up early Saturday morning, the one that was supposed to be my birthday party. Everyone is still asleep, and Baily is snoring softly beside me.

Under my bed is a special box shaped like a small ancient treasure chest. Inside I keep a variety of precious items essential to keeping the Dictator at bay. One such charm is an amulet, a glassy turquoise eye my grandmother brought me from Greece I sometimes wear around my neck. It's supposed to protect me from the *evil eye* (Grandma can be a little superstitious). There are other special items, like geodes and sea glass, but those are mostly things I collect. They do not have special powers.

There is one particularly powerful charm I also keep in the box.

I reach under my mattress and retrieve my chest. Carefully opening the curved lid, I pull out my latest hidden treasure: my enchanted eraser. To anyone else, it's a normal rectangular white eraser any kid would have on their desk. Nothing of value. However, this one is special to me.

It helps me tell the future.

Like Merlin the Magician, this is my own crystal ball that gives me insight into important matters.

On one side of this eraser, I've written the word YES. On the other, NO. Every time I flip it in the air, I call out a question that requires an answer.

Will I grow up to be a soccer legend?

NO.

Will Baily live a long time?

YES.

Does Amy have a secret crush on me?

YES.

Ewww!

Will Mom and Dad buy me a python for my birthday?

NO.

Does Mom love me?

NO.

Does Mom love me?

NO.

Does Mom love me?

YES.

I do this over and over and over until I feel some relief.

I decide to quietly sneak downstairs to where Mom and Dad usually gather a pile of presents for my birthday. It's still too early to wake them, but maybe I can have a peek and count how many I have. Usually there is a bunch of balloons too . . .

As I approach the seventh stair on the landing, I know I have to make a difficult jump quietly so I don't hit the squeaky spot and wake everyone up. For a terrible moment, I find it hard to move.

If you don't make this jump, you'll have an awful birthday.

I clamp my eyes shut and try to ignore him.

I'm so busy concentrating, I don't hear Baily padding up behind me, waiting to pass the narrow landing to be let out to pee. His cold wet nose touches the back of my knee and I let out a yelp as my leg buckles. As I lose my balance, I pitch forward and tumble into a heap on the landing.

In a flash I jump up and gasp, as if I'd just fallen in a pool of molten lava. Panicked, I jump from the landing over the final four steps onto the basement floor. The stone stings my bare feet and I wince.

Baily observes me in amusement. His head tilts with curiosity as he tries to understand my agitation. His floppy tongue hangs from his mouth and his tail wags around in giant circles, because it's far too long to wag sideways like a normal dog's.

Silly boy, he seems to be thinking.

I let Baily out, then head to the back room to peek at my presents.

There's nothing there.

Nothing.

No balloons.

No cheerfully wrapped packages with coloured ribbons Mom has carefully adorned, but that only slow down the unwrapping process.

Nothing.

This is the *worst* birthday ever.

Did Mom forget? Dad might, but Mom? Never!

Did they find out about the failed math test?

I told you if you didn't follow my instructions about jumping the step on the landing you would have an awful day.

I swat at my forehead in frustration. Go away! I think. Tears begin to sting my eyes.

Baily begins scratching at the door to be let in. Disappointed, I turn to open it. Baily's scratches become more urgent; something seems to be bothering him.

I open the door fully and encounter an enormous and unexpected surprise: a large trampoline has been set up at the end of the garden!

I dash down the lawn barefoot to test it out.

Bounce, screech, bounce, screech, bounce screech . . . up and down I go, higher and higher

with my face tilted to the sky. I forget I'm not wearing a mask in the moist morning air.

"Happy birthday, Louie!"

I turn to the chorus of Mom and Dad's voices. They are huddled at the back door in their robes, laughing.

"Now come inside and have pancakes before you wake all the neighbours with your bouncing, you silly goose!"

It looks like the Dictator was wrong about my day after all.

Chapter 6

THE POISONED PEAR

Breakfast is the hardest meal of the day. Mom is usually in a rush to get ready for work, and this morning is no exception. Plus, the Dictator has really slowed me down today. Mom's job is *really important* right now. She reminds me of this often when I'm too slow to get ready. She works in healthcare and her team has to help the homeless find places to safely lock down or self-isolate to prevent the spread of the virus and stay safe and warm.

Today is particularly pressing, as she needs to meet others to inspect some buildings in the community that they plan to convert into homeless shelters. Ice rinks, churches, and old hotels are all being considered. Mom keeps reminding me it is *crucial* she be on time and that she is very lucky to have a job when so many people have lost theirs.

When she keeps saying it's *crucial*, I know she means it's *very important*.

Mom has been going into work later than usual this week, and it's my fault. She doesn't realize that lately the Dictator has insisted I must follow even more rituals to keep her safe from the virus.

"Are you dancing, buddy?" she asks. I look up hastily. I've been tiptoeing and bouncing between the floorboards to avoid the cracks from my bedroom to the dining room. For some reason it's taking me longer than usual. The Dictator's power has grown, and the path from my room to the table is becoming more complicated.

"Remember, sweetheart, Dad's on another search and rescue call-out, so we have to get out the door a little earlier today so I can drop you off to school and get to work on time. It's *crucial* I'm on time."

The emphasis on the time makes my heart pound. I look at my watch and my chest squeezes. It's the bad number again: 7:07. I freeze and hold my breath for as long as I can until the second hand makes its way around past the unlucky minute. I exhale with relief when it turns over to 7:08.

Mom quickly passes me my breakfast while taking a call. It used to be my favourite meal: peanut butter waffles and sliced pears. Don't get me wrong, I love waffles, it's the fruit that's been bothering me lately- and breakfast is when I get served the most fruit.

I used to love fruit, especially crunchy green pears. Now when I look at the pear I can't help but notice the spots, the brown imperfections on the skin—they gross me out and make me think they are poisoned.

I look down at my plate. The pear slices have marks on the skin. They are also touching the waffles, which means I can't eat those, as they too have been infected with poison. I can see the Dictator's shadow sliding across my breakfast, seeping poison into my food. He grimaces. I push the plate away.

"Louie, ten more minutes, love. I need you to finish your meal and be dressed. I cannot be late today."

Five minutes later, she walks over to the table.

"Louie, why haven't you eaten yet? This is your favourite!"

"Because it's poisoned," I explain.

Mom breathes in sharply.

"It's not poisoned, love. Please, just eat your waffles," she pleads. "I have to be out the door in five minutes." I can hear the panic in her voice.

I refuse.

"Just eat *something*!" She picks up a waffle and guides it to my mouth. I swat it away and it lands on the floor.

"Louie, what's wrong? Why won't you eat?" she asks hysterically.

I explode in frustration.

"It's because it's poisoned! It's because you *poisoned* my pear!"

I don't know why I said that.

Stunned, we stare at each other. Mom's eyes are wide with shock. As she turns away, I notice her face crumple in a silent sob.

NOW YOU'VE DONE IT.

***

Later that evening, as Mom tucks me into bed, she gently touches a red mark on my forehead and asks me about it. I ignore the question and ask,

"Mom, when you had to have the operation two years ago, did you feel anything?"

"No, sweetie, they put to me sleep using anesthesia. I wasn't aware of anything and I woke up feeling fine. Why do you ask?"

"Do you think you could ask those doctors to put me to sleep and drill into my head?"

Mom looks at me quizzically.

"I want them to drill a hole in my head and take the Dictator out. He's always there, every moment of the day." My lips start to tremble and my eyes sting. "I don't know what to do," I whisper.

Mom kisses the tender spot on my forehead. "Louie, is this why your forehead is red?"

I tell Mom I smacked my head a few times to try to knock the Dictator out in the hopes it would stop the bad thoughts from always coming. I just don't know if this is me anymore and it makes me so afraid.

"Oh, honey!" she sighs, wrapping her arms around me and kissing me again. "How exhausting and scary this must be for you. I want you to know those thoughts are not you, no matter how bad or scary you think they are. We are going to get help to figure this out. You are so brave. Dad and I don't quite understand what is happening, but I promise we are going to get you help and we are going to stand beside you, whatever this journey looks like."

Mom tells me about all the crazy thoughts that pop into her head when she's mad, sad, or tired, and we giggle.

She holds me close and sings me my favourite bedtime song until I nod off.

As I fall asleep, I can hear Mom and Dad's worried whispers on the other side of the wall and know they are talking about me.

Maybe Mom and Dad will leave you tonight because they are upset with you. You have caused so much trouble lately. Just wait and see. You will wake up to a world with no one there.

The Dictator's unwelcome message is the last thing I hear before falling into a troubled sleep.

Chapter 7

THE MIND WIZARD

"**W**e have wonderful news for you, Louie!" Mom and Dad chatter excitedly. "You know how you wished for an operation to take the Dictator out of your head? Well, we found a mind wizard who helps children experiencing similar things to you. He is an expert who can teach you how to fight back."

A wizard does sound like the only person who can help me right now. I imagine Merlin casting spells to protect Arthur and I listen.

When the appointment day comes, I'm nervous. I have put on my favourite mask, my extra-thick marigold gloves, and have slipped my magic eraser into my pocket. When we arrive at the wizard's office, I tell Mom and Dad I don't want to go inside. There is nothing magical about this place on the outside. It looks like any typical office building.

"Let's give this a chance, Louie," Dad pleads. "For being so courageous, you get an extra game of sword fighting with me on the trampoline tonight. Watch out, buddy, because I'm on fire today!" He squeezes my shoulders and gently leads me to the door.

Reluctantly, I enter what looks like an office with a desk and a few extra comfy chairs. Mom and Dad get to come with me, which makes me feel better. When Dr. Sander introduces himself, he does seem a little magical. With his white beard peeking out from under his own mask and his knowing way of looking at me over his spectacles, it kind of feels like I may have met him before. Like maybe he's one of those Santa Clauses whose lap I sat on when I was a little kid.

Dr. Sander asks me hundreds of questions. Some of them seem really strange. He reassures me he's heard everything and there is no wrong or bad answer. I'm relieved I haven't experienced all the things he's asking about. Other questions I answer match things I can relate to. This makes me feel a little more reassured, as I'm clearly not the only one experiencing this.

As we near the end of our meeting, Dr. Sander explains he knows what is causing the Dictator.

Leaning in from across the table, he confirms I have obsessive compulsive disorder, or OCD for short.

"Do you know what that is, Louie? It's like a little computer glitch or a hiccup in your brain. A worry or a fear might just pop into a kid's head and be hard to get rid of. OCD can make kids feel like they have to do certain things to feel safe. Does this sound like your experience?"

I nod my head vigorously. I totally understand this. It's exactly like some of those rituals that I just *have* to do to prevent bad things from happening, as if they have power or magic. I learn from Dr. Sander that these glitches are just mind tricks that make the worries seem bigger than they are.

Mom and Dad have many questions. Dr. Sander reassures us that OCD is not something that happens because of anything a child or parent has done. He tells me one out of forty people in the whole world has OCD. These are often talented, smart, successful people.

"Sometimes," the mind wizard explains, "smart, ambitious, sensitive, and imaginative kids can have these experiences."

I start to feel better. Just because I have OCD doesn't mean I'm sick, bad, or abnormal!

Dr. Sander then explains *how* the Dictator likes to play tricks on me.

"Louis, I hear you like King Arthur. I loved those stories when I was a kid too. Can I tell you something? Arthur was a master tactician in battle. This means

he could imagine what the enemy was up to in advance, and then plan a crushing counterattack. I'm going to tell you the Dictator's dirty tricks so you can fight back."

He begins to explain. "OCD likes to attack you in three ways:[1] by sending your brain false alarms to trick you into thinking you are in real danger; by making you think something bad *might* happen to frighten you, and then making you do all sorts of things to waste your time; and by making you feel funny if things aren't just right."

I nod again, because this is exactly how I've been feeling.

He explains these experiences are like optical illusions, and he promises to give me tools—he calls them my *weapons*—to fight back against the Dictator's tricks.

I start to feel lighter and more hopeful in my chest. This means I'm not bad. It's not my fault this is happening and I'm not weird or brain-damaged. Best of all, it means nothing bad will happen if I don't follow the Dictator's orders!

Dr. Sander asks my parents to go grab a coffee for fifteen minutes. I watch them leave and look back at him.

"We are going to spend a little time today preparing your arsenal. And together, in the coming

weeks, I'm going to teach you how to use the power of your brain to shrink Mr. Lousy Dictator."

He goes on.

"Did you know our thoughts create our feelings, which then affects our actions or behaviours? When the Dictator is lying to you and saying you are in danger and need to obey its commands, you feel really scared, right? Your heart starts to pound, or you start to breathe really fast, or your palms get sweaty, or your feel like you want to throw up?"

I'm nodding at every word.

"This scary feeling then makes you do things to feel better. Am I still right?"

It's like this wizard can read my mind. He understands!

"Did you also know your brain is kind of like your muscles? If you exercise your muscles a certain way, they grow powerful and strong."

"Yes!" I laugh, and I tell him about the one hundred push-ups I have to do for my Taekwondo exam.

"Exactly," exclaims Dr. Sander. "Think back to the first time you were asked to do ten push-ups and how hard it seemed, even painful. Then remember how often you had to practice to build your muscles to get to one hundred. Well, I'm going to teach you some exercises to give you *new* power. *Greater* power. Think of the tools as your armour and spells to ward

off and counter the Dictator's attacks. They might not work right away, but you must promise to keep practicing them, and I promise you will see results!"

I am getting excited. I like the sound of this.

"I'm going to give you the first weapon today and I want you to practice it until we meet again, OK? The more you practice, the more power you take from the Dictator."

He leans in as if imparting a great secret or magical spell.

"Next time you are worried or scared, ask yourself if this is the kind of emergency where you have to call 911, or if it's a false alarm."[2]

We talk about 911 emergencies, the kind where you need to call the police or fire department or get an ambulance to come. Or the kind where you have to run away to escape danger.

"When you know it's a false alarm, in that moment I want you to pause, take a deep breath, and close your eyes."

Mesmerized by his voice, I lean into the softness of the chair and close my eyes.

"Imagine you are flying on the back of your favourite dragon over the sea towards a beautiful mountain range bathed in the golden light of the sunset. The Dictator might be screaming at you, but keep imagining something that makes you feel happy and safe.

"By pausing to take a moment to *not* do what the Dictator asks, you are defying him. In that moment, his power is diminished. The first few times you do this might feel really uncomfortable, like the first time you had to do ten push-ups."

He pauses, and then says, "This might seem impossible right now, but I've spoken to your mom and dad and they've agreed to be part of your army."

He opens the door to his office and calls my parents in.

"Let's practice something now. I've asked Mom and Dad to bring you some of your favourite treats— pear slices with the skins on them."

I look at the hopeful faces of my parents and gulp nervously.

"Remember, one of the fastest ways to beat the Dictator is to *defy* his orders!"

Mom hands me a pear slice. The skin has brown marks on it.

"Now, Louie," coaxes Dr. Sander, "I don't want you to inspect the food. I'd like to see you just pick it up and take a bite. Can you do that for me?"

I nod uncertainly, but my heart is pounding.

Here goes . . .

I pop the pear into my mouth, chew ferociously, and swallow quickly. I feel a little shaky, but it wasn't so bad.

Mom and Dad cheer. The wizard nods and smiles. For the first time I feel a little powerful.

***

That night, when we settle down for bedtime reading, Mom hands me a list of names.

"What's this?" I ask.

"It's a list of a whole bunch of smart, successful, and famous people who have OCD."

I glance at it and am amazed.

World-famous soccer player David Beckham. Brilliant scientists like Charles Darwin and Nikola Tesla. Celebrated actors like Leonardo DiCaprio. TV personalities like Howie Mandel and pop stars like Katy Perry.

"OCD didn't stop them," says Mom as she kisses me and tucks me into bed.

Chapter 8

BAILY IS MISSING

Baily is a rescue dog. He's not a fancy pedigree or designer doodle-oodle-noodle dog. According to his adoption DNA test, he's some odd mix of coonhound and poodle and something indeterminable. He looks like a scruffy cow with large black spots, a giant nose, and soulful chocolate-brown eyes. He even smells like a cow because you'll always find him rolling in some kind of manure. Whatever his is, he is 100 percent perfect and I love him with all my heart. I met Baily at a puppy adoption event three years ago, and since I don't have any siblings I kind of think of him as my furry brother.

I can talk to Baily about anything and he totally understands. I can tell from the way he looks at me with his serious eyes, and the way he bats me with his paw when I talk to him about important things. He's

also a little anxious, like me, and that's OK because it means we can share our worries. Baily's start at life was an unhappy one. He and his siblings were found together in a box, abandoned at the dump when they were just tiny puppies. Luckily, a nice man heard their whimpers as he walked to work and brought them to the local dog rescue centre. By the time Baily came home to us, he was five months old and afraid of everything.

A few things spook Baily: baby prams, blowing leaves, garbage bags, backpacks, postal workers, kittens, tiny dogs, ladders, men, hats, men wearing hats, bicycles, umbrellas, and shopping carts. If he encounters any one of these items on his walk, he'll back out of his collar and bolt home in terror.

Over time, and with a lot of patience and love, Baily has learned to be brave, and a few of these items have come off the list.

Today Dad is on another call-out to a rescue near the local waterfall. I overhear Dad on the radio as he prepares his gear. Some teens decided to go cliff jumping in the river near the falls. The swollen spring runoff and frozen temperatures meant someone had gotten into trouble and needs help. Because Dad is a volunteer with the local mountain search and rescue team, he is often interrupted at dinner and on weekends to help.

Mom decides this is the perfect time for the two of us to walk Baily and pick up some bread for supper—get two chores done at once, she says.

As we approach the store, we decide to tie Baily to the railing near the entrance.

Mom and I put our masks on before we go in. I jam my hands into my pockets, as I realize I have forgotten my gloves. The Dictator is hissing again and my stomach is starting to rumble uncomfortably. If we could just hurry through the shop, pick up the baguette, pay, and leave right away, I won't have to touch anything with my ungloved hand.

It takes unusually long for us in this shop, as we have to stand on one of those spots on the floor marking a safe place to ensure physical distancing to protect customers from the virus. I try holding my breath for the duration of each move to the next step. The customers ahead have enormous carts filled with what seems like their weekly shops. I begin to feet hot and dizzy. My heart is pounding in my chest and I am running out of air as I struggle to hold my breath for the time in between each customer's turn.

"Are you OK, kiddo?" Mom asks. "We'll be done soon." She points to the next cashier, who is opening a new stall.

Finally, it's our turn. I pull Mom to her spot, eager to get out of the store and into the cleaner air of the outdoors.

"Hold on, Louie!" She drops her debit card and stoops to pick it up. I can see the Dictator eying it with distaste. I can imagine all the germs and viruses crawling on the card as her bare hand taps it against the cash machine. I make sure to use extra hand sanitizer while she pays.

Finally! It's time to go.

Just as we turn to leave the shop, the store manager comes rushing in.

"Was that your black and white dog tied up outside the door?" He asks breathlessly.

"Yes!" Mom and I reply together.

"Well, he just bolted out of his collar and ran away!"

"*What?*" I scream.

Mom grabs me by the arm before I can dash out into the parking lot.

"What happened?" she asks.

"I was collecting all the shopping carts and bringing them back into the store," he replies. "I'm so sorry! I had no idea he was so frightened, or that he could get away!"

I look at the train of carts lined together like a giant grating centipede and can only imagine the terror that gripped Baily. My heart is pounding again and I feel like I am going to throw up.

"Which way did he head?" shouts Mom. I can feel her rising panic too. Baily could get hit by a car.

He has no common sense, no road sense, no sense of direction to get home— no sense at all!

The manager points to the back lane behind the store. This is reassuring and horrifying at the same time. If Baily bolted in this direction, the good news is he was not heading across the busy road in front of the shop, where he could get hit by a car. The bad news is this trail network leads deep into the forest and eventually into the backcountry. There are several signs on the telephone poles outside the shop with hurriedly laminated posters of desperate pet owners asking for information for their lost dog or cat. Next to those pictures hang posters declaring cougar or bear sightings in the area.

Our community sits on the edge of a mountain range. Though this is great for quick access to the endless nature of the backcountry, people and pets often get lost and need Dad's team to come and rescue them.

I think about the bears, cougars, and coyotes that are regularly seen on the trails, and I feel so worried for Baily. I run ahead of Mom, screaming his name up the path.

"*Baily! Baillllyyyyyyy! Baiiiiilyyyyyyyy!*"

"Louie, don't go too far!" Mom is calling frantically for him too. "Let's take a second and think. Where could he go? He can't have gotten far!" Mom begins to furiously jab at her phone. "I'm

calling Dad. Maybe his team can help once they deal with those teens."

I ignore Mom and run deeper and deeper into the woods, calling out for my dog. I run so far and fast my breath becomes ragged. I can no longer hear Mom calling after us. It's getting darker the deeper I head into the woods. Twilight turns into darkness quickly in the mountains, and Dad always reminds me to be prepared, bring a light, and tell someone where I am going when I head into the forest.

I haven't done any of these things, but I can't think about that right now.

My voice hurts from screaming Baily's name. As I wipe the tears and snot running down my face, I barely realize my mask has broken or that I've been wiping snot and dirt on my bare hands. My heart is gripped with icy fear for my friend. I *must* find Baily!

Scrambling down a ravine ledge, thorn bushes and loose branches cut my hands. I trip and roll farther and farther down. When I come to a stop, I shudder. The only sound is the pounding of my heart, my hiccups, and my sobs. A moment later, I hear some chatting noises. I spot a gathering of squirrels chirruping in a tree ahead. Baily loves to chase squirrels, so I head towards the tree. As I race over, I trip over a root and land face down in the dirt. Winded, I suck my breath back and realize the back

of the tree extends over a steeper ravine overlooking the rapids.

Below I hear a voice and my heart explodes with joy. Not the *dreaded* voice, but Baily's deep bray! Forgetting my pain and my fear, I jump up to race towards the sound. Suddenly, another voice stops me—my Dad's warning about ravines and cliffs. I pause to review my surroundings. Carefully I make my way towards a dark clearing without trees. I inch forward on my hands and knees as I realize I must be near the edge of the falls.

I hear the braying again and lie flat on my stomach, peering into the void. In that moment, I spot him! Baily is trapped on a ledge near the waterfall and has no way of scrambling up the cliff.

"*Baily!*" I scream as I look down the cliff's edge. "I'm over here, buddy. Stay right where you are, Dad's coming!" Baily bawls back joyfully, his tongue lolling out and his tail wagging round and round in giant circles.

"You silly, silly dog!" I laugh, tears streaming down my eyes. "You couldn't resist those pesky squirrels, could you?"

A crash rumbles behind me. Rocks and broken branches start to fall on me. For a moment I freeze, remembering the posters about the cougar sightings. I hear a screech and my blood freezes. A second later I realize it's Mom running down the ravine

and releasing a pile of scree as she slides towards me, screaming my name over and over. Before I can call out, she's crushed me to her chest and we sob together.

"Never, *ever* go into the woods without telling us where you are heading again! Promise me!"

"It's OK Mom. Look, I found Baily!" Mom peers down and looks like she's going to faint. Overhead, a powerful wind whips our hair and the sky suddenly roars. It's Dad dangling from his helicopter's long line. His search and rescue team have come to save Baily!

Baily is oblivious to the helicopter's roar. The mighty wind from the rotors is ruffling his fur and tugging his ears in circles. How he is not terrified of a helicopter is beyond me. I guess his tail is just wagging like crazy because he sees Dad. There is little space on the ledge for both Dad and Baily, and I worry the silly dog will fall off. As soon as Dad's toes touch the ledge, Baily jumps onto his lap. Gripping him by the collar with one hand, he attaches him to a special harness made for dog rescues with the other. When he has secured the dog to his own harness, Dad circles his forefinger around his head and I watch as the helicopter pulls them both out of the ravine and up into the night sky.

Mom is still clutching on to me long after the helicopter has left, until the only sound we hear is the rushing falls.

***

That night, after promising Mom and Dad a thousand times I'll never run off into the woods alone again, I fall asleep spooning Baily on my bed. Much later, I realize that the Dictator did not visit me that night.

Chapter 9

JUST AN UNINVITED GUEST

After the rescue, Baily goes about life as if nothing scary happened. He seemed to forget about the whole thing and was back to snoring beside my pillow. Dogs are inspiring this way. Baily continues to teach me to enjoy the good moments now, and not think about what bad things *could* happen.

As for me, I remembered something important about that day. During the rescue the Dictator was silent. I was so focused on finding Baily there was no space for anything else.

He's quieter now, the Dictator. Like an uninvited guest, he sometimes pops by occasionally. After some more visits with my wizard, I can now imagine my scary thoughts as bubbles: I can watch them float

by, and then I can pop them with the pointy sword I've created in my mind's eye. Just like King Arthur in a joust, I can ride my dragon when I need to calm myself, and I can strike back in defiance when attacked by an annoying thought.

Mom and Dad are noticing a difference too. They have been my coaches, helping me practice my new skills. The voice is quieter and less insistent. I am stepping on cracks in the floorboards, and I can *quickly* step on the landing. I can go out with a different mask, and even without one, if I'm outside and standing two metres away from others. These are the public health rules right now, and *not* the Dictator's. Every small victory is celebrated. When I ate my pear slices at lunch, we went out and ordered french fries full of potato skins with brown spots to celebrate. I ate them all.

At my last visit with my mind wizard, I told him the rescue story. He smiled knowingly and shared that sometimes when we are called to heroic action, an all-consuming focus will put fear on the back burner, and this is what makes ordinary people heroes.

"So what can you learn from this experience to help you in the future?" he asked.

"The Dictator might come again, but I have weapons to beat him." I replied.

"Yes, indeed, my young knight. You have a wizard's mind to push back bad thoughts, you have a knight's will to fight back and defy his commands, you have a mental sword to pop the frightening thought bubbles as they come, and you have a dragon's spirit to breathe fire on the untruth spells or mind tricks."

Epilogue

The morning of his black belt test, Louie felt a different kind of worry. This was an ordinary worry, the nervous kind when you get butterflies before a test, not the kind where you *have* to do something to make the worry go away.

During the exam, Louie performed all of his skills from each of his previous eight belts. These included all his kicks, self-defence movements, eight distinct *poomse*, plus his own creative pattern, all in front of a live, masked audience of fellow students and parents. Though Louie was nervous, the Dictator didn't bother showing up. Louie left his amulets at home but still wore his favourite mask, because he likes how the shark teeth make him look scary.

The meditations and breathing exercises taught by his wizard helped him to focus during his test. As he performed his creative pattern, he found joy in the movement, his newfound power, and his sense of freedom. For the finale, he twirled his wooden bo staff over his head, and launched into a tornado kick

finished with an acrobatic roll - all in one direction only! The audience stood up and applauded wildly.

Bowing before his masters, he beamed when presented with his black belt. This time, it was a very proud Mom and Dad who winked back at him from behind their masks.

Glossary of Taekwondo Terms in Korean

Taekwondo is a Korean martial art that dates back over 2000 years. It means "the way of the hand and the foot" because of its use of both punching and kicking as forms of self-defence.

Here are a few terms you encountered in *Louie and the Dictator*.

Dobok: This is the uniform worn by practitioners of Taekwondo. "Do" means way, and "bok" means clothing.

Dojang: Refers to a formal training hall or place of gathering for students of martial arts to conduct training and examinations. This is where Louie goes to take his lessons.

Chariyot: Pronounced like the word chariot, this is the instruction to pay attention.

Kyung-nae: This is the instruction to bow.

Shee-jak: This is the instruction to begin.

Kihap: This describes the shout a martial artist makes. *Kihap* is a combination of two words in Korean. Together, they mean a gathering of force, energy and power.

Endnotes

My deepest thanks to Dr. Robert Selles and his team

For more information about OCD visit:
https://kidshealth.org/en/kids/ocd.html

[1] What to do When Your Brain Gets Stuck: A Kid's Guide to Overcoming OCD. By Huebner, Dawn; Matthews, Bonnie [Illustrator], 2007.

[2] In recognition of therapeutic interventions developed by Sharon Selby, registered clinical counsellor, supporting children with anxiety. *(Reference to 911 emergency versus perceived emergencies)* www.sharonselby.com

Manufactured by Amazon.ca
Bolton, ON

20921771R00037

Contents

Dedication

Dedicated to my son—my hero.

In honour of all children battling anxiety, compulsions or intrusive thoughts. You are each heroes of your own stories.

Tellwell Talent
www.tellwell.ca

ISBN
978-0-2288-5768-6 (Paperback)
978-0-2288-6334-2 (eBook)

Louie
and the Dictator

LISA BOURNELIS

Contents

Prologue

We eased through the noisy crowd of overheated bodies surging through the heavy air. Elegantly robed men, their embroidered tunics sweeping the ground, brushed past us. Ragged T-shirts, damp with perspiration, covered bony shoulders. Wrap skirts of once-vibrant African cloth, licked colorless by the sun's harsh rays, hung limply against sinewy limbs. Our white skin stood out—a stark contrast with the rich, deep brown of those streaming around us.

The village's sun-hardened compounds burst with people. With their backs propped against rough clay huts, some of the villagers drank home-brewed palm wine. Some ate bits of animal parts hidden in a hot pepper sauce. Others danced to pounding, multifaceted rhythms that sprang from the hands of a group of drummers. The drummers' solemn expressions transformed into wide, toothy grins as a young girl, her hair twisted into a multitude of long black spikes, laid a gift of roasted pig heads at their feet. Jarring, unintelligible music exploded through huge, generator-powered speakers.

Makeshift shanties constructed of palm branches mounted on limbs created bits of undulating shade in a sea of hot light.

It was the tenth anniversary of Etienne's father's death. In life his father's birthday had never been celebrated. No one's birthday ever is. But voodoo custom mandated the celebration of his death to respectfully honor him. He was to be remembered and his spirit appeased. Family members believed that without a memorial ceremony, they would suffer great harm from his father's dissatisfied, angered spirit.

We watched as traditional dancers, their faces devilishly masked and bodies costumed in skirts made from torn paper, mounted tall, wooden stilts that were incautiously tied to their legs. In wild bursts of energy, dictated by frenzied drumbeats, they recklessly kicked their legs high into the air, nearly striking the rowdy crowd. Shrieking fear and pleasure the spectators tossed coins to the dust-shrouded dancers. One sweaty stilt-walker plopped himself onto the weather-beaten tin roof of a nearby hut, his wooden legs extended to the ground far below him, to watch yet another spectacle—the pole dance.

Raised in the middle of the dirt compound was a 30-foot, slender, bamboo pole, with a tiny crossbar nailed at the very top. We stared in shock as a young, masked man climbed the pole and performed acrobatic stunts from the flimsy bar. No net protected him from a sudden fall. No rope secured him to the trembling pole. With abandon he stood, flipped, and hung on one leg from the dizzying height. His grand finale was to descend, head first, in a slow slide to the ground. People in the raucous mob roared their approval and lifted their arms to catch him in the final feet of his descent.

My husband, Jeff, and I had hoped to share Christ with these people. Instead, we found ourselves unable to utter a single, understandable word to one another, let alone to anyone else, above the din.

We couldn't blend in. Our every body movement glaringly contrasted culturally with the tide of African revelers. Yet, we somehow felt completely comfortable in these bizarre surroundings. That was God. Several years before, if someone had told me that we would be standing one day in the middle of what seemed to be a *National Geographic* special and loving it, I'd have laughed.

As the day fell behind the palm-treed horizon and cooler temperatures crept across this remote corner of the earth, Bernadette invited us into her simple home. Quickly she brought in two chairs. She scraped them around until they were almost level on the uneven dirt floor, then dusted them with a shredded piece of cloth and offered them to us. Her tiny tin lantern, made of a battered, tomato-paste can, barely illuminated the space where we sat.

She owned nothing but a hand-sawn, wooden table and the mat on which she slept. Yet, she set before us a gracious gift—two warm, syrupy Cokes. Her greatest gift, however, was her spoken greeting—one we would carry in our hearts the rest of our lives.

"Greetings in your love for people."

We hadn't spoken a word. Christ's love had spoken through us.

That is what being in Africa is all about—living out our love for Christ and the adventure of loving people to Christ.

Come, walk the adventure with us.

ONE

Stepping into Abundance

Having grown up a bona-fide Michigander, the South seemed like a foreign land of confusing words and bizarre foods. If I needed a pin, I'd have to ask for a "pen." If the search was for a pen, the word was a multisyllabled "pi-i-n." I soon discovered that a "fanger" is where you wear your "wedd'n rangs," "You guys", the global statement in the North for "everyone", referred only to males! "Pop", which we called carbonated beverages, was a sound made by a car backfiring, while "Coke" referred to all carbonated drinks. Long, purple things that looked like color-blind green beans weren't beans at all but were "peas." They sure looked like beans to me! You weren't to chop them. You were to "hull 'em." A thoughtful gift was a cooler of dead fish, most commonly, long-whiskered catfish. Home Economics 101 in my high school never taught what to do with fins, heads, skin, scales, or freshly killed squirrel or duck.

Duck-hunting season was bigger than Christmas and almost more important than a wife giving birth! Ducks, in my life's experience, were for feeding in the park, not for the plate. Then the South had cornbread. If it didn't suck your mouth completely dry, it was not made quite "ryight." Butter, alone, graced its "innards." What a ghastly mistake of protocol to request a bit of honey! We breakfasted on grits, yet no one could explain what a "grit" was. Southerners would only laugh, ridicule the question, and say, incredulously, "Ain't no such thing!" How odd that you can make a food out of something that does not even exist.

Southern iced tea tasted like carbonated syrup without the fizz. Drinks made of tea bags dipped in heavy sugar water and flavored with wild mint leaves were unheard of in the North. We took our iced tea straight and simple and never in winter. Southern life was different. Never before had I imagined that an American could have culture shock in America.

Yet, this was the beginning of the adventure of my life—our lives. Amazingly our voyage to the South was one that would lead into the wilds of Africa!

Jesus said, "I am come that they might have life, and that they might have it more abundantly" (John 10:10 KJV).

An abundant life, I once believed, was a life overflowing with good things. I defined "good", of course, solely by my perspective of good; what made me happy—what was without difficulty or pain. Yet, in promising an abundant life, Christ did not promise to pour into and over my life just what I considered good. He promised abundance—more life in life. A deeper, richer life. A life overflowing with joys that propel your hands upward in abandoned adoration. A life with grief profound that compels you to your knees, weeping over lostness. Abundance is released when the toughness of life drives an empty, weak, struggling spirit to entwine itself with the very heart of God. Life abundant is a life of abandonment. Abundance is realized only through complete abandonment.

My Michigan life ended abruptly during the final days of my first year of college. After 12 years of ministry in Port Huron, my father changed pastorates—to Tabernacle Baptist Church in Chillicothe, Ohio. I came home to a new home, in a smoke-stacked, paper-mill town, surrounded by ancient, wooded hills.

In my homecoming, a whisper of excitement feathered around my heart, for in my father's ministry, for the first time, he was to have a youth pastor. The thought of that youth pastor greatly intrigued me. The intrigue had little to do with the spiritual growth and development of the church's youth.

Over the summer I grew to know Jeff Singerman, the physical-education director at the local YMCA. While considering going to seminary, he volunteered to work temporarily with the church's youth until a youth pastor could be found. After a few months the church's search committee approached him. Jeff accepted the job.

Jeff and my father respected each other deeply. My father became Jeff's friend and mentor in the ministry. Jeff became my father's right-hand man.

When I returned home from college for Christmas break, Jeff proposed. We glowed. Jeff would read the morning's announcements from the pulpit, glance at me, and broadly grin. I'd blush and break into an uncontrollable grin. The choir members would nudge each other and grin. The watching congregation would grin. We could have been the storybook prince and princess, for all the entertainment we gave! Within a year we married.

I thought I had discovered Jeff, but after our engagement, my mother told me the real story. Weeks before I arrived home to Ohio for the first time, my mother had met Jeff in the receiving line at church. When he took her hand to greet her, she looked into his eyes and thought, "Do you know I have a daughter?" She claims she chose Jeff for me first.

Jeff's version of the whole story, however, is altogether different. When he was offered the full-time youth pastor position, only one hitch was involved. He had to marry the pastor's daughter to get the job!

After five years of ministering with my father, Jeff sensed the need for a theological education, to be prepared for whatever God would call him to do in the future. In obedience, we packed up our lives; tore our two-year-old son, Ryan, out of the arms of his grandparents, and moved 14 hours away to attend Mid-America Baptist Theological Seminary in Memphis, Tennessee, in the heart of the South.

In our journey into the South, we only had one weekend to find a place to rent. Hour after hour we wearily searched the ads and pounded the streets, looking for suitable housing, but we kept coming up empty. At the end of a very long Saturday, while gazing through the dirty windows of an empty rental, we noticed a house across the street that was posted, "For Sale, Assumable Loan." We had the necessary ingredient to assume a loan—cash. We had just sold a house. We scribbled down the number of the real-estate agent, found a phone, and contacted her. That same evening we walked through the house and signed a contract. Without a job, without insurance, we had purchased a comfortable little house in a pleasant Memphis subdivision, with payments equaling the price of a small rental! We were certain we had experienced God's miraculous leading. As an added plus we had noticed that Memphis, unlike the church-less streets of the North, had a church on every block. We assumed God intended to give Jeff a ministry position on someone's corner.

Weeks passed. We became quite concerned. Our home was set up. Our little vegetable garden was growing, but our savings was running fearfully low. We prayed. We waited and prayed some more. Then the call occurred. A Baptist church in a little town 70 miles west of Memphis, in Arkansas, needed a family-life minister. Would we visit them?

I didn't even want to consider it. We would have to move. We would take a great financial loss on reselling our house that quickly. We hadn't even had a chance to get to know our new neighbors. "God," I thought, "could not be serious about this!" But we went.

My first glimpse of Brinkley was disheartening. Shacks blatantly stood next to manicured homes. The town's hauntingly empty buildings and vacant window fronts gave evidence to times of great economic difficulty. Worst of all, the closest mall was more than an hour away! "No, Jeff, we're not going to live here," was my emphatic response as I glanced around during a stoplight.

Then I met the people of First Baptist Church and encountered their fervency for Christ. Before we returned to our brand-new Memphis home, God's intentions were clear. Jeff was to be their family-life minister. I would repack our lives into boxes and say "goodbye" to my freshly refurbished cottage. We would once again start the search for a home. Jeff would travel to Memphis four days a week to attend seminary classes and then would work at the church late afternoons.

The lifestyle was difficult. But the people in that small town, surrounded by acres of waving wheat, flooded rice fields, and zillions of fat, hungry mosquitoes, would become among the most precious on earth to me. In Brinkley God began calling us to missions.

God put our faith and obedience to the test. Our faith was challenged when following His leading hurt, when it meant significant financial loss coupled with the emotional pain of giving up our treasured home. Our obedience was challenged when moving to Brinkley meant losing honor in others' sight. No one believed God had led us to buy that fine, little house when we placed it immediately back on the market. God further challenged our obedience when it resulted in the loss of our personal comfort. The only available place to live in

Brinkley was a tiny, three-room, paper-thin-walled, furnished apartment, with no laundry hookup, an ugly carpet that reeked, and an abundance of disgusting roaches of numerous varieties. That was not the abundance I had expected in Christ. In my cool-climated, Northern upbringing, I had never even seen a roach before! Nothing in our move to Brinkley was easy, but we obeyed.

Tests of faith and obedience are not rational to our human minds. In fact, the Christian life seems pretty irrational. The one who selflessly serves is the greatest leader. The desires and ambitions of others are to take complete precedence over yours. Love those who despise you, who would dance with abandon on your grave. When your life is crumbling tragically around you, practice praising God. Rejoice! Dying in Christ means true Life. Abundance in Christ occurs only through complete abandonment—the emptying of all that we have, all that we are, and all that we hope into His consuming hands.

Abandonment. That our hearts might beat with God's heartbeat. That Jesus might have first place in our lives. Fullness, abundance in life is secreted in an intimate relationship with Christ.

We step into abundance on our knees.

I am come that they might have life, and that they might have it more abundantly (John 10:10, KJV).

TWO

Right Down to the Bugs

When we did finally move, our new, unfurnished apartment was still exceptionally confining. Most of our belongings stayed heaped up in a gracious church member's cold-storage space while I struggled to survive the limitations of three, tiny, dark-panel-walled rooms. We couldn't take a deep breath and exhale energetically without knocking a picture off the wall!

The carpet stank as terribly as did the last one, although diligently cleaned and daily offered perfumed, incense-type offerings that were sacrificially purchased and shaken over its entirety from wall to wall and closet to corner. It didn't work. The stink-god just laughed at my feeble attempts to appease him and continued to odiferize the apartment. He particularly loved to reek on damp, rainy days.

Fetid carpeting aside, those filthy, loathed, roach menaces were more numerous than before. I discovered realities about roaches I'd never longed to learn: that a little brown trail of dots in my mug cabinet weren't coffee grounds but roach goo; that another empty, brown, crunchy egg smashed under the flour canister meant there'd been a release of another 30 vile ogres into my home that would in turn hatch out more miniature reproductive monsters!

The rank carpeting fouled the air. The roaches were stealing the cutlery. And we were expecting our second child. Where would we put a baby? The only possible place for a crib, I realized with dismay, would be in the combination living room/kitchen. I was already teaching piano lessons in Ryan's bedroom in a space so cramped, I could not push back the piano bench sufficiently to adequately access the pedals. When I grievously complained to one of the most respected, godly women in the church about my horrible plight, she looked around and smilingly stated that we had plenty of space for a baby in our over-scrunched apartment. Smoldering after her visit, I left for the Laundromat, uncomfortably hefting large, heavy clothes baskets around my expanding belly. Once again I was more than disgusted as I battled for space with those six-legged horrors that were determined to crawl across the clean laundry I was folding.

As I folded and flung the wash into its plastic prisons, I stewed over my life. I resented our housing condition. I was angry at the detestable, multitudinous roaches. I was enraged at having to do laundry at the grungy Laundromat. I was hurt that Jeff's salary only amounted to part-time pay due to the hours he was away at seminary, although he accomplished full-time work. It was all so frustrating!

The people at the church were loving, kind, and caring, yet not one seemed to see the difficulties we were encountering. We needed more room. We needed a house. We needed a better salary. Quickly my accusations moved beyond the church and straight to the Creator. I whimpered, "Don't You care about our needs? Your Word promises that You will supply all our needs according to Your riches in glory in Christ Jesus" (Phil. 4:19).

To me it didn't seem like God was being faithful to His Word. In fact, it seemed that Paul, who had written these words, had experienced just the opposite of having his needs richly supplied. He, himself, mentioned that he hadn't only been hungry but often had substantial hunger that was not satisfied (Phil. 4:12, 2 Cor. 11:27). He blatantly admitted he knew what it was to be thirsty. Sleepless. Without adequate clothing. Cold (2 Cor. 11:27). As a captive, Paul had been subjected to the relentless, punishing winds of a raging tempest that tore at his prison ship for days (Acts 27:14-44). He knew the physical shock of plummeting into frigid, hostile waters during three shipwrecks.

Once he endured a starless night and trembling day in the water with the wind-whipped waves beating against his body while he clung to a shattered board and awaited rescue (2 Cor. 11:25). Although he was a man of position, he humbled himself to the level of a common slave and served others by helping gather firewood to dry their sopping-wet clothes from a Mediterranean drenching. His reward? Picture this: Paul moved from the rain-tossed and tangled brush surrounding the sandy shoreline with a mound of rough sticks in his shivering arms.[1] As he dropped them cautiously onto the fire, his outstretched hands lingering a moment to catch a breath of warmth from the flickering flame, a poisonous viper slithered out of the rough sticks and drove its sharp fangs deep into his hand.

Paul, the man who wrote, "my God shall supply all your needs", was bitten by this venomous snake because of his service to Christ (Acts 28:1-10). This is a man who had desperate needs. He even admittedly wrote about personally "suffering need" (Phil. 4:12).

I was confused. Is not safety a need? Is not food a need? Is not warmth a need? Is not sleep a need? Is not health a need? Is not possessing adequate space in which to live a need?

The questions bounding around in my brain finally boiled down to one specific question: What is a need?

I realized the bottom line in any dilemma is this: God always acts in complete accordance with His Word. Yet, even with this belief, I took a while to realize that what seemed to be an oversight on the Almighty's part in failing to meet Paul's needs or my needs was actually the greatest meeting of those needs. God just happens to be more passionately concerned about our spiritual than physical needs.

Let me put this into perspective. If we need to learn patience, He will put us in as many frustrating situations as necessary to teach us patience. If we need to learn endurance, through life's tough encounters He will teach us to endure. If we need to learn simple, obedient trust, we may remain sick, although we've earnestly sought healing. If we need to learn contentment, He will allow us to live in challenging conditions to urge us to surrender our will to His. Paul knew the secret of having his real needs richly supplied.

Gradually God caused me to realize that He had blinded the eyes of the people at our church to our physical circumstances because of me. They weren't intentionally overlooking our housing situation or our financial difficulties. What we were enduring wasn't their fault. It was mine. It was because of my greater spiritual need that they weren't seeing. God wanted me to start learning what Paul had learned: to be content in any situation (Phil. 4:11-12). And Paul's situations were exceedingly more drastic than mine were. He was content to have his stomach cramping with hunger pains, to drag his body through the day because of sleepless nights, to endure extreme conditions that caused his thin body to tremble, to know the power of unquenched thirst for his Lord. I had everything Paul didn't have except contentment.

I had a choice to make: continue in anger, or yield and be willing to be made content. That gentle, quiet Voice nudged me, "How will I ever ask anything greater of you if you won't live here, in this place, for Me?" Desperate for relief from the agony within myself, I finally fell on my face before the Lord, right on that disgustingly smelly carpet, and poured out my heart. "Jesus," I prayed, "if you want us to stay in this awful apartment for the rest of our lives, I am willing."

Do you know what happened? I became content. The apartment's frustrating limitations hadn't changed. The roaches hadn't croaked; instead, they continued to multiply voraciously. The carpeting hadn't ceased emitting obnoxious odors. Our dollars hadn't doubled. I had changed. I didn't have to love unpleasant circumstances, but I could live through them with His joy, yielded to His will. Amazingly, surrendering my will to Christ made the awfulness shrink in magnitude.

Now, with laughter in my heart, I can recount my roach encounters in our hot and excessively humid corner of Africa. These flying fiends are enormous in size, resistantly undefeatable, and sport incredibly fertile reproductive organs! When one climbed in my shoe, I had no room for my foot. When one wore my robe, my arm wouldn't slide down through the sleeve. God's preparations in our lives exude humor and are awesomely complete, right down to the bugs.

Small steps of surrender were necessary to bring us slowly to the big step out of America and into the world. And we stepped with confidence, knowing that Jesus would always meet our needs, even if they included bugs.

I know how to get along with humble means, and I also know how to live in prosperity; in any and every circumstance I have learned the secret of being filled and going hungry, both of having abundance and suffering need. I can do all things through Him who strengthens me. And my God shall supply all your needs according to His riches in glory in Christ Jesus (Phil. 4:12-13, 19).

---

[1]Jefferson White, *Evidence and Paul's Journeys* (Hilliard, OH: Parsagard Press, 2001), 79.

THREE

Beyond the Littleness

It started out like any other seminary day. I rose long before dawn, fixed Jeff's breakfast, packed his sack lunch, and dove back into bed to the sound of our old car's engine revving, to catch a few more moments of sleep before Ryan and baby Kevin woke up. Hours later, Jeff zipped back in after his 140-mile, round-trip commute to his classes, dropped off his books, and grabbed a chocolate-chip cookie or two before heading to his office at church. That's where the similarity to an ordinary day ended. I was completely unprepared for the question.

During chapel that day, world missions was once again preached. Mid-America Baptist Theological Seminary's heart is evangelism, but its heartbeat is missions. Jeff, sincere in his walk with the Lord, had decided, from the moment he'd given his life to Christ, that he was God's. Lordship was a settled issue. God could ask anything of him, and he would do it. He never felt compelled to respond to a mission invitation, knowing that if God prompted him that direction, he would go.

But this day guest speaker Dr. John Floyd spoke. His words challenged Jeff and appealed to his practical nature. "Maybe you're sitting there in that pew, ready and willing to serve the Lord in any capacity. How will you know He does not want you to be a missionary unless you knock on the door? If it opens, walk through it. Get in touch with the Foreign Mission Board (now known as the International Mission Board, SBC)." To Jeff it was a logical proposal. He experienced no special revelation from the Lord. No pounding heart or assuredness of a direction. Just the presence of a door. Jeff was willing to knock.

Few words can be more shocking to an unsuspecting wife than the question Jeff posed in his homecoming:

"Want to be a missionary?"

At the brink of seminary graduation with endless hours of commuting, midnight-hour studies, 5 a.m. breakfasts, and all-night paper-typing falling behind us, I thought we could ease up, concentrate solely on ministry demands, and rest. Then Jeff popped the question.

The actual question he asked was, "Do you want to get in touch with the Foreign Mission Board?" But it meant the same thing. I said, "You can get in touch with the Foreign Mission Board, but we're not going to be missionaries." That meant, "No."

I had my life all planned out. Jeff was to become a famous youth pastor with such an incredible ministry, he would fly around the country as the guest speaker for massive youth rallies.

We would build a beautiful home with a spacious front porch on which we would relax on cool summer evenings or snuggle together for quiet moments during the rain. We would rear our children in Christ. I'd have a flourishing women's speaking ministry. Pride runs strong in my family. So strong is it, it had convinced me that all these were God-given goals. My pride and I didn't have any problem with any of them. But God did.

Being a missionary just didn't fit. I had never even spent a moment of my life considering it.

Early on I surrendered to Christ as fully as I knew how. I lived seriously for Him, but I never wanted to be a missionary. I knew missionaries. My parents entertained them frequently in our home while I was growing up. Frumpy-looking missionary ladies, with their tight, fuzzy perms and muumuu dresses, had included in the initiation to their order a multitude of shots. I despised doctors' offices. I hated shots. Be a missionary? That was out of the question.

Jeff's contact with the Foreign Mission Board turned into an avalanche of paperwork, which resulted in our receiving an invitation to a week-long foreign missions' conference at Ridgecrest Conference Center in North Carolina as potential missionary candidates.

An aura of holiness permeated the mountain setting. The sharply angled pathways, immense dining hall, and conference center were dotted with missionaries sporting name tags and long, bright red ribbons denoting their otherworldliness. In an awed whisper I turned to Jeff and said, "We don't belong here." I felt like an unholy person walking on holy ground. The soul-shaking words of William Carey were heralded at every turn, "I must venture down, but remember that you must hold the ropes."[1] Gradually my sentiments turned from one of not belonging to a curious longing to belong, tinged with a heaping of fear.

Late one romantic evening we walked toward our dorm room to the rhythm of gentle raindrops cascading from the fragrant fir trees that lined our path. I confided in Jeff, "I feel like we're dating missions, and if we do not get out of here, we're going to get married."

That Thursday night, alone on a pine-scented balcony, I fell on my knees before the Lord. I sensed that a great wall existed between me and a call to missions: a thick, impenetrable wall that consisted of all the plans Pride and I had made. There, weeping, I died to the ministry ambitions I had fashioned for us. I surrendered my dreams of building a house with a large front porch. Drenched with my tears, I placed at the feet of Jesus my private desires and future hopes which didn't seem to fit a missionary call. In those moments the wall crashed into dusty ruins around me and blew off the porch in the breeze.

The Call came.

For me it had started with a question that turned into a vow as solemn and serious as our marriage vows. Jeff and I are committed to the Call, for better or worse, for richer or poorer, in sickness and in health. We have already tried to accomplish the "until-death-do-us-part" section several times on the mission field. In our marriage we have covenanted together never to breathe the word *divorce*, not even in jest. Neither will we allow the thought to play on our minds. It is forbidden. The word "resign" is treated with the same vital significance. We do not think it, joke about it, or speak of it. We are in this for the duration.

During our furloughs, Jeff and I have been confronted with many people who say:

"Even if God called me to missions, I wouldn't go. I could never live without McDonald's."

"I couldn't give up my TV programs or my house."

"Did you say 'snakes'? Then count me out!"

"I couldn't stand the heat!"

"But my children might get sick!"

"No missionary job possibilities fit my skills, so God couldn't want me to be a missionary."

Their words slice through our hearts like sabers. We grieve for them. These people are saying they would rather stay in the familiar and comfortable than to step out into an awesome adventure with Christ, possibly to suffer change and discomfort. But these are minor matters compared to earning the privilege of sharing Life with someone who is dying to hear.

We believe that anything that would keep you from going on the mission field is standing between you and a deeper relationship with Jesus. At whatever juncture you say "I can't, couldn't, or wouldn't be a missionary", is a breaking point between you and Christ. You will never grow beyond it until you die to it. Whether God would call you or not, whatever would keep you from surrendering to the possibility of the call, you love more than Christ. Give it up. What riches in Christ Jesus are waiting for you beyond surrender! Only in surrender does God begin to move us beyond our fears.

God's calling—God's will isn't directing you into personal disaster but personal wholeness. God has designed your heart's desires to be incredibly granted, but only as you daily commit to His Lordship. Resistance brings emptiness; surrender brings immeasurable depths of fulfillment.

Our calling to missions has been the thrill of my life. An incredible completeness and sense of God's presence are in our lives as we share Christ in Benin. God has granted the desires of our hearts, beyond what I imagined, in our following Him. After dying to a women's speaking ministry years ago, God has opened special opportunities to me that, now, I walk into with a right heart! On furloughs, I have been invited to speak to many women's groups, to expand their vision and compassion for winning the world for Christ. During our Stateside assignments, Jeff and I travel (sometimes flying) across America, to share about God's work in Benin, to challenge others to deeper commitments to Christ, to missions, and to prayer.

My early mornings in the African bush are spent contentedly sitting on my expansive front porch, with my Bible in my lap, looking out over orange trees, leafy palms, and beautiful flowering bougainvillaea. Jeff and I even sit here in the sweet privacy and intimacy of the rain.

Don't hang on to the littleness of your life and deny God the privilege of surprising you with your deepest, richest, grandest, most secret desires.

I count all things to be loss in view of the surpassing value of knowing Christ Jesus my Lord, for whom I have suffered the loss of all things, and count them but rubbish in order that I may gain Christ . . . that I may know Him and the power of His resurrection and the fellowship of His sufferings, being conformed to His death in order that I may attain to the resurrection from the dead (Phil. 3:8,10-11).

---

[1]Mary Drewery, *William Carey* (Grand Rapids, MI: Zondervan, 1979), 46.

FOUR

Stages of the Call

So, we immediately packed up all we owned and flew to the wilds of Africa. That's how you might think this next chapter would begin. But that's not what happened. We weren't quite ready yet. In our lives the "Call" had an infancy stage that needed to grow into maturity before we gained our wings. It was fundamentally necessary. We needed to know our Call and the foundation of that Call before venturing out.

The Call is an incredible thing. It begins, and as you feed it, it builds in fervency. To this day we continue to grow deeper and deeper into the Call. If we hear an appeal for Christians to dedicate their lives to missions, to winning yet another people who have never heard, we can barely restrain ourselves from running down the aisle and consecrating ourselves to this new task. If someone preaches about the needs of a lost world, tears will stream down our faces. I even hear the Call in the Christmas story! "And the angel said unto them, 'Fear not: for, behold, I bring you good tidings of great joy, which shall be for ALL people'" (Luke 2:10 KJV).

With each passing year the zeal God has given us for winning the unreached does not diminish but threads itself more intensely through every fiber of our beings.

In the months following "the question", I'd discover Jeff in his easy chair, his lap piled high with books, researching "What is a Call to missions?" The responses were as varied as the people who wrote them. Some say no specific Call exists but that everyone is a missionary. Our responsibility and duty are to go, based on Matthew 28:18-20. The fault lies in not going. Others say that the Call to missions is a special endowment from the Lord given to those He appoints to cross-cultural ministries. Another says, "If you're willing, then go." Jeff was willing, but was that enough? Was he really "Called" to go? I could not answer that question for him. All I knew was that God had moved me deeply about personally reaching a desperate world for Christ.

One wise man, Glendon Grober, a Southern Baptist missionary to Brazil, advised us, "If you can do anything other than being a missionary, then do it." We understood his meaning. Only if being a missionary compelled us with such a force that we could be nothing less, pursue it. Jeff was not sure he was there.

During this time of searching we had been placed "on hold" in the missionary application process due to two-year-old Kevin's allergy problems. We were discouraged and puzzled. At the same time, although we didn't desire to move or change ministries and hadn't even sent out any resumes, Mt. Juliet First Baptist Church, a congregation in the Nashville, Tennessee, suburbs, began seeking after Jeff to fill its youth-minister position. This large church was situated in the middle of a housing explosion with easy access to two populous high schools. It was kicking off a family-life-center building program, which included a gymnasium.

Jeff's idyllic childhood growing up at YMCA's Camp Kern under his father Jack's directorship propelled him to acquire a degree in sports education. He loved ministering on high school campuses and discipling youth in the Word. The Mt. Juliet position was the ministry of Jeff's dreams.

We were so torn. We spent weeks talking, praying, and searching for God's will. The closed door on missions broke our hearts. We reasoned together, "Maybe God only meant to give us a zeal for missions that we could instill in the youth by taking them on mission trips." We pleaded, "God, if You are going to keep us here in the States, allow us the privilege of inspiring hundreds to surrender and go."

We had kept our journey into the realm of missions a secret, yet I was asked at this time to speak to a woman's missionary society associational meeting. I wept before them as I shared, "If you once surrendered to missions and weren't terribly disappointed when God shut the door, you were never really surrendered at all."

We didn't pack our bags and head to the ends of the earth. We moved to Mt. Juliet.

We bought a beautiful home in a lovely housing development. Jeff vigorously trained youth, took them on U.S. mission trips, and preached. I hung wallpaper, taught Ryan kindergarten, played piano for the youth choir, led a senior-high ensemble, and happily discovered myself pregnant with Kari. God had given back to me a portion of what I had laid at His feet. I was happy with the state of our lives.

Early in January 1989, barely a year into our ministry in Mt. Juliet, Kari was born. She followed on the heels of the church's December emphasis on missions. My mind had been singly directed toward her impending birth. I had turned a deaf ear toward the mission's appeals.

But Jeff hadn't. Soon after Kari's arrival, night after night Jeff started returning home from the church, heavily burdened. "Is this an adequate use of my life?" he would question. "The youth here have a right to have someone love them and teach them about Christ. But how much more do those have a right to hear who have never heard, and are dying to hear, but have no one to tell them? Many men are capable of doing a good job in this position. Many men applied for this position. But who else will go?"

The searching had ended. Jeff knew the Call.

The question I thought settled towered before me. The goals I had died to were nearly secured within my hands once more. Now God was demanding them back again. Without emotion, but with my will, I opened my hands and released all that lay there to the Lord. The moment is marked in my memory forever. I paused while vacuuming and just stood there, thinking, when the Lord gently spoke to me. He promised, in whatever He demanded of me, that He would give the wisdom and courage necessary.

I bowed my head and simply responded, "Lord, I'm willing."

From those moments on, every Scripture we read shouted missions to our hearts. Every song sung had missions as its theme. Sermons all bore down upon us the necessity to "Go!"

God "desires *all* men to be saved . . ." (1 Tim. 2:4).

"You are the salt of the *earth* . . . You are the light of the world" (Matt. 5:13-14).

"Everywhere I send you, you shall *go* . . ." (Jer. 1:7).

"You did not choose Me, but I chose you, and appointed you, that you should *go* . . ." (John 15:16).

"As the Father has sent Me, I also *send* you" (John 20:21).

Emotions no longer were the root of the Call for me; God's Word was. My secondary surrender hadn't been based on my feelings but on my will. As the Word and the willful decision to follow God's leading to the mission field formed the foundation of our Calling, we began to step from infancy toward maturity.

With this necessary foundation firmly in place, God rushed us along through the rest of the missionary application process. Kevin received immediate health clearance. Suddenly we were caught in a flowing current of power that enveloped our lives and carried us toward the mission field with a great sense of urgency. We needed to go and go now.

We spoke to the Lord concerning our children. We prayed that He would prepare their hearts for the future changes. We believed that God didn't just call parents to missions; He called families. One Sunday evening, shortly after praying in this way, Ryan, just seven at the time, approached me with a serious expression.

"Mom," he confided, "during that last song I felt Jesus tugging at my heart. My heart is on fire. No water can put it out. God wants me to be a missionary." With tears flooding my eyes, I hugged him with all my might and told him God might give him that opportunity soon!

How exciting it has been to watch Ryan on the mission field! He has led friends to Christ, gone compound-to-compound witnessing in villages before dawn, and joined in countless prayerwalking experiences. He has given time during his summers, without our personal involvement, to work with volunteer construction teams: to dig holes, haul bricks, and translate from English to French for the sharing of their testimonies.

At 17, due to the great need we had for men to preach in our constantly growing number of church starts, he began to preach on a rotation basis. I teasingly told Jeff that Ryan preached better in French than Jeff started out preaching in English! I am moved to realize that Ryan's style is a carbon copy of his dad's.

Ryan has joyfully worked in medical clinics, even gladly learning to do glaucoma testing and triage. As a translator for volunteer doctors he has been asked to assist in minor surgeries. This propelled him to choose a college medical major. Even at the university his heart for ministry continues. During his first spring break, when I chanced to fly to the States for a conference, we never saw each other. When I arrived from Africa to America, he flew from America to France to spend his break walking through icy rain to distribute Arabic Bibles and the Jesus film to Moslem people. No water has put out that fire!

Kevin and Kari are following in Ryan's footsteps. If a chance exists for them to minister with a volunteer team, I cannot convince them to stay home and rest despite their extreme exhaustion. They will cut and package medicines, explain to patients their usages, tell them of Christ's love, translate between English and French for physicians, distribute eyeglasses, fit them on patients, prayerwalk, greet people in the villages, clear land for new preaching points, and do whatever is asked of them—from making sandwiches to inventorying medicines, so that people can hear about Jesus. Kevin and Kari have been thrilled to be a part of leading many people to Christ by sharing with patients His message. Jeff and I are not the only missionaries. We are a family of missionaries.

I discovered these words in my journal, "The Call! How powerfully it comes and cannot be denied nor set aside. It has ceased to be a word but lives and breathes and beats inside me. It consumes my thoughts, and my energy is directed to answer it." We were compelled.

Less than a year after re-contacting the Foreign Mission Board, we were on a plane bound for language school in France.

During a furlough in the States I once heard a man in Sunday School say, "God won't send to hell all those people who haven't heard. Besides, it's not our fault if they haven't heard. It's His responsibility, not ours."

Oh, he is so wrong! The people who have not heard will go to hell, and it is our fault. Jesus said, "No one comes unto the Father, but through Me" (John 14:6). If He said, "No one," that means no one. Jesus also commanded, "Go into all the world and preach the gospel to all creation" (Mark 16:15).

In response to these words Ryan says, "The Great Commission is not the Great Suggestion. It is a *command*!" That command was to our forefathers. That command is to you and me. People are dying and going to a Christ-less eternity because we have not gone. We have not sacrificially given. We have not engaged in informed, intercessory prayer for the nations. If the thought of literally billions of people around the globe dying in abject spiritual darkness and despair does not put you on your knees in tears, then repent and ask the Lord to give you His heart.

Once an elderly African man confronted me with a question to which I had no answer, "If your people have known about Jesus for all these hundreds of years, why didn't you come sooner?"

That hurts. The spiritual responsibility Jesus has placed on us is awesome. It extends to every dusty, cold, hot, dry, humid, buggy, urban, jungly, disease-infested corner of the world. People want to know. They are dying to hear. They just have not been told.

And it's our fault.

How then shall they call upon Him in whom they have not believed? And how shall they believe in Him whom they have not heard? And how shall they hear without a preacher? And how shall they preach unless they are sent? (Rom. 10:14-15).

FIVE

Going Pains

I thought they would be excited. But they weren't, and I really felt puzzled. They were my spiritual heroes. Dad had surrendered to be a missionary pilot, to fly over hazardous jungles carrying desperately needed supplies to faithful, suffering missionaries. He had geared his life toward that end. He even attended airplane-mechanic school so he could repair his own plane.

But, in the end, or rather the beginning, God called him to be a pastor. Out of obedience, he gave his airplane mechanic tools to a missionary friend and fellow pilot leaving for Zaire. Instead of being a missionary who piloted his craft through foreign skies, over unfamiliar landscapes and coconut-laden trees, he was pastor of Baptist mission churches in the U.S. He guided them to becoming self-sustaining, mission-supporting churches. He loved people to Christ and nurtured them in God's Word.

Mom, my other spiritual hero, led me to Christ when I was age five while we sat on the creaky, wooden back steps of our old two-story parsonage. She was aiming for my older brother, Bill, but got us both instead.

The life Dad preached from the pulpit was lived in our home. By example my parents guided my brother and me into daily quiet times and a willingness to pray anywhere, anytime, with anyone. I had seen this trait over and over in my father. If someone told him of a need while he and the person shook hands at the church door, Dad would say, "Let's pray right now." They did. With people milling around, Dad would lift his voice earnestly, compassionately, in prayer.

Dad has never been ashamed of his Lord. If he was in a hospital, restaurant, exposition hall, elevator, or airport, and someone mentioned a need, Dad would graciously pray, right then—right there. Once a woman with a terrible leg pain called him over to pray as he hurriedly walked out of a convention center. Seeing the need, he paused to pray, then ran to his pressing appointment. Later he learned that God had instantaneously healed her leg. I grew up challenged to make prayer an immediate response.

Mom always had fun with God in prayer. If we were traveling in the rain with our pop-up camper, she would ask the Lord to clear the skies so we could set up. As we would enter the campground, the sun would suddenly burst out from behind the storm clouds, right over our selected camping spot. We would hastily work as a team to pop up its canvas top and secure it down with ropes. Without fail, just as we finished, the waiting clouds would obscure the sun. Rain would pelt down with renewed vigor!

Because of my mother's prayer example, at ages nine and seven, respectively, my brother and I specifically prayed for three feet of snow to fall while we visited my great-aunt and -uncle for Thanksgiving. As Uncle Lloyd locked the doors of his little white country church (he was a Baptist preacher, too) after Dad had spoken that Wednesday night, huge flakes of fluff started hurtling down from the darkened skies above and continued throughout the starless night. A crisp, blazing, blue morning greeted us. Laughingly, we could only make out our car, lost pitifully in the snow, by its lonely antenna held coldly aloft! Three feet of delightful, unforgettable snow covered the ground.

The monster-sized, New York snow plows took several days to find us on that one-lane, tar road, but once they did, our family continued our journey. Ten miles from Uncle Lloyd's house the snow barely covered the ground. Astonished, our eyes grew wide at the sight of the grass stubbornly poking its blades up through the cottony fluff, creating the illusion of a lacy, white blanket. God had dumped the snow right on our uncle's house! Bill and I were awed. What a way to encourage a child's prayer life! Obviously God has fun with prayer, too.

Dad taught and still teaches people to walk in the power of the Holy Spirit, not as an emotional experience, but as a daily way of life. As a young boy he surrendered to Christ but every morning recommits his life to the Lordship of Jesus. He empties himself out before the Lord that the Holy Spirit may control him completely. He believes that a life surrendered to the empowering of the Holy Spirit results in the person hungering deeply to read and study the Word of God, thereby being grounded firmly in the Truth. He preaches that the Holy Spirit impassions a person to be disciplined in his or her prayer life and tenderly diligent in evangelism. These truths are evident in my parents' lives every day. They know the Word, live the Word, and pray in power. Any opportunity to share Christ is always lovingly embraced by both of my parents. Anyone they meet with the slightest thirst for Christ will later walk away with a river of Life flowing up from within them!

We knew missionaries. They were often in our home. I remember a visiting missionary from India who gave me a little sandalwood elephant on a key chain. I wasn't more than six. She taught me an Indian word for elephant, which sounded like "hot tea." She left her mark on my life, for I have never forgotten that word. I heard my father pray for missionaries, their ministries, their difficulties, and their warring countries. He gave so that Christ would be preached around the world.

Dad served on their convention's mission board. He was part of the body which commissioned people to go and enabled missionaries to stay on the field. He led a mission trip to Nicaragua and was deeply touched by the spiritual hunger and poverty of the people. (He was amazed that parrots could speak Spanish!) When home-video cameras were invented, Mom and Dad attended a mission conference and became among the first to videotape interviews with missionaries— videos that they later used to inspire their church members at home. My parents are exceptional people, consecrated to God, mighty in spirit, warriors in prayer with a heart for missions.

I thought they would be excited.

But they weren't.

Jeff and I, enthralled with the calling Christ was placing on our lives, drove from Tennessee to Ohio and exuberantly shared our hearts with my parents. After our visit, they walked us out through their garage to say good-bye. Little did I know then, that as we drove our young family away, they clung to each other in the garage and wept. They knew what, in our innocence, Jeff and I didn't. They had seen the suffering. They had heard the difficult and sometimes tragic stories of missionary life. And they grieved. God could call anyone else to the mission field, but not their daughter. Not to that life.

I didn't understand. Suddenly my mom, who has always been my closest confidante, grew distant from me. Conversation became strained with unspoken words and unexpressed emotions. They didn't want me to join in sharing the storehouse of intense trials and difficulties known by their missionary friends. They had just purchased a spacious home in a charming neighborhood with old cracked sidewalks (the memory-makers of childhood) so all their grandchildren could come to stay. But we were taking half their grandchildren away. I was going away. Far away and out of their lives. I didn't understand then; I was too excited about the Call. But I do now.

Sometime in those months between our telling and our parting we were sacrificed by them on the tear-stained, bloodied altar of the Lord. I can still remember the pressure of my mother's arms around me as she held me close and said, "I may not have you in this life, but we will have eternity together."

Our last Christmas before winging away, my brother, Bill, and his wife, Wanda, joined us in a solemn moment as Jeff and I knelt before my parents. Mom and Dad read from a piece of parchment containing precious words which they had composed. They spoke these over our lives as an act of blessing and consecration. Then they laid their hands on us and prayed.

And they continue to pray. Every day they engage in spiritual warfare prayer over our lives and ministry. That is why we are still on the field. That is why we have had the power to stay in spite of incredibly hard times. They represent the key to why God moves where He has planted us. It is not because of our lives. It is theirs. It is the power of prayer battles being fought on our behalf by two precious, sacrificial warriors a half a world away.

During one of my parents' visits to Benin, Josephine, an African friend of mine, took my mother's hand and spoke solemnly to her. I haltingly translated, for tears were clogging my heart. Josephine said, "Thank you so much for giving up your daughter so that I could know Christ."

Someday in heaven we will have the tremendous joy of introducing my parents to the thousands that were won to Jesus because of my parents' pain, sacrifice, and prayers.

Those who sow in tears shall reap with joyful shouting. He who goes to and fro weeping, carrying his bag of seed, shall indeed come again with a shout of joy, bringing his sheaves with him (Ps. 126:5-6).

SIX

Go Tell This People

If you ever become a missionary, don't go without the Word. Unless your Call is solidly grounded in the Word—undoubtedly, unwaveringly—you will quit. The Call holds your feet on germ-infested soil when your emotions have flown away. The Call drives you with passion when your sweat and strength have puddled at your filthy feet in the baking heat. The Call, through God's Word, becomes life's consuming fire.

The Call is a living contract with the Creator to be His messenger, His ambassador, His sacrificial offering to a people who do not acknowledge Him as Lord. The Call is not singular. It may start as one but leads to many avenues of Calling, blocked by altars of personal surrender. We are called to be missionaries, then called to a country, called to a ministry, and maybe called to a people. God calls us within a Calling. The Call to missions is just the starting point of surrender, not the end!

During our missionary training we worshiped with songs that yielded ourselves as offerings and sacrifices to the Lord. Every person present sang those words with conviction. We knew we were heading out and might possibly never return.

"Gather to me my consecrated ones, who have made a covenant with me by sacrifice" (Ps. 50:5 NIV). The Lord uses us as we lay ourselves on the altars of God's Calling.

As God called us and we labored through the missionary appointment process, we were burdened to offer a twofold prayer. We prayed that God would send us to a country where the gifts He had given us, along with our personalities, would work in harmony with the people. Secondly, we prayed that He would send us to a harvest field.

The day arrived when we received our first job request in the mail. The missionaries in each country prayerfully considered the needs of their people and wrote requests for new missionaries. The requests that matched what we believed God wanted us to do would filter down through the system and be sent to us. Excitedly, we tore open the huge manila envelope and started reading. We were immediately astounded. In this job description the missionaries had included a list of character qualities that would be useful for the missionary husband to have to be able to work well within their host country. The words described Jeff. We turned the page and read the few words that described the gifts and interests which would be helpful for the missionary wife to have. They described me.

The job request was for a youth worker for the African nation of Benin, a small country of five million, in which 50 percent of the population was under age 15. Benin was a nation of youth! With Jeff's passion for winning youth to Christ we had an instant, electrifying attraction of our lives toward Benin. The requested missionary youth director would not only work with the established churches to start youth programs, train leadership, hold retreats, and host camps but would also develop an evangelistic outreach on Benin's sole university campus. If we accepted the position, we would spend a year in France to learn the national language—French. Then we would study one of Benin's local languages, Fon (pronounced like phone).

Reading those two brief pages was like falling in love. It just felt right. Bewildered at our joint, immediate, positive reactions, we held that flimsy piece of paper in our hands and wondered out loud, "Where in the world is Benin?" We had never even heard of the country. We didn't even know how to pronounce its name!

In our calling to missions the Lord used the words of His call to Abraham:

"Go forth from your country, and from your relatives, and from your father's house, to the land which I will show you" (Gen. 12:1). On faith Abraham obediently went, not knowing where he was going. Now God was setting before us the same faith challenge, to go in Him, not really knowing where we would go.

From the answered prayer evidenced by the job-request descriptions and the peace of God in our hearts, we believed Benin was where God was leading us. Yet, we asked for confirmation.

The next day, Sunday, while sitting in the third row of our plush, suburban sanctuary, I half-listened as a woman from the mission society gave a plea for home missions during the Sunday morning service. I was too lost in prayer and awe over the content of the job request to center my concentration on her appeal. Only one thought, one prayer consumed my thoughts. Over and over in the secretness of my heart, I repeated, "Lord, do you want us to go to Benin?"

As the speaker began to read the vibrant, piercing words from Isaiah 6:8, "'Whom shall I send, and who will go for Us?' Then I said, 'Here am I. Send me!'" my ears perked up. My heart began to beat with the pain of a world suffering without Christ and with my earnest willingness to respond to that suffering. Again I whispered, "Lord, do you want us to go to Benin?" At that exact moment she read half of the next verse, words that I've never heard read before, nor since, in conjunction with these verses. Then she sat down, leaving me in stunned amazement. I longed to throw myself on my knees between the crowded pews and cry out to the Lord in adoration. She had read a direct command in answer to my inquiry.

"Go, and tell this people."

This people.

Benin's people.

Jeff and I immediately notified the mission board of our decision. Officials there said, "You can't accept the first and only job request you've received. Let us send you some others." We said, "You may send us more, but we are going to Benin." One or two other descriptions arrived within the week, but our resolve stood firm. We had been called to Benin. We were Benin-bound.

"I am sending you to open their eyes so that they may turn from darkness to light and from the dominion of Satan to God, in order that they may receive forgiveness of sins and an inheritance among those who have been sanctified by faith in Me" (Acts 26:17-18).

Before we knew Benin was the birthplace of voodoo; before we witnessed the idols' grotesque forms, stained black and hideously misshapen through years of oil and blood sacrifices poured liberally on them, God lifted these powerful words from the pages of the Bible and imbedded them in our hearts. These words became the cornerstone for our ministry among Benin's people. From intense darkness, they would turn to the brilliance of the Light. Now living in abject slavery in Satan's evil kingdom of hate, deception, and treachery, they would be freed to live in Christ's Kingdom of love, peace, power, and hope. Their sins, which destroy them from the inside out, would be completely forgiven and lifted away. From the horrors of eternal death and suffering, they would be released through Christ's blood to unparalleled, eternal joy in heaven. From darkness to Light. From Satan to God.

Only one thing remained.

We had to go.

I am the Lord, I have called you in righteousness, I will also hold you by the hand and watch over you, And I will appoint you as a covenant to the people, as a light to the nations, to open blind eyes, to bring out prisoners from the dungeon, and those who dwell in darkness from the prison. I am the Lord, that is My name; I will not give My glory to another, nor My praise to graven images (Isa. 42:6-8).

SEVEN

A Love Affair with Benin Begins

Snow had fallen. It rarely snows in France, but layers of sparkling fluff blanketed the roofs of the ancient stone buildings. It nestled on signs that swung lightly in the frigid breeze and covered the majestic, bare tree limbs with a robe of shimmering white. The kings and queens that had passed along those paths were never so radiantly adorned. The pristine, wintry scene beckoned us. We hastily abandoned any further thoughts of packing and headed our young family out into the icy splendor. We had no idea when we would see snow again. Benin rests six degrees north of the equator. Pictures we'd found of Benin had been desert-like in appearance. Long stretches of coarse sand held scraggly, bent palm trees. It was not pretty. The esthetic nature of my surroundings is very important to me. I found the barrenness appalling. Therefore, with our impending departure, I accepted each enchanting snowflake as a special gift from the Father.

Several days later with the excitement of a first-term missionary, my arms laden with two-year-old Kari; an oversized shoulder purse packed tightly with bibs, diapers, baby toys, candy bars, GI Joes, and Ninja Turtles; and with an overstuffed carry-on squeaking along behind me, I boarded the plane.

After a long night of confinement in uncomfortable, squishingly compact airline seats, the airliner's wheels screeched across the runway. We had touched down. We were in Benin. Cotonou, Benin (koh-tohn-new, behn-in).

It was 5 a.m. An early thunderstorm had struck, completely cutting off the limited electrical power. Everything was enshrouded in palpable black. Forced to leave the cool, dry air of the cabin, our winter-adapted bodies were physically slammed into a wall of excessive humidity. It was the difference between strolling through fresh, spring air and sludging through odiferous, hot gelatin.

We slogged down the slippery metal stairs placed at the airplane's massive door while we struggled to breathe the thick air. The thickness gripped us so tightly, it was as though our feet stepped forward twice but ended up one back. The blackness before us was faintly illuminated by light filtering through the cabin's open door.

As we shifted the packs, parcels, and carry-ons for our trek into obscurity, we were startled by the presence of a vicious-looking soldier sporting a menacing rifle. He stood stock-still under the jet's massive, dripping wings. He eyed us ominously as though we were unwanted intruders as we cautiously crept across the broken tarmac and nearly tripped into a water-drainage system lying open directly in our path. The only light that lit the still-sleeping city was an occasional sizzling flash of lightening. With trepidation we retreated toward the cavernous, urine-scented terminal.

As we inched toward the warehouse-like structure, six-year-old Kevin cried out, "Mom, where is my Ninja Turtle hat? It was right here, attached to my backpack." Somewhere his precious possession had disappeared. I was too frightened in this strange, deeply shadowed environment to go back to search for it. That speechless soldier holding his intimidating rifle had spoken volumes. To Kevin's dismay we left the hat behind and forged on.

Within the vast, empty, terminal, lanterns brought circlets of illumination to the faces of the custom officials who stood behind ruggedly constructed, wooden booths. Each humorously mumbled a strange, African French, totally incomprehensible to our France-trained ears and tongues. Their Benin French was guttural, the rhythm choppy, and the pronunciation—beyond different. It was wholly dissimilar to what we had learned.

Somehow between language bobbles and Jeff's patient spirit, our passports were stamped. We were waved on. I held sleepy Kari. Kevin and nine-year-old Ryan restlessly stuck by my side. They were anxious for us to give them permission to explore this strange environment.

The large, barren structure they called an airport was filthy, stifling, and incredibly noisy. We waited. The growing scents of body odor crowded in around us along with the mass of shoving, insistent humanity that filled the airless space. Within minutes our clothing clung to us like a second skin. Still, we waited. The heat increased.

As the dawning sun flitted across our new world, unseen hands rudely shoved our footlockers through a large hole in the wall. We snatched them up and eagerly turned toward the doorway. Baggage inspectors, like an impenetrable wall, blocked the only exit. With grim faces, indecipherable commands, and irritating manners, they frowned at our excessive luggage, scrutinized the contents, and scribbled chalk markings across each case before eventually waving us on.

Finally we found ourselves lovingly, joyfully engulfed in the eager, waiting arms of our new mission family, who had prayed for us and for years had anticipated our arrival! They enthusiastically greeted us into our new country and new life.

As we bounced away from the airport and into the thousands of bottomless potholes that studded the dirt street, sunlight flitted teasingly across the treetops. Its gaze unveiled trees laden with foreign-shaped leaves, vibrant blossoms of pink and yellow, majestic palms, and flowering walls of brilliant purple and fuchsia bougainvillaea.

Benin was more than just sand! As an amazed adventurer exploring an uncharted land, I drank in the sights around me. Tearing my eyes from the visual feast, I excitedly turned to Jeff, "I can see flowers and trees! If I can see green, I can live here!" Benin was not the barren wasteland I had expected but a tropical land of savage beauty. God had placed me in a floral kaleidoscope bursting with delightful varieties of living emerald. Even seeing a destitute, naked man bathing in a huge, freshly created mud puddle at the end of our new street didn't dissuade me from my resolve. I had decided. I'd never know until years later, after seeing many missionaries come and go, the stability that decision made in our first minutes in Benin gave me. It created a foundational part of my ability to stay.

"I can live here." So began our love affair with Benin.

Finally, brethren, whatever is true, whatever is honorable, whatever is right, whatever is pure, whatever is lovely, whatever is of good repute, if there is any excellence and if anything worthy of praise let your mind dwell on these things . . . practice these things; and the God of peace shall be with you (Phil. 4:8-9).

EIGHT

Something Out of a Movie

Eager worshipers crammed into the overcrowded, cement-block building. Their bright African attire created a refreshing sea of color against the drab, unpainted walls. We ushered our family onto the bench furthest in the back and wondered how we would contain the buoyant energy of our three children during the long service to follow. In the short week we'd spent in Benin, we'd already noticed that when African children sat, they just sat.

Suddenly voices began to sing loudly and fervently from an entrance next to the wooden platform. It was the choir, robed in aqua gowns down to their ankles. As they boisterously cried their traditional music, they swayed slowly to their places with a shuffle-dance. Engulfing smiles shone across their faces. Their hearty voices shook the wooden, slatted windows in exuberant praise. Tears flowed down my cheeks. It wasn't my culture. It wasn't my language. It wasn't familiar. But it was right. My spirit had come home.

At some point during the extended hours of worship, Kari voiced a need. Turning to missionaries Richard and Carmela Bartels, who we had accompanied to the Cotonou church, I asked, "Where is the bathroom?" I quickly learned that was an inappropriate question. The real question should have been, "Is there, possibly, an outhouse anywhere close by?" Carmela waved in the same manner the custom guys had waved and said, "Just take her over there by the garbage."

Hearty in heart Kari and I made our way across the muddy dirt road to the community garbage-strewn, public restroom area. An enormous, hairy pig, looking more savage than tame, rooted angrily up close to us, as I encouraged my newly potty-trained baby to perform the task at hand. She looked at the pig, clearly three times her size, and then at me, with wide, incredulous eyes. Nature overcame fear!

So many aspects of our new life were bewildering. Little about the country felt familiar. Nothing about us fit them.

In a pile of old letters I had written to my parents and friends, I discovered these words about those early days:

"My skin always feels clammy from constant perspiration and humidity.

"We brush our teeth with bottled water and keep our mouths tightly closed in the shower against any stray, impure droplets.

"I scrub Kari's hands each time I see her begin to put her fingers in her little mouth.

"I keep demonstrating to the boys what it means to wash their hands with lots of soap.

"I wonder how to get Kari's fine hair dry. It is constantly wet and plastered with sweat to her precious head.

"I wonder how to avoid the aggressive, burning heat rash Kari is developing.

"I praise God that, after struggling for two weeks to force Kari to take the incredibly horrible-tasting, liquid anti-malaria medication, she begged for the capsule form after seeing Kevin toss a pill in his mouth and swallow! I handed her a pill, and, amazingly she tossed it in her mouth and likewise swallowed! How I have been praying about this deadly problem!

"When we brake for one of the few stop lights in Cotonou, Wal-Mart walks by, draped over the arms of the hawkers. Geometry rulers, huge radio/cassette players, tablecloths, wrenches, sweat suits, super glue, extension chords, chandeliers. I even saw a man with a ceiling fan on his head!

"The streets are lined with vendors selling a wide assortment of things: green oranges and bananas, as well as an amazing variety of others—yellow, red, tiny and sweet, long and tart; loaves of hot, golden French bread in baskets perched on women's heads; cashews and peanuts stuffed into old whiskey bottles; black-market gasoline sold from enormous, globular, glass containers (which is openly sold without consequence); fried fish (with the heads); a pineapple drink served from a large gourd; hand-woven baskets of all shapes and sizes, and even used baby clothes, to name a few.

"Beggars approach the car regularly. They are usually crippled in some way—no fingers due to leprosy, no arm, no leg for some other reason. They don't become hostile if you don't have change. They smile and say, 'see you next time.'

"I took only one week to realize I couldn't handle the house alone. It needs to be mopped daily—entirely—and all the louvered windows need to be cleaned several times a week. That will be impossible for me to do when I'll soon be studying Fon full time, teaching the children, chasing a t w o - y e a r - o l d, cooking, shopping in the portable Wal-Mart, and managing the household.

"Boiling water for 20 minutes takes forever. Just boiling enough water for the day is an incredible chore. I never realized before how much water it takes to fill ice cube trays, mix powdered milk, make ice tea and Kool-Aid until I had to make the water myself!

"Mail goes out only on Fridays.

"On Wednesday morning the car wouldn't start and the phone was dead. So we couldn't tell anyone that we couldn't go anywhere.

"We have lizards in the house.

"We have to take a 2:30 p.m. nap. That's when it's the hottest and most humid.

"The heat makes me dizzy. The temperature in the house is 93 degrees. At night the heat is significant but not as oppressive as during the day.

"I saw a man rifling through the garbage on the side of the road today. At the same time I realized the man who is working for us took a broken, partially shattered mirror out of our garbage. The other missionaries say our house help will go through every bit of garbage before disposing of it. That makes me think twice before putting something in there.

"Driving here is suicide. The rules are that there are no rules. Bicycles, mopeds, and scooters zoom around you every which way but straight. People cross the road at random intervals, causing you to brake and dodge. He who has his car nosed out first, goes first. It's like driving through a continuous moving traffic jam of people hurrying away in every direction from a fiercely erupting volcano. Our Atari Frogger and Asteroid games of our early marriage had a higher purpose—to prepare us to drive in Benin! The stakes here are just a bit higher than squishing frogs!

"We went to the ocean today and just stood there and let its roaring waves sweep over our feet. Just beyond us was a bamboo-and-thatch fishing village nestled under a grove of palm trees. It was like something out of a movie."

A movie. Over the years we would change our language, our customs, our clothing, our mannerisms—our lives under the plan and scrutiny of the Director, until we did feel like we fit. Until the rightness was all-consuming. We have so immersed ourselves in our role that we forget, at times, our true nationality and skin color. The God-driven script unfolds moment by moment as a comedy, tragedy, or action-adventure. We are the real-life actors working against time to prevent our co-actors' deaths. Our production has one purpose—to draw them into Life. In the scheme of eternity we only have one reel to shoot. The cameras are rolling.

For though I am free from all men, I have made myself a slave to all, that I might win the more . . . I have become all things to all men, that I may by all means save some (1 Cor. 9:19, 22).

NINE

Throne Rooms

I have stood in majestic castles in France and Germany and let the history of their cold stone walls wash over me. I have studied the ancient architecture and intricate tapestries which marked the chambers of power from which kings ruled. Then I was taken from the throne rooms of men to one of the throne rooms of Satan—Benin. Benin is a power center in Satan's domain, for it is the birthplace of voodoo.

The deadly threads of voodoo worship are woven in a tangled web throughout the culture. Every event, from birth to death and beyond, is marked by the bloody stain of voodoo. Its claws permeate all of life. The extensive Satan-worship practiced binds the country in a tangible darkness. At times this darkness is so intense and weighty, I have physically felt a heaviness fall from my shoulders when I fly out of Benin. Those ensnared in voodoo are fearfully, destructively enslaved to the very gods from which they seek blessings.

The Beninese believe that everything in the world that cannot be explained must be set aside as holy, as untouchable. These things become voodoo. Among these things are water, the ocean, fire, wind, thunder, spirits of large trees, pythons, smallpox, twins, children born with deformities, or those who were born feet first. These, among others, are feared and worshiped. We have heard the stories and seen the realities of these deadly forces ruling over the lives of the people God has called us to love.

The presence of voodoo worship is everywhere. As we walk through the markets or villages, the abundance of ugly voodoo idols, flags, dolls, rings on fingers, physical scarring, and ragged symbols hanging in fields mark the evil defilement of their land and lives.

If a mother gives birth to twins and either or both dies, the mother must carry a wooden effigy of the dead child with her every day for the rest of her life. Wherever she goes, whatever she does, she must carry the child tucked protectively into her skirt. She dresses the doll-child in festive cloth for its trips to the market. At mealtime she sets it at a special, handmade, wooden table and places food offerings before it in tiny, painted, metal dishes. If she fails in her responsibility to her dead baby, the child's angry spirit will return to spread sickness and death among family members. Through the death of her child, the mother's life is reduced to living to appease the god she birthed.

Ancestors become honored gods to which the Beninese offer sacrifices during ancestral ceremonies. Immediately after the death of a loved one, the entire family and extended family must come together to walk from mud hut to mud hut of the surviving husband or wives, brothers, sisters, and children. Under makeshift palm-branch shelters, furnished with rugged, wooden benches, the visiting family is greeted. At each home the guests must receive drinks and food, in bounty, from those who are, like themselves, greatly impoverished.

Each long day of the ceremony women slave over cooking fires dawn to dusk neither resting nor complaining. Drums must be beaten. Dancers must dance. Chants must be shouted. And songs must be sung in respect of the dead. Little honored or celebrated in life, one is greatly feasted in death out of fear that the departed spirit will return to rain havoc upon those still living. Money that could not be found nor spared to save the life is now spent to protect the family from the spirit's hostility after death.

When death takes the breath from a body, the family quickly consults the departed spirit to learn the demands he now makes on the living. The spirit will dictate the frequency of the ceremonies that must be held in his honor to keep him at peace. The initial funeral ceremony is never enough. He must be remembered at yearly intervals and appeased. The money family members would invest in crops, goods to sell, medicines, and in educating their children is cast upon the bones of those long dead.

In areas of Benin, dead family members are buried under the hard-packed dirt floor of the central family house. Any visitor entering will be offered a bowl of water from which to cool his or her burning thirst. But first, the hostess will drink deeply from the tin to show it is not poisoned. Then, after she has poured some out on the clay floor for the ancestors, the visitor may quench his thirst. The dead are remembered first; the living, second.

After giving birth a mother will guard the placenta of her child and bury it so it can't be used in a curse against her or her infant. A person's fingernail and hair clippings are carefully discarded so they can't be concocted into evil sorcery spells to destroy him. If someone falls ill, he or she will seek out a *Bokono* (boh-koh-no). *Bokonos*, through magic, discern which god has been offended and how to placate its anger. They determine the sacrifice to be given.

Even doctors, when their diagnostic skills fail to detect a medical cause of a patient's sickness, will send the person home from the hospital with the prescription to discover who cursed him or her. When the sickness still remains, the family will place a basket or large gourd sacrifice of live chicks, money, and voodoo spells at a crossroads to stop the spirit of sickness from continuing to attack their home.

Although human sacrifices have been officially forbidden by the government, strange events continue to happen to this present day. During our second term, I shopped with an African friend, Alima, in the city of Cotonou. A frantic mob suddenly rushed by. Intrigued, with boldness overcoming caution, we stepped out onto the street to see what was happening. A few inquiries later we discovered that a woman had stolen a newborn from a birthing clinic. The angry crowd was running to apprehend her. Her actions made absolutely no sense to me. Children in Benin belong to the husband's family. If the husband should die, his family decides with whom and how the children will be reared. It is their cultural right. The mother isn't even involved nor consulted in the decisions. Children are kept within the father's extended family. Adoption is not accepted and rarely practiced. Children not belonging to the family bloodline are rejected. A woman's stealing and keeping of a child that was not her own would not be permitted.

"What could she possibly want with the baby?" I asked Alima. She quietly explained, "She is going to sell the baby to the sorcerer for parts."

Emanuel, now a man of Christ, was once part of the Zangbeto (zang-beh-toe) voodoo group. The members consider themselves night guardians who protect the people from criminal activity. At festivals they dance in bizarre outfits that flounce around like horned, walking haystacks. After Emmanuel witnessed the midnight, cold-blooded murder of a fellow Zangebeto for possibly telling some of the sect's secrets, he fled. If they had found him, it would have cost him his life. No one quits the Zangbetos. Emmanuel did. Instead of death he found Christ and was given true Life.

When dancers for the Revenant appear in their glittering fabrics and eerily masked faces, a crowd of curious spectators quickly forms. When they erupt into a furious spin and whirl into the dense assembly, the people scatter in terror. To touch one would mean certain death. Each dancer's accompanying guardian attempts to keep the unseeing haystack from the people with a stick he sports in his hand. If he fails to keep an unwanted body from brushing against his god, this guardian of evil will insure that a touch results in death—if not by the god he worships, then by poison.

The followers of the voodoo Xevioso (hev-ee-o-so), the god of thunder, traditionally do not permit the burial of a person who has been presumed killed by lightning. The body remains where it has fallen, whether for hours or for days, until the faithful can discern the absolute cause of death. If the person was killed by lightning, the body is supposed to be slowly smoked in the open, from twilight to dawn. Xevioso once required his followers to bring pieces of the dead person's flesh to their mouths in pretense of eating it, in order to honor their vile god.[1]

Another voodoo group, the Oros (or-os), during their secret, fear-instilling ceremonies, take over a village at night and threaten to kill any who would venture to leave their huts. By swinging a special carved stick in the air above their heads, they warn people of their presence. The whirling noise it produces causes people to flee and the strong to tremble.

The Tolegba (toe-leg-bah), the guardian of life, is represented by huge, earthen idols. At times their mounds rest over the graves of human victims who had been buried alive in their foundation to awaken the power of the god. They stand, silent and menacing, as sentinels at the entrance of large villages. Tolegba is the prince of gods who allows the presence of all the other gods into Benin. No other voodoo god can be worshiped until one of Tolegba's faithful followers, wearing a palm skirt and male phallic symbol, walks the paths of the village to announce the ceremony and sacrifice. No other mouth can make the proclamation. The Tolegba empowers the Legbas, who mark the entrances of smaller villages and compounds. They guard all who live there and must be offered a yearly sacrifice of goat's blood, food, and drink.

Villages have idols. Markets have idols. Families have idols. Individuals have idols. All must be appeased. All must be maintained and their hunger fed. The people seek to manipulate the favor of the gods by abandoning themselves to these demons of death who rule them through horrific fear. Idolatry flourishes. Bokonos thrive. Sorcerers, who kill people for satanic power, abound. Voodoo priests rule. Voodoo priestesses to demonic entities are numerous beyond imagination. Each person lives his or her life in search of a spiritual blessing but gain a life of poverty, misery, and slavery instead.

The situation looks bleak. Without hope. Without a solution. But we know Satan's throne room is trembling. Its walls are beginning to crumble. The power of prayer and the preaching of the Author of True Life is demolishing Satan's dominion in Benin, one person at a time.

Thy throne, O God, is forever and ever; A scepter of uprightness is the scepter of Thy kingdom (Ps. 45:6).

---

[1]Robert Cornevin, "The Dahomeyan Pantheon", *Ouidah Petite Anthologie Historique* (Coutonou, Republic of Benin: L'Imprimerie Industrielle Nouvelle Presse, 1993), 80.

TEN

Into the Darkness

One day, while we traveled from one village to another, Jeff and I encountered a group of women walking to a ceremony. The women were dressed in voodoo-worship attire. Multiple strands of tiny beads adorned their bare necks. Their costumes consisted of colorful cloth wrapped around their torsos and attached at one side. Powder covered their upper chests and exposed shoulders. But their dress was not the thing that caught my attention. It was their faces. Each looked drawn and sorrowful. No joy. No purpose. No love gleamed from their countenances; just despair. With tears blurring my vision, I prayed for them that they might turn from darkness to Light and from the dominion of Satan to God.

A close friend of mine used to be numbered among these women. As a mere child she was given by her family to be the bride of the voodoo god, the Nesuwe (nay-sue-way). After going through the rights of initiation, her responsibility was to live for the god. Her father had made a request of the Nesuwe and promised to give it one of his children when the request was granted. Roberte was the chosen one. She had no choice but to serve. Anything less than explicit obedience released evil spirits upon her family. Her initiation included a month-long stay in the coven of the Nesuwe. There she learned its secret language and dance.

The process of initiation into a voodoo coven changes from sect to sect. But many have a common theme—the symbolic dying of the person and his or her coming back to life, possessed with the spirit of his or her god. In the Ogoun (oh-goon) voodoo group, which worships the god of war and of iron, the initiate falls into a deathlike trance. The body is wrapped in a shroud and then carried into their temple, as into a tomb. The secret rites and rituals that take place within a temple are never disclosed. The resurrection of the initiate takes place a week later. The seemingly lifeless body is carried from the temple and stripped of the shroud to now live a new life consecrated to the demon god.[1]

On a magic mat placed within a triangle drawn in the dirt and covered with red and white spots, the high priests of Sakpata (sahk-pah-tah), the voodoo god of smallpox, offer a sacrifice of chickens. They invoke the god to accept the blood sacrifices in place of the lives of their initiates. The initiate is carried from their temple by six people. Three times they transport the body around the temple. Three times it is presented to the gods who protect the temple. Then the motionless body is placed on a mat and bathed by women. When the cleansing is complete, the high priest seven times cries out the name of the initiate. On the seventh cry the seemingly dead body shows signs of life. The initiate is once again carried back into the coven. From that time the person's personality is altered. He or she loses everything that the initiate was in "death", to become what the god makes him or her to be. The initiate is no longer considered solely a human being but a creature. In the person's death and resurrection he or she is stripped of the power of speech. Seven to eight months pass before the person is allowed to return home. During these months the initiate is taught the language of the Sakpata. Each voodoo god has a language known only by its followers. The resurrected initiate receives a new name, a name of this person's god. The person is called by this name until the day he or she dies.

During their ceremonies the Sakpata worshipers experience states of delirium, which cause them to act with animalistic impulses. They kill goats with their teeth and bathe themselves in the blood. During high ceremonies the worshipers kill a cow, drink its blood, and baptize themselves in it.[2]

Some women, to show their absolute dedication to Sakpata, tattoo their bodies with designs made of raised welts. The scarring is permanent.

A skinny, elderly woman with little fists of gray hair crowning her head stepped forward to be baptized in the village of Gomey. She was a voodoo priestess but had recently surrendered to Jesus Christ. Before stepping into the chilly water she lifted her shirt for the crowd from the village to see the thousands of voodoo scars that marked her body. She wanted everyone to clearly understand her former level of devotion to her voodoo god. Then she said, "Never again! I've given my life to Jesus!" Spontaneously the Christians shouted chants of praise. She continued, "I had been searching for Jesus all my life. Now that I've found Him, I'm going to tell my entire family about Him."

Looking at the gathering of curious onlookers she requested one of the men to read John 3:16. Then she testified, "I believe this with all my heart!" She was so old and weak that Jeff and another man had to lift her into the portable baptistry. During the communion service to follow, she fainted. The Christian brothers carried her out of the burning sun, into the shade, and laid her gingerly on a reed mat. I joined other believers around her prostrate form. We began to pray and sing. As she came to, she feebly began to lift her hands to the Lord and to join us in song. During her baptism, the communion, prayer, and praise, Christ had dramatically released her from the remaining chains of her former bondage. The freedom was sweet. She kept her promise. Every Sunday thereafter she had family members with her in church. She was only to experience living in Christ on this side of eternity for a few years. But she remained faithful to the Lord Jesus until her death.

Roberte, completely consecrated to the service of her god, danced at ceremonies and festivals to invoke its spirit to possess her body. It is considered an honored experience to have the god gyrate your body in convulsive movements. Roberte was in bondage.

One day her older brother, Bienvenu (bee-en-veh-new), came excitedly to see her. He was different. Jesus had come into his life. "This Jesus," he said emphatically, "is completely unlike the voodoo gods." He told her about Christ's sacrifice, His blood that poured out onto the cross and the ground because of her sins. He spoke of Christ's true death and His awesome physical and spiritual resurrection from the tomb. "All this happened, Roberte, to purchase our freedom. Your freedom. Jesus' Spirit fills a person with holiness, not evil," her brother said. Roberte knew the words her brother was telling her were true. She turned her back on the wrath of the Nesuwe, emptied herself out before Jesus, and was filled with Christ's Spirit.

Roberte once told me, "You'll never know freedom like I know freedom, because you were never enslaved like I was enslaved."

God has called us into the darkness that we might call others from darkness into His marvelous Light. But we can't do it alone. Too many people are dying in bondage, searching for Christ but never knowing Him.

We need your help.

They need your help.

He brought them out of darkness and the shadow of death, and broke their bands apart. Let them give thanks to the Lord for His lovingkindness, and for His wonders to the sons of men! (Ps. 107:14-15).

---

[1]Pierre Berger and Roger Bastide, "Les Deux Afrique", *Ouidah Petite Anthologie Historique* (Coutonou, Republic of Benin: L'Imprimerie Industrielle Nouvelle Presse, 1993), 88.

[2]Ibid.

ELEVEN

Please, Teach Us More!

Jeff crawled out of bed and looked down from our two-story rental into the cramped yard of the African family living next door. The squawking of hundreds of chickens being delivered in the dead of the night had once again awakened us.

However, also as before, when morning arrived, he couldn't spot as much as a feather in their yard. Where the chickens originated and to where they were secreted remained a mystery.

The usual sight of our neighbors' motorcycle occupying their tiny, exquisitely tiled kitchen no longer surprised him. He'd grown accustomed to the fact they found their kitchen a useless room, except as a garage, and preferred instead to do all their cooking over a charcoal fire outside.

In fact, the sight of the candle sitting on our windowsill in a contorted position like a gymnastic instructor who was illustrating a backbend but couldn't straighten up didn't raise a reaction out of him, either. As the blazing rays from the sun unsheathed by a cloudless dawn burst upon our room, the temperature quickened in its ascent from uncomfortably warm to hot within minutes.

With the searing light illuminating the millions of once-invisible dust particles before our eyes, the question of the candle was answered before it was posed. A glance at our curtains, which had been a delicate blue when they were pulled from the crate but were now nearly completely white, answered the rest of the question.

Still unaccustomed to the heat, Jeff moved slowly toward the tepid shower awaiting him in the next room. The water, even though piped up from below the foundation, couldn't achieve anything reminiscent of "cold." Water had two temperatures: lukewarm and scald-

ing. Lukewarm would have to do. Jeff had a Herculean drive on nearly non-navigable roads ahead of him. He was finally delving into his
ministry after long months of study to earn a basic level in the Fon
language. He was eager to be on his way.

When Jeff, frustrated from the length and difficulty of the drive,
arrived at the appointed meeting place, the area youth were already
waiting. Some of their faces were smudged and their clothing damp
with perspiration. Going to the rickety, dusty bikes parked under the
trees, they eagerly retrieved their Bibles from worn plastic sacks.
Looking at the tires' bare tread, Jeff questioned, "How far did you
travel on those bikes?" The answer shamed him. These young men
and women couldn't produce 50-cents to rent a place in a taxi.
Instead, in their zeal to learn more about Christ, they had borrowed
bikes from villagers and peddled the 17 miles to the rendezvous spot.
After the day-long retreat they would peddle the 17 miles home. Jeff
never again complained about the distance or the difficulty of travel
by car.

They dug into Bible study. Hours passed. The students posed
question after difficult question. They wrote notes in their notebooks
and translated for those who couldn't understand French. Needing to
feed the body as well as the spirit, they took a break for lunch. Each
person grabbed his battered tin plate; gratefully received the white
corn mush, spicy sauce, and smoked fish portion; found a seat on the
ground, and began to eat.

As the youth finished, Jeff went to the car and tossed soccer balls
and a volleyball to those already standing around. Incredulously they
asked him, "Pastor, what in the world are you doing?"

With the enthusiasm of an American youth pastor he responded,
"I thought we'd take a break from Bible study for some recreation."

"Pastor, put these things away," they implored, handing him back
the balls. "We didn't come all this way to play. We came to learn
more about Jesus."

Jeff was overcome with their passion for Christ. He put the
unused balls back in the car and locked the door. Picking up his Bible
from the hood, he took his place among them once more.

The sun would set in three hours. Jeff had a two-hour, bumpy
drive ahead of him and wanted to be home before dark. Driving on
Benin's roads is a challenge of dexterity and alertness and requires

intense prayer during the day and is nothing less than a nightmare at night. He told the people in his group, "I need to leave." They said, "No. Teach us more."

Jeff was concerned for the young men and women who would ride bikes back to their villages on black roads and unlit paths. "I need to go, and so do you," he said. They responded, "Please, just teach us a little more."

The sun was dipping down below the fields as he put the key into the ignition and watched the youth mount their bikes. They talked and laughed easily among themselves. Clearly they faced with joy the toilsome journey ahead of them.

Jeff had taught but had learned more. He had given but had received more deeply. He went to grow men and women in Christ, but he, himself, ended up growing.

Blessed are those who hunger and thirst for righteousness, for they shall be satisfied (Matt. 5:6).

TWELVE

Death Threat

Shadrach, Meshach, and Abednego knew what it meant to surrender themselves to God, to empty themselves upon Him in a conscious disregard of their physical self. They fully realized that their spiritual connection with the Lord Most High was their true life. The death-throwing flames of persecution became their greatest source of freedom as it disintegrated the ropes that bound them and catapulted them into the presence of Jesus. Unbound, they encountered the living Christ and walked with Him in the midst of the fire. As these great men of faith decided, often the followers of Jesus in Benin must decide that their physical lives aren't the essence of life. Being faithful to Jesus, no matter what the cost, is.

I watched the suffering form of my husband in the bed next to me. His gaunt skin was a ghastly color of yellow. He couldn't eat or drink without violent repercussions. Any light filtering into the room pierced his overly sensitive eyes. Nothing soothed the sickness that ravaged his body. Medicine only made the hepatitis worse. Although the doctor didn't seem overly concerned, I was. As I lay there, knowing the intensity of the disease which tormented his body, I thought he was going to die. "Jesus," I whispered with a breaking heart, "Jeff belongs to You. I release him completely into Your hands."

In the short time we had ministered in Benin, I had witnessed God working through Jeff. Weekly, on the sparsely equipped Benin university campus, he had shown Christian films. Voodoo worshipers, Moslems, agnostics, and atheists gathered in the suffocatingly hot room to debate the Truths they viewed. Some were won to Christ. A Sunday-morning service was started.

Jeff was often seen walking across the carefully swept dirt of tree-lined, high school courtyards as he sought the director's permission to lead Bible clubs and to project films on the assembly grounds at night. Permission was always granted. Many responded to Christ.

Jeff often zipped along the hazardous village roads, the dust swirling in billowing clouds behind him as he traveled to various regions of Benin to train youth leaders and lead one-day youth conferences. He returned home excited. "They aren't very strong in biblical knowledge," he said of his young youth leaders, "but they have a heart and a desire to grow—that is very refreshing!" The fervency of the Benin youth to know Christ deeply marked Jeff's life.

When the week for the first national Baptist youth camp arrived, he was there. None of the buildings had fans. The temperature hovered at 100-degrees Fahrenheit without the mercy of rain. Jeff slept and ate on campus. He carried his plate and fork with him, as did the campers. He spent exhaustive amounts of time driving back and forth to the decrepit outdoor markets to purchase food for the large assembly. He had engaged Christian women to cook the meals. With swollen hands they stirred huge cauldrons of bubbling corn meal in a tiny, smoke-filled room over excessively hot fires. Thirty minutes of scooping out boiling mush with a fire burning at my back while bending over another was all I could take. I lasted much longer scrubbing down, with laundry detergent, the bald, glassy-eyed chickens. Every plucked chicken got a bath before boiling! I stayed for a day. Jeff directed, preached, prayed, and hung out with his youth for a week.

We were stirred to watch these young men and women approach their relationship to Christ with an energy and seriousness we'd rarely seen matched during our U.S. ministry. To our prayer partners back in the States Jeff wrote,

"Have you ever had 93 live chickens in the back of your station wagon? How about a very live pig tied to the top of your car? How many campers have you seen give up their free time to kill and clean those squawking chickens for supper? How often have you seen 325 young people start each day with Bible study at 7:30 a.m. and continue sitting until 1 p.m. through preaching, seminars, and more Bible studies? How many youth camps have you heard of where there were only two one-hour periods of recreation in the whole week because the students wanted to study about Christ rather than recreate?"

Such experiences filled Jeff's life with grateful joy.

Other times Jeff came home heavily burdened with stories of the persecution and suffering of his youth.

Elizabeth, a 17-year-old girl living with relatives in the port city of Cotonou, accepted Jesus as her Savior. Her parents, who lived two hours north in Benin's voodoo center of Abomey (ah-boe-may), were furious. In a rare telephone call they demanded she return home immediately. Obediently, she waved down a bush taxi, squeezed in beside the other four occupants of the back seat, and endured the pot-holed, dangerous drive from the coast to her family compound. The voodoo Legba beside the tall mud walls of their concession was ominously covered in fresh blood. She pushed open the rusting corrugated piece of roofing used as a door and stepped inside. Seeing her mother bending over a basin on the ground scrubbing clothes, she called out a greeting. Her eagerness was met with anger as her mother maliciously threw down the wet, twisted cloth she held in her hands, stood up, and shrieked for her husband to come. Together they faced Elizabeth. "You may not serve this Jesus! It is forbidden. You will worship our ancestral gods!"

Their thundering voices promised that a spectacle was at hand. The entire family ran to watch: her father's other wives, brothers, sisters, aunts and uncles, cousins, and even her decrepit grandmother hobbled out to participate. Grabbing Elizabeth's arms her father tried to force her to her knees before their family idol. Elizabeth refused. She would not bow.

A family meeting convened. The older members flung insults at her and vehemently ordered her participation in a voodoo ritual that would reinstate her into the worship of their god. Again Elizabeth refused. In desperation the elders brutally hauled her to her former coven. There she was locked into the sacred temple. Trembling, she crawled into a corner and sought the Lord, for dreadful, unspoken things happened within those walls.

After a time men, in freakish outfits, the physical representation of the spirit they worshiped, entered and stood before her. She expected the worst and was surprised when all they wanted was money. She emptied her pockets onto the dirty floor and was allowed to go. Relieved, Elizabeth walked the footpaths through cornfields and tall, rustling, teak trees back to her parents' home.

The youth of her family spotted her while she was still outside the compound. They had witnessed her ordeal and began to ply her with a multitude of questions about her faith. Empowered by the Lord Jesus Christ, she shared. Soon, three bowed in prayer and joined her in her new life. Curious about her time within the sacred walls of the voodoo temple, they asked her to tell everything she had experienced. Because she knew Christ, she no longer felt bound by the voodoo secrecy taboos. She told them all she had seen and heard.

A neighbor, knowing all about the earlier commotion, gradually crept forward until he discerned Elizabeth's subject. A bloodcurdling scream bellowed from his mouth. He rushed upon her, scattering her powerless peers. With a length of cutting, plastic rope, he tied her hands together and dragged her into the compound before her parents. Vexed beyond reason, they bound her feet as well and beat her with a wooden rod. But her heart was steadfast. She would not renounce Christ.

Like Elizabeth, Beatrice surrendered her life to Jesus. Her father, a village voodoo priest, was horrified at her decision. The spiritual harmony of the household had been disrupted. The voodoo worshipers and gods would be angry. Her father ordered her to recant her alien faith. Beatrice graciously refused and begged him to listen to what Jesus had done in her life. Throwing his hands over his ears to drown out her words, he then pointed a long finger at her and said, "If you ever dare to tell anyone in this family about Christ, I will kill you." This was no idle threat. He had the power. He threw her from the household and proclaimed her dead.

Destitute, but rejoicing in Christ, she traveled to Cotonou, where a Christian family took her in.

One day Jeff, with a car full of youth, headed across the unpaved, pocked streets of Cotonou. He and the youth had an extensive list of young people they hoped to visit. As the car bumped along, one of the youth called out, "Hey, there's Beatrice!" Jeff braked and eased to a stop. Beatrice waved and walked over. "What are you doing?" she inquired. "We're going out to tell some kids about Jesus," Jeff responded. "You are?" Beatrice exclaimed. "Oh, may I please come with you? My sister just lives two blocks from here. We must go tell her."

Under a death threat she climbed into the car.

For the freedom they had found in Christ, Elizabeth, Beatrice, and countless others suffered without complaint. They were faithful, no matter what the cost. They had embraced all of Christ from blessings to sufferings. Christ was enough.

As Jeff's head lay on the pillow, he knew, too, that Christ was enough.

His youth suffered persecution for Jesus. Jeff suffered physically and shared, in part, in their suffering. The privilege of discipling these ardent youth had its price. Like the youth, Jeff was willing to pay.

To fervently follow the Lord Jesus Christ costs.

What is it costing you?

God . . . sent His angel and delivered His servants who put their trust in Him, violating the King's command, and yielded up their bodies so as not to serve or worship any god except their own God (Dan. 3:28).

THIRTEEN

Our Adequacy

I arrived on the mission field full of excitement at what God would accomplish through me. Between the paper mountains of the application process my faith had been dissected, my gifts categorized, my relationships scrutinized, and my psyche psychoanalyzed. I had been called by God, approved by humankind, and sent by the Foreign Mission Board. I believed that if the Southern Baptist Convention said I could do it, then I could! And God has spent the past 13 years stripping me down to a daily realization that I can't. Life, let alone ministry on the mission field, is impossible.

We landed in this African country of extremely difficult tonal languages and unbelievable grammar structures. Our target language, Fon, divides verbs in two, pronouns in two, and sets them at opposite ends of the sentence. Nice. We have to think in halves of pieces extending from the inside out before we can begin to speak. Fon also delightfully splits some nouns in two, so that you, the owner, end up in the middle of the house in the middle of the sentence.

No similarities exist between our two cultures except that the people walk upright on two feet and smile. You can say it incorrectly. You can offer it incorrectly. You can wave incorrectly. You can do nothing and be incorrect. The only thing you can do well in Benin, on your own, is sweat. The water from the pump is too filthy to use for washing clothes many months of the year. Bugs reign over the floor, walls, tables, cupboards, and even clean-underwear drawers. Major diseases stalk our lives. Driving conditions are seriously life-challenging. Privacy is a distant memory. The schedules we set are ripped apart by needy people knocking on our gate who've walked long, hot distances just to talk with us. They don't have access to phones, so they use their feet. Communication in Benin is only one step above the Dark Ages. The Pony Express would be a welcome relief.

I discovered I could not live this life. It is much bigger than I am and demands more of me than I have to give.

Since arriving in Benin these words have begun to ring in my heart with absolute clarity: "Not that we are adequate in ourselves to consider anything as coming from ourselves, but our adequacy is from God" (2 Cor. 3:5).

I can't. I am inadequate. Yet, the state of inadequacy is the best place to be, because Christ is adequate. He can through me. God delights in our impossible, uncomfortable situations, which thrust us beyond our capability because they force us to Him. When we collapse on our faces before the Lord and discover we are still breathing when the storm abates, He gets the praise. When we think we have had a hand in what was accomplished, in living or ministry, we guard for ourselves a portion of praise. God is tired of us stealing His glory. When we are taken beyond ourselves, we know that what has been accomplished has been God at work, not us. When we know it is Christ at work, He gets all the glory.

If you feel you are capable of doing the job you have been appointed to do, you are going to find out that you can't. If you are comfortable, watch out! God is about to make you very uncomfortable. If you feel inadequate to accomplish the task to which God calls you, you are just the person for the job.

After living a year in France, performing oral gymnastics with the tongue and lips to master the proper pucker and accent, we were plunged headlong into Benin's incomprehensible French and the Fon language, one of 53 spoken throughout the land.

Three times a week Momono arrived at our home. Balanced on top of her tightly braided hair was an enormous platter of precariously stacked, scrubbed, and shining vegetables. I'd leave the boys supposedly studiously studying at their school desks and with Kari toddling at my side, walk to the gate to greet her. I'd help lift the incredible weight off her head, and we would sit on the tiled steps of our terrace to talk.

She was illiterate. She knew no French. I knew no Fon. Communication was difficult at best. But I could somewhat pronounce the Fon alphabet. Together we stumbled through a Fon Bible study, a simple one covering the basics of Christianity. I attempted to teach her to read, while I struggled to learn vocabulary.

One day, during a particularly arduous study for me, she grabbed my knee and said, "Let's pray."

I hadn't understood the lesson. I didn't understand the words of her fervent prayer. But pray, she did!

Months later, as our communication skills developed, I questioned her, "Momono, when did you give your life to Jesus?" "Oh, don't you know?" She responded, "That day when we prayed together on your terrace."

I never knew. I was inadequate.

But Christ is our adequacy.

During our second term illness terribly depleted my physical strength. Dengue fever, Epstein-Barr virus, infections, recurring bouts of malaria mixed with an undiagnosed blood-sugar problem, left me weak and constantly ill for more than a year.

In the middle of all this sickness—during a bout of malaria that announced its presence with extreme muscle aches—I felt compelled in spite of the drizzling rain to greet my neighbors in the compound across our rutted, muddy road. Greetings are extremely important in Benin. You can be greeted in your waking, in your existing, in your troubles, in your work, in your giving, in your grieving, in your walking, in your sitting, in your travel, and in your preaching. They even have special greetings for when it is windy, cool, or rainy.

Due to illness, I hadn't greeted my neighbors for several days. This is considered quite rude. When I walked over, they enthusiastically welcomed me and invited me into a crowded, steamy room shut tight against the rain. Entering, I ran through a barrage of greetings which expended all my energy. Desiring to return to my bed I culturally correctly said, "I beg permission to leave."

But one woman stopped me by saying, "Wait. You told us to read John 10:9-10, but you've not explained it. Please, tell us what it means." Seven women and one boy were cramped together in that tiny, dimly lit room, waiting on what I'd say. Too weak to be able to remain standing, I knelt on a straw mat and prayed for the words to come. It is difficult to speak English when you are ill. Imagine struggling for the right words, with fatigue and sickness chasing your every thought, in your third language.

The Lord faithfully intervened. I shared with them in my beggar's Fon what it meant to entrust their lives to Jesus. Wearily, tentatively, without any hope, I asked if anyone desired to give his or her life to Christ.

One by one each quickly, quietly slipped onto his or her knees before me. Dazed at their responsiveness I led them in a prayer of confession and surrender. Absolutely powerless and weak, I understandably experienced for the first time the words, "My grace is sufficient for you, for power is perfected in weakness . . ." (2 Cor. 12:9).

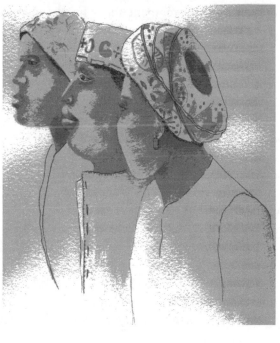

I could not take the credit for the rebirth of these lives. I could not boast in what I had done, for I knew, really knew, I had not accomplished a thing in my own strength. Christ had taken control. His strength had flooded my aching, shaking, empty body. Christ's strength is most evident in our weakness. We are to cry out to the Lord the words of Paul: "Therefore, I am well content with weaknesses, with insults, with distresses, with persecutions, with difficulties, for Christ's sake; for when I am weak, then I am strong" (2 Cor. 12:10).

I am to be thoroughly content in every circumstance that would leave me helpless in myself but abandoned to Christ. Not adequate, but inadequate. Not capable, but incapable. Not strong, but weak, having nothing in myself, but everything in Christ.

During our furloughs I have grown to wonder what would happen if churches didn't choose pastors and youth and music ministers based on their diplomas and credentials but on their inadequacies, on their willing desperation to stay on their knees before Jesus to get the job done. Interesting thought.

As the days pass into years here on the mission field, I do not feel more confident of my own abilities or more capable of successful ministry. Rather, God always demands more than I can give and places me constantly in situations beyond my capacity and strength. We live always on the edge. Why? To keep us crying out to Him. To keep us on our knees pleading for wisdom and power. To keep us knowing, at every moment, that Christ, and not us, has done the work, for we could not.

And He gets the praise.

"But we have this treasure in earthen vessels, that the surpassing greatness of the power may be of God and not from ourselves" (2 Cor. 4:7).

We lumps of clay have a hidden treasure, a Power Source far beyond ourselves. We find this only when we are not relying on self. We find this only through our inadequacy. Stay inadequate. Reach out beyond yourself into Christ. Surprisingly He will accomplish the work thoroughly through you, while you watch with a grateful, joyful, humble heart.

We can't.

He always can.

Whom have I in heaven but Thee? And besides Thee, I desire nothing on earth. My flesh and my heart may fail, but God is the strength of my heart and my portion forever (Ps. 73:25-26).

FOURTEEN

Open Their Eyes

Dr. Jim Butner, a volunteer ophthalmologist from Oklahoma, drew his ophthalmoscope close to the eye of his next patient in the darkened, craggy, clay-walled hut. Perplexity knit his eyebrows together as he struggled to discern the reason. Here was yet another.

Since early morning patient after patient had stood before him. Each was mostly blind. Their retinas had been severely burned. Jeff, standing by Dr. Butner's side, knew Jim's heart was heavy. Frustration was etched in his face and evident in his voice, for he could do nothing for them. He could not determine the cause. No cure was available.

These men and women would live the rest of their lives with only peripheral vision.

Baffled, the doctor finally asked the man he was examining, "What have you done to your eyes?"

The villager responded, "As part of our voodoo worship we stand and stare at the sun."

This story grips our hearts. Neither Jeff nor I can tell it without weeping. If you were looking at my manuscript, you would see tear stains—tears for the people of Benin—for they are blinded through their worship of Satan, blinded physically and spiritually. How appropriate the words, "The god of this world has blinded the minds of the unbelieving, that they might not see the light of the gospel of the glory of Christ" (2 Cor. 4:4).

God said, "I am sending you to open their eyes that they may turn from darkness to light and from the dominion of Satan to Christ" (Acts 26:17-18). He didn't say, "You go and I will open their eyes." He commanded, "You open their eyes."

But how? What surgical instruments do we hold in our hands to open blind eyes? What weapons do we possess to wield in battle against the god of this world? Has God commanded and then left us defenseless? No. He has empowered us to act in the authority of our Lord Jesus Christ, imbued us with spiritual armor, endowed us with the sword of the Spirit, and granted us the power of prayer!

Jesus Christ said, "All authority has been given to Me in heaven and on earth" (Matt. 28:18).

Why does Jesus possess this awesome authority? Jesus is the Creator. The creation, the things which have substance and things which do not, can never have authority over the Creator.

The invisible component that holds all atoms together, the invisible glue the nuclear physicists are still trying to discover, is Jesus (Col. 1:16-17). If He holds it all together, then without Him it all falls apart. That is a position of great authority. While He is keeping everything in our dimension, and beyond, from self-destructing, He pours Himself into the greatest and most minute parts (Eph. 4:9-10). No places in time and space exist that Jesus doesn't fill. He is "I AM." That's authority!

God the Father placed Jesus physically in the position of absolute authority through Christ's resurrection. Jesus' authority extends exceedingly beyond all earthly and spiritual rulers, regardless of their power source or the name that they name (Eph. 1:20-22).

Furthermore, Jesus displayed His authority when He disarmed Satan and his demonic forces and made a mockery of them. He stands with His feet firmly squeezing down on their necks, triumphant in His authority (Col. 2:15).

Nothing can take preeminence over Christ. Jesus is the ultimate authority from galaxy to galaxy, from the seen to the unseen. His authority is omnipotent. What would be the result if we would dare to believe completely in His overcoming, overwhelming authority?

July 2001. Paul, one of the few in his family from Azoe Cada (ah-zoe-aye cah-dah) to believe in Christ, entered the heavily oppressive air of the hut. The sweaty bodies that crowded the cramped area had escalated the temperature in the room from uncomfortably warm to stiflingly hot. But the oppressiveness had a wholly different source. His family was tightly gathered around one of their children, his nephew, just a young boy, who was deathly sick. The boy's still, pale form lay stretched out over a thin reed mat on the dirt floor. Rays of light, which filtered in through the door and flitted about the millions of dust particles hanging heavily on the motionless air, dimly lit the anxious scene. Each person stared intently at the Bokono (boh-koh-no) before them, as he spoke mysterious incantations and prepared to apply a sacred, magic ointment to the rapidly heaving chest of the child. They believed. They'd paid the required fee. The Bokono was the only one who understood the voodoo gods and could do what was necessary to bring health to their son.

Paul eased in with a grieving heart. His family refused to accept his testimony of Jesus. Silently, he prayed.

The Bokono dipped his magic stick into the potion and reached carefully across the suffering form to apply it to the child's chest. At that instant, before he could touch the boy, the child's labored breathing sharply stopped. The men and women present gasped. His mother started to wail, "No. No. No. Not my child! Not my son!"

The Bokono laid his head on the boy's chest. Empty silence resounded within the cavity. Resolutely he called for a lemon to be brought. Someone quickly pushed through the crowd, ran from the room, and raced back with a lemon and sharp knife. The Bokono took the lemon in his hand, sliced it in two, then squeezed it over the boy's eyes. If they flickered, life was still there. He watched and waited. Nothing. The child was dead. A mighty struggle ensued of man and woman against the tears that scalded their eyes. Yet another of their family was dead, but they refused to allow themselves to visibly yield to the grief that gripped their hearts.

As the Bokono slipped out, Paul stepped boldly forward. "Wait," he cried. "I want everyone to leave the room, except you," he said, pointing to one of his brothers. The room immediately cleared. Paul commanded, "Hold him up in front of me." His brother did so. Paul stood before him and prayed. He prayed in the authority and name of the Lord Jesus Christ. He prayed for a miracle. He prayed for the Lord to restore the child's life. Time passed. Yet, he prayed.

Startled by a sensation of movement, Paul's brother's heart started beating wildly. He looked down on the dead form he held. "Paul! Paul, look!" he shouted. The child's chest was moving. The boy opened his eyes, looked up into the face of the one who held him, stretched, and stood up, completely well!

Paul believes in Christ's authority.

God, in His love for us, has allowed us to share in the very authority of Jesus. Through our submission to the lordship of Christ, our feet may be sloshing through the mud puddles on earth, but our spirits are seated with Jesus, on His very throne, next to God in heaven (Eph. 2:4-6). That is a position of authority. We have done nothing to merit this fantastic seating arrangement. It is completely an act of Divine grace.

Instead of trembling in fear we can stand firm in the absolute, undefeated, indisputable Authority of the universe. Jesus gave us "power and authority over all the demons, and to heal diseases" (Luke 9:1) and "authority to tread upon serpents and scorpions, and over all the power of the enemy" (Luke 10:19). We are to speak, live, and act in the same authority that Christ has, for He has given that privilege to us. It is our right. It is our responsibility. When we stand in Jesus' authority, we are greater than the mightiest army, visible or invisible, that exists.

The apostle Paul, in 2 Timothy 2:3, calls *soldiers* those who trust in Christ Jesus. No soldier joins the battle without acting under the authority of his commanding officer. Once the command has been given, the soldier executes his orders with authority—the authority that has been accorded him. As soldiers we obediently move in the authority of our Commander. Jesus praised the centurion from Capernaum who said. "Lord, I am not qualified for You to come under my roof, but just say the word, and my servant will be healed. For I, too, am a man under authority, with soldiers under me; and I say to this one, 'Go!' and he goes, and to another, 'Come!' and he comes, and to my slave, "Do this!' and he does it" (Matt. 8:8-9).

Why did Jesus praise this man? Because the centurion understood authority, not only in the physical realm but also in the spiritual. The centurion was a man who not only received orders and explicitly obeyed them, he was also a man who gave orders that were explicitly obeyed. Through faith he related the human system of authority to the spiritual system. His words revealed his belief in Christ as the Supreme Authority, as God Almighty. He knew that Jesus only needed to say the word, and it would be done, because everything that existed was under His authority. His insight amazed Jesus! It is a tough thing to amaze God.

The clarity and depth of the centurion's perception must become our own. We need to acknowledge, through faith, that Jesus has all authority. We need to daily practice living in the spiritual authority He has extended to us.

Before I left the United States, I had a dream. I was riding in the back seat of a car with other missionaries as we passed a forest of tall trees with skinny trunks. Scattered throughout the forest were many short, white creatures, which greatly resembled children dressed as ghosts. In the name of Jesus I began to come against these satanic apparitions. Suddenly I could not breathe. It was as if I was being angrily choked by an unseen hand. A voice spoke to me, saying, "You are not strong enough to rebuke us on your own." I woke up startled and resumed breathing. I never forgot that night.

Not long after our arrival in Benin, we drove up-country, to explore the land and to visit some of our missionary colleagues. Along the way my spirit was confronted by an idol, boldly standing by the roadside. I knew him. He was the spitting image of the creatures in my dream. Unafraid, I stared right back into his ugly, Tolegba face. The scare tactic hadn't worked against me. I had continued to pray against Satan's power over Benin, for one with Jesus is greater than an army of spiritual adversaries. I had never been standing alone but had been praying in Christ's authority. If Jeff and I didn't believe these words, we would have fled from Benin years ago.

Many volunteers arrive in Benin and see miraculous things. We pray together, in Christ's authority, for Satan to be bound. We pray for salvation to be revealed and accepted and the sick to be healed.

In October 2000 Fred Orcutt, from First Baptist Church, Woodstock, Georgia, led a volunteer medical team to Benin. The days were hot, the work difficult. We set up the portable clinic in schools, huts, and bamboo churches in an attempt to gain large audiences who would listen to the words of Jesus Christ. Crowds followed us wherever we went. Children clung to our hands. Mothers pleaded for their babies to be seen.

A man on a black, wobbling bicycle rode up to the clinic we were holding in the village of Tanu (tah-new). He had ridden miles to get there. He pushed through the noisy multitude and begged the Christian brothers to give him an opportunity to see one of the doctors. Although he moved with the energy of a healthy person, his face was intriguingly covered by a large bandanna. Once the mysterious man walked into the makeshift examining room, he pulled off the cloth. Shocked, Dr. Jim Lindsey hesitated for a moment. The man's skin was rotting off his cheek and jawbones. Cautiously he examined him but could not name the disease that was tearing the man's flesh from his face.

With a prayer he handed the suffering man some antibiotic cream and capsules and called for the next patient. The contingent of African workers witnessed to him and prayed for him.

One week later we were holding a clinic in yet another village when a man on a black, rickety bicycle rode up. He was sweaty from his long ride over rough paths and through scraggly brush. He walked urgently up to those staffing the clinic and said, "Please, I must see the doctor. I have to thank him."

Dr. Lindsey was examining his 50th patient of the day when commotion behind him caused him to turn around. The man moved toward him, hand extended. "Thank you, doctor," is all he said. Jim took his extended hand, nodded, and returned to his patient. But one of the Christian men grabbed his arm and said, "Wait, Dr. Lindsey, you don't understand! This is the man with the face!"

Incredulous, he urged the young man to take a seat and examined him. His skin was perfectly well. "This is impossible," Jim repeated over and over. "Even if I had diagnosed the disease correctly and had given him exactly the right medicines, this could not have happened in a week." With waves of chill bumps flowing over his body he exclaimed, "This is God!"

The man explained, "After seeing my face all my village proclaimed that I had been cursed and would die within a week. I was desperate, so I came to your clinic for help."

The last we heard, he had given his life to Jesus and was faithfully attending church. He wasn't healed through medical knowledge but through the power of prayer prayed in the authority of the Lord Jesus Christ.

Jesus has privileged us to participate in His authority for a specific purpose. In Matthew 28:18-19 Jesus said, "All authority has been given to Me in heaven and on earth," which He followed with a clear, simple, command, "Go therefore and make disciples of all the nations, baptizing them in the name of the Father and the Son and the

Holy Spirit." We have been given Christ's authority that the world may know Him.

Take up the responsibility of your position. Be bold in Christ's authority. In Jesus' name come against that which has blinded the people, over that which keeps them in darkness. Then win them for Christ. God has granted this to us, not only as our privilege but also as our responsibility.

You are from God, little children, and have overcome them; because greater is He who is in you than he who is in the world (I John 4:4).

FIFTEEN

Battle Array

To fulfill God's command to "open their eyes", we must stand in the authority of Christ and prepare ourselves to enter the battle, for those who have been blinded by Satan are also enslaved by Satan, held captive by him to do his will (2 Pet. 2:19). They can only be set free—unblinded—by those under Christ's dominion. That means you and me. They have no other source of escape. Their freedom in Christ is won when we willfully place ourselves in the conflict.

No soldier enters the battlefield without his gear in place. Ephesians 6:11 exhorts us to "Put on the full armor of God, that you may be able to stand firm against the schemes of the devil." Ephesians 6:13 instructs, "Therefore, take up the full armor of God, that you may be able to resist in the evil day, and having done everything, to stand firm."

In the original Greek the word denoting "to resist" in verse 13 emphasizes the final result, that the armor gives us the ability to remain strongly steadfast during the heat of battle and to maintain our position victoriously until the end of the conflict, "neither dislodged nor felled."[1] Verse 14 admonishes us to "Stand firm then, with the belt of truth buckled (NASB girded) around your waist . . ." (NIV).

The Roman soldier, from whom Paul took his analogy, wore a loose-fitting tunic made from a large, square piece of cloth, belted at his waist with a weighty leather belt. Loose is comfortable, but it is also extremely hazardous in combat. You can well imagine the excess cloth of a long, flowing tunic entangling itself around the soldier's legs and tripping him in the heat of battle. It would be the trip of death. To "gird" meant to tuck the dangerous extra fabric into his belt so the soldier obtains maximum freedom of movement. The belt was essential for maintaining his readiness and mobility.[2] The belt also served another extremely important purpose. It held the sheathing for the soldier's sword. Without the belt the sword had no place.[3]

Without truth the Word has no power.

Jeff and I pray daily that the Lord will strap around us the belt of Truth, that we may always speak the truth, share accurately the Truth, and that we may be able to discern the truth.

Deviousness exists in every culture. In fact, some dishonesty is culturally applauded. In Benin, for example, if a person unexpectedly dies in a village distant from his own, a messenger will be sent to his family. This messenger will not inform the family that the person is dead. He will begin by gently saying, "Your son is very sick."

After the family weeps over this painful thought for an hour or more, the messenger pushes a little further and says, "In fact, your son is critically sick." These foreboding words sink into the minds of the family members. Finally, hours after he arrives, he will say, "Actually, your son is dead." The cultural mindset is to gradually work up to the horrible fact of the death without springing it suddenly on a person or family. They believe that simply stating the fact would be unbearable. I have decided that if anyone ever tells me Jeff is sick in a village somewhere, I will just accept the fact that he is dead and spare myself all their stages of emotional trauma.

Apart from cultural dishonesty, we are often plunged into situations demanding a clear understanding of what is the truth. For instance, we daily have people arriving at our gate in search of financial help. They need money for seed to plant corn to feed their family. Their mother has died, and they need money for her funeral. Their motorcycle taxi is broken, and they have no money for repairs. Without the bike they have no income. They are hungry. Their child is on the brink of death. They want to send their son to school but do not have the $20 necessary for the school uniform and supplies. They have just completed training as a seamstress, or mechanic, or weaver, but now need a sewing machine, tools, or loom. They want us to get them an American wife and buy them a car. The list goes on and on. We desperately need discernment of the truth to know whether the situation is real or fabricated. No matter what culture surrounds us, we must have Truth to guide and uphold our lives. Without the Truth we have no sheath for the sword. Put on the belt of Truth.

"And having put on the breastplate of righteousness" (Eph. 6:14). The breastplate covered the back, shoulders, and chest of the soldier. Sometimes it was fashioned of hammered metal plates. These plates, once large pieces of misshapen metal, were held over an intense flame in weighty tongs by the massive hands of the forger. Once they glowed a shimmering red, they were beaten over an anvil with a punishing, oversized hammer into just the right shape to protect the life of the soldier. Jesus was beaten for you and me that we might be protected by His absolute righteousness.

God expects us to wear Christ's righteousness. Every morning we ask for Jesus' righteousness to cover us, in complete knowledge that we have absolutely no goodness of our own. Scripture makes this very clear, "I have no good besides Thee" (Ps. 16:2).

In Isaiah 64:6 God states, "For all of us have become like one who is unclean, and all our righteous deeds are like a filthy garment." That "filthy garment" refers to rags used for women's monthly cycles. This illustrates that our absolute best is disgusting to God—not a pleasant thought. What a great danger to think we have any right standing with God apart from the Lord Jesus Christ or that any good thing we do arises from within ourselves, from our "filthy garment."

The world teaches that people are basically good. This belief is a satanic deception. This idea has lulled us into believing that the good thoughts we think, the good thing we just said, or the good action we just accomplished originated from within ourselves. Therefore we proudly accept the applause, the acclaim, the pat on the back.

The reality is that we have no goodness in ourselves apart from Christ. The truth is, the mistakes are ours. The good is His. Jeremiah boldly declared, "The heart is more deceitful than all else and is desperately sick" (Jer. 17:9). The longer I live, the more I know the horrid reality of these words. Nothing of any worth comes from my heart. Any good, creative, or spiritual thought, word, action, reaction, or accomplishment does not originate from within but from Without, from the Source of all Good. All good—any good—is inspired by God. Any goodness found in the world is because of God's abiding presence. Take God out of the world, and all that is left is hell.

No good thing is in me. That's why I desperately need a Savior. That's why I need His grace to live out each day. This realization puts the praise justly back on the only One worthy of it.

We come to God through Jesus Christ completely empty-handed and unworthy, but this does not mean that we are worthless. We are of immeasurable value to God, who proved this fact through shedding the blood of our Savior—His Son, Jesus Christ—for us, individually and personally. Our imaginations cannot conceive how greatly God treasures us. Even though we are leprous beggars before an awesome God, we do have the thrill of experiencing God's Spirit consuming our lives and expressing His character through us. We can exchange our repulsive attempts at righteousness for His perfect, pure righteousness. Through the bounty of the Holy Spirit we can be loving, giving, gentle, kind, caring, moral, patient, selfless, humble, and able to think positive thoughts, to understand Scripture, and to share Christ with others. What an awesome exchange!

When we stay aware of the vastness of our personal sin along with our utter unworthiness before Him, God can use us. When we forget who we are and begin to think we have something in ourselves to offer to God, we step into pride. Pride easily enters our lives through self-righteousness. We need to daily exchange our self-righteousness for His righteousness. We need to confess our sins and ask that His purity be our protection. We must ask the Lord to reveal our sins to us, for we easily become insensitive to sin. I am amazed at the multitude of sins the Holy Spirit can dredge up from my heart when I invite Him to examine my life. Praying that God will place on our lives the breastplate of righteousness reminds us of who we are and Whose we are.

Put on the breastplate of righteousness.

Pursue righteousness, godliness, faith, love, perseverance and gentleness. Fight the good fight of faith; take hold of the eternal life to which you were called (I Tim. 6:11-12).

---

[1]Rev. W. Robertson Nicoll, M.A., LL.D., editor, *The Expositor's Greek New Testament,* vol. 3 (Grand Rapids, MI: Wm. B. Eerdmans Publishing Co., 1993), 385.

[2]John MacArthur, Jr., *The MacArthur New Testament Commentary on Ephesians* (Chicago: Moody Press, 1986), 348-349.

[3]Warren W. Wiersbe, *The Bible Exposition Commentary,* vol. 2 (Wheaton, IL: Victor Books, 1989), 58.

SIXTEEN

Battle Boots

Soldiers exist because the enemy exists. The soldier's purpose is to take his stand against the enemy. Ephesians 6:14-15 states, "Stand firm then . . . with your feet fitted with the readiness that comes from the gospel of peace" (NIV). *The New Testament An Expanded Translation*, from Greek, states, "Stand therefore . . . having sandalled your feet with a firm foundation of the good news of peace."[1] Paul binds two separate images together in these few words. The first is the foundation of the gospel—the good news. The soldier in God's army stands on all that is God's Word. The salvation, the power, the truth, the promises, the absolutes, the character of God Himself found in the Word create a rock-solid, unshakable base for all the activity of the soldier. The proof of the living, transforming Word of God is His peace, only known by those who live in Christ Jesus. This peace which owns us and which we own gives us security in our sonship, security to stand firm as soldiers. To attempt to stand on the gospel without God's peace is treachery. If we have no peace, we have no relationship with Christ. We have no foundation. Peacelessness is a bottomless quagmire.

Paul speaks of our foundation and also of shoes. A soldier taking his stand must have his feet fully protected. The Greek clarifies that the sandal mentioned in verse 15 is not just a common, everyday sandal or shoe, but it is military equipment. John MacArthur, in his *New Testament Commentary on Ephesians*, gives us a vivid glimpse of a soldier and his footwear. He states:

"A soldier's shoes are more important even than an athlete's, because his very life could depend on them. As he marches on rough, hot roads, climbs over jagged rocks, tramples over thorns, and wades through streambeds of jagged stones, his feet need much protection. A soldier whose feet are blistered, cut, or swollen cannot fight well and often is not even able to stand up—a perilous situation in battle. He cannot very well handle his sword or shield and cannot advance rapidly or even retreat.

"Besides being made tough and durable to protect his feet, the Roman soldier's shoes, or boots, were usually impregnated with bits of metal or nails to give him greater traction as he climbed a slippery cliff and greater stability as he fought."[2] When a soldier's feet are protected, he can move quickly and confidently.

Not only is the soldier to stand on the firm foundation of the gospel, he is also to wear it. Here Paul's imagery takes on surrealistic dimensions. When Jesus walked on the water, he walked on liquid, yet it was rock-solid under His feet. It was liquid with rock's properties. The inverse is true in this case. The foundation on which we stand is absolutely impregnable—stronger than granite. Yet, it is liquid rock. Our feet are not only fixed on this foundation but are also encased in it. This fluid, flexible granite wraps itself with might around our toes, ankles, and calves and forms impenetrable, empowered battle boots.

Paul desires us to grasp a twofold reality of our foundation. We stand on it. We step out in it.

When we place our feet on the foundation of God's Word, armed with military-issue boots that are created for marching and for warfare, we are propelled into the battle to win people from the bondage of Satan to God.

Based on these truths, Jeff and I invite Christ to make us ready at all times to share His message of salvation with others. We pray that He will guide our steps during the day that we physically will be where He desires us to be.

If you pray this way, expect your schedule to be disrupted with unexpected appointments. Expect to sacrifice your pleasure, your solitude, and your need of rest to have the exceptional experience of leading others to Christ. Expect to use those metal bits to dig in during the tough situations of life, to help you to remain and to fulfill God's task for you.

After praying in such a manner, I have been astounded at all the encounters that Jesus lines up for me to share my faith. Opportunities occur at the market, in stores, or as I walk along the road. They are not always convenient, but they always have eternal value!

After a sun-drenched day at the beach, where we celebrated Ryan's 18th birthday, I was exhausted. At our mission guest house I showered the sand and salt away and walked down the shady dirt road toward our American Embassy's Recreation Center to join Jeff and the children. I looked forward to the rare comfort of sitting in air-conditioning and watching the news on the Armed Forces Network before we headed back up to our village of Allada. I longed to regain contact with world events. We easily can become lost to what is happening outside Benin since our daily lives don't always include radio and television.

Along roadsides sellers set up shabby, crooked tables from which to sell a myriad of things, from vegetables and shoes to plastic basins, rope, and backpacks. Between our mission headquarters and the Recreation Center, Rose had built a small shanty. Teak seedlings, procured from the bush, held up a tilted, tin roof. Every morning, underneath this shaking shelter, she carefully arranged several benches and stacked her table with large, painted tin basins. Each held African rice, meat, or sauce to sell—Benin's equivalent of fast food. In fact, little shanties like this one comprise the only type of fast food found in the country. The ambiance and the flies are quite unlike McDonald's and Pizza Hut!

When I was young, we often heard unfounded rumors that someone at a Stateside fast-food restaurant bit into a rat-stick instead of a drumstick. Here rat is a favored meat sold at roadside restaurants. We just make sure to pick out the piece with the tail, or we may end up eating dog instead! Barbecue it, and it all tastes the same.

Weeks before, I had given Rose a pineapple. She was ecstatic at the small gift. Ever since, she made it a point to warmly greet me when I passed her way. This day, as I strolled by, Rose was packing up all her assorted dented and scratched bowls to head home. I paused to say hi. But the conversation continued much further than that. She commented, "Most white people who walk by here ignore me. But you Americans greet me."

Knowing that the "Americans" she was encountering were missionaries staying temporarily at the guesthouse who made the same trek as I did, I quickly corrected her. "It isn't Americans who are greeting you but those who love Jesus and have given their lives to Him. God's love is within them and compels them to be kind to others."

She took this to heart. I questioned her, "Where do you go to church?" She replied, "I'm not going to church yet; I'm searching for one that will give me peace." You and I know that a church cannot give a person peace; only Christ can. But I needed to explain this to her. Honestly, I wanted to escape to the Recreational Center's cool air. My legs were weary from trudging through sand and from battling waves. The afternoon sun scared my shoulders. Yet, I could not leave her without sharing Jesus.

As we talked, she became excited. "I want to follow Jesus," she emphatically stated. I was surprised at her immediate embracing of the Truth. Not sure she had completely understood, I gave her a tract written in French, which clearly presented the steps of surrender to Christ. Rose didn't speak French. She couldn't read French. But she promised to have someone in her household read it to her.

A week passed before the need of groceries propelled me back to Cotonou. There I found Rose eagerly waiting for me. With a huge smile she said, "My son read the booklet to me. I understood it all. I slept well that night!" I rejoiced! Her statement revealed a new Life within her. Fear dominates the Beninese; therefore, most have great difficulty sleeping. Since Satan rules their lives, they have no peace. They are terrified of spirits and sorcerers that nightly roam the earth. A Beninese who has come to a relationship with Christ sleeps well!

Pray that God will make your feet ready to go where He guides or to stand still in the face of fatigue, so that others may have peace in Christ. Then watch the way He leads you into amazing faith-sharing encounters. They are more refreshing than air-conditioning on a blistering hot day!

Know on what foundation you stand; then, on that foundation, move forward into the battle. Know that you can step forward aggressively with confidence because you have been given all that is necessary for the fight.

For by Thee I can run upon a troop; and by my God I can leap over a wall. He makes my feet like hinds' feet, and sets me upon my high places. Thou dost enlarge my steps under me, and my feet have not slipped (Ps. 18:29, 33, 36).

---

[1]Kenneth S. Wuest, *The New Testament: An Expanded Translation* (Grand Rapids, MI: William B. Eerdmans Publishing Co., 1961), 457.

[2]John MacArthur, Jr., *The MacArthur New Testament Commentary on Ephesians* (Chicago: Moody Press, 1986), 354.

SEVENTEEN

Wall of Power

"In addition to all this, take up the shield of faith, with which you can extinguish all the flaming arrows of the evil one" (Eph. 6:16 NIV). The picture Paul paints in this verse is not of a lightly armored soldier about to prove his skill in an easy contest. It is not the Roman soldier often seen in old movies who straps a small round shield to one arm to fend off the enemy's blows while he attacks with his sword in the other.[1] Rather the picture is of a heavily armed soldier[2] who has raised before him a massive wood shield finished with metal or oiled leather which nearly covered his body's height and width. These shields were only carried by soldiers on the front line of battle. If we had been alive during Paul's time, his words would have evoked an image in our minds of disciplined, confident, powerful soldiers standing shoulder to shoulder on the field of battle with their shields extended before them as a mighty wall of force stretching as far as the eye could see against the might of the enemy.[3] That is the shield of faith.

Jeff and I daily pray that God will place firmly in our hands such a shield of faith, and above all, to strengthen our faith. The shield of faith defeats ALL the attacks of Satan. When placed side by side with other shields of faith, its capacity is limitless. No modern defense system can equal the force of a solid shield of faith. It radiates power.

As we bow in prayer with our African brothers and sisters over one who is sick, the leader will often tell people not to pray if they do not have faith that Jesus can heal the person. In those moments, within the quietness of my heart, I always question my own faith and confirm my belief in Christ's healing power. Then I pray for Christ to increase my faith. I may have education and biblical knowledge that these Christians do not possess. But they outfaith me. They do not have money. They do not have medicines. They just have faith. A great faith. They must rely on God, because God is all they have. Even when they do hold a packet of medication in their hands, they will pray that God will empower the medicine. We hear endless stories of mothers spending the night in prayer over a feverish child and seeing God calm the fever and heal.

A special naming ceremony is held among voodoo worshipers for a newborn. All the family members attend. During the first part of the ceremony they sacrifice a chicken and smear its blood over the family's idol. Following this they invoke the ancestral spirits to indwell the child. Afterward the mother and baby are banished to her hut for seven days, if the baby is a girl, and nine days, if the baby is a boy. Since this is a polygamist society, wives have their own one-room dwelling. During the days of her banishment, a wife is forbidden to eat salt. Depending on her family's rules, she may have other dietary restrictions during this time for her purification.

At the end of the required days the second portion of the ceremony takes place. Another chicken is slaughtered. The baby's soft birth hair will be completely shaved off. Then a thick piece of wood is placed before the mother, and she is presented with a machete. She must, with a single blow, completely chop this wood in two. If she does, she is pure. The baby will live. If she does not, this indicates her impurity and signifies that the child will die. The father offers a name for the baby, often based on any suffering he has endured since the child's birth.

Christians refuse to participate in this ceremony. Instead, they publicly consecrate their little ones to Christ and give their child a godly name based on how God has blessed their lives. In the past they would have invited everyone to the voodoo ceremony. Now they invite their entire family to church for the baby dedication as a witness to them.

In July 2000, Clement, a new Christian, was excitedly walking the narrow footpaths through the village to invite his family members to the church for the dedication of his newborn baby. Suddenly, the stick he stepped on reared up and latched itself on his leg. Shaking the poisonous snake away, he proclaimed, "No! This will not happen! In the name of Jesus, this poison will not harm me!"

Arriving at his compound he called his family and explained what had happened. Terrified, they insisted he drink a special voodoo oil prepared for snake bites and then massage it into the wound. Because of his faith in Christ, Clement refused. The news of the snakebite quickly spread through the entire village. It brought a huge crowd of people to his door. Fearfully, urgently, they kept repeating, "Clement, you're going to die. You are going to die right now!"

Clement prayed.

The wound began to hurt and then stopped instantly. He announced to everyone that he had already called on Jesus to protect him. He told them to go home and go to bed. He turned from the gathering, went into his hut, lay down on his mat, and went to sleep. The people sat on Clement's doorstep and listened to his breathing all night long. They were sure he would die before dawn. As the rays of the sun etched lines of light through the sky, Clement rolled off his mat, stood up, and walked out the door of his house, alive and well. Word spread everywhere about what God had done. The people had never seen anything like this before! Death always won.

Georgette, though, died. She had accepted Jesus Christ in the village church of Toffo. From that moment on she faithfully attended the ragged, three-walled church which sat on a forested little hill engulfed in thick, verdant bushes and vines. She diligently struggled to learn to read Fon so she could read the Bible for herself. Her sweet spirit was a testimony of her faith.

Georgette became violently ill. In an unusual act of love her father, a voodoo worshiper, took her to a private clinic, St. Pierre, in the town of Allada. Her heart was beating her life away at 160 beats per minute. The doctor tried everything he could, but it wasn't enough. Georgette's form suddenly convulsed and went still. He placed his stethoscope against her chest and listened, waited, and listened again. Georgette was gone. Her father stood and watched, broken. As the doctor slowly walked to his office, scrounged around for the death certificates, and painstakingly filled one out, her father stumbled from the room to find a coffin maker. Georgette would be buried at midnight.

A Christian woman stood in the clinic courtyard. Seeing the distress on Georgette's father's face, she approached him. "What has happened?" she gently asked. "My daughter has just died," he bluntly responded. "May I go in and pray for her?" she requested. "Why? She's dead! But, do what you want," he curtly replied through his grief.

The woman drew a few other Christian women together. As one, they got on their knees on the hard cement floor, before the quiet form on the bed. They began to pray. After a time the lifeless body sneezed three times. Georgette sat up, fully well, fully alive!

"I'm hungry!" the once-dead young woman called out. Instead of searching for coffin builders, her father ran, in utter amazement, to find her some meat. The doctor rushed in, Georgette's death certificate in his hands, and stood in speechless wonder.

Georgette's father, although he hasn't yet surrendered his life to the Lord Jesus Christ, shows visitors, with trembling hands, Georgette's death certificate. He has living proof that Jesus is the Resurrection and the Life.

Late one breezeless afternoon Jeff and I walked through the village of Sekou (say-koo) to visit the people. It was rainy season, yet the entire area was suffering from the lack of rain. Several old men, sitting on a log, waved us over and told us about the voodoo ceremonies they were about to perform to cause a storm. Compelled, we told them that we would instead pray for Jesus to send rain. We did pray, right there, with the men. We trembled slightly at our own boldness. The Lord answered. Before we left the village, growling thunder sounded a storm's approach. Its rumble thrilled my heart. Before the night had passed, before they could perform their ceremony, rain fell. Jesus' rain!

We often find ourselves in faith-challenging situations. Within myself I know my faith is not sufficient. I don't even have a mustard-grain's worth, yet. But I pray to have the faith that will move mountains.

Take up your shield of faith, so that shoulder to shoulder we may form a moving wall of power that stops cold the enemy's attack.

And I searched for a man among them who should build up the wall and stand in the gap before Me for the land, that I should not destroy it; but I found no one (Ezek. 22:30).

[1]John MacArthur, Jr., *The MacArthur New Testament Commentary on Ephesians* (Chicago: Moody Press, 1986), 357-458.

[2]Rev. W. Robertson Nicoll, M.A., LL.D., editor, *The Expositor's Greek New Testament,* vol. 3 (Grand Rapids, MI: Wm. B. Eerdmans Publishing Co., 1993), 387.

[13]MacArthur, 358.

EIGHTEEN

First Line of Battle

With truth you have tucked the excesses of your life in around your waist so you can move quickly, easily, unencumbered. You are sporting your breastplate against attack. Your battle boots are laced tightly in place. Your armored shield is held out unwaveringly before you. You appear ready for battle. Although the shield nearly covers your body, your head remains exposed to enemy attack. No soldier would purposely enter the field of combat without his helmet firmly in place! Therefore God, in His need of fully equipped soldiers, exhorts us to "Take the helmet of salvation" (Eph. 6:17 NIV).

The Roman soldier's helmet, which was molded to cover the soldier's head and cheeks, was created by the forger or made of thick leather covered with large pieces of metal.[1] Just as the breastplate of righteousness guards the portion of our bodies over our hearts, the helmet of salvation guards our minds. As we put on the armor we need to realize that before our feet hit the battlefield, spiritual warfare begins in our minds. The spiritual battle is first waged, won or lost, in the mind. The thoughts we allow to enter our minds determine the direction of our lives.

We must ask the Lord to fill our minds with His thoughts. The natural outcome is, if we have His thoughts, then our words will be His words, our responses, His responses, our actions, His actions. 2 Corinthians 10:3-5 deals with spiritual warfare and points the reader to the core of the matter—our thoughts.

It states: "For though we walk in the flesh, we do not war according to the flesh, for the weapons of our warfare are not of the flesh but divinely powerful for the destruction of fortresses. We are destroying speculations (arguments NIV) and every lofty thing (pretension NIV) raised up against the knowledge of God, and we are taking every thought captive to the obedience of Christ."

The piercingly bright sun burst through the crystalline blue sky, warming the early morning air. The sounds of rustling palms and vibrant green ferns floated into the room. Beyond my window brilliant bursts of fuchsia and violet flowers scattered across my vision. The loud noises of neighbor's radios, clanging cooking pots, crying babies, and bellowing goats, were unusually quiet. Even our children were playing calmly.

Yet, I was frantic. Never having suffered from claustrophobia, I suddenly felt caged, trapped, and unable to breathe. My prison was not my bedroom, even with its security bars on the windows, nor my house contained within the small, walled compound, but the confines of Benin. The sensation of needing to immediately escape overwhelmed me. To run. To flee. I felt that I could not tolerate staying in this country another minute without literally clawing my way up the walls.

The emotion was so intense, I thought I was losing my mind.

With all the self-control I possessed, I sat myself on the bed and evaluated my thoughts. "What is bothering me?" I asked myself. Usually, at any given moment, I could recite a list of disappointments, grievances, and cultural frustrations that gradually build up in my spirit through our cross-cultural living. I know that if these stay in my spirit, I will feel broken and unable to handle life. With determination I reviewed, honestly, the contents of my heart. Surprisingly, nothing was lurking there.

I realized then that these unreasonable, consuming thoughts and emotions were stemming from a direct satanic attack. I needed to resist them, for they weren't from the Lord. I needed to take responsibility for what was in my mind and make my thoughts submit to Christ.

Out loud, in the name Jesus, standing in His authority, I resisted Satan—specifically, a spirit of insanity. I demanded in Jesus' name that it leave me alone.

Instant calm flooded my spirit. Just as Jesus rebuked the roaring wind and the raging waves and they instantly stilled, so did the wild thoughts of my mind. I stood and joyfully continued with the day's tasks.

Our thoughts need to be placed under the authority of Jesus Christ and made obedient to Him.

As I mentioned earlier, Jeff and I have refused to allow ourselves to joke about, talk about, or to even think of divorce. This is forbidden. We willfully slam the door shut on any such stray thought that enters our minds. Once a mind starts down that path just once, it becomes more and more easy to walk that path. Sin originates in our minds. The thought of sexual immorality is a sin. The thought of disobedience to Christ is a sin. The thought of running away from God's calling is a sin. The physical manifestation of sin is simply a re-enactment of what was conceived in the mind. God compels us to take every thought and make it obedient to Christ. It is an exercise of our will and takes concentrated effort. We can more easily run down the path of escape in our minds than to walk past temptation or through distress with Jesus. In fact, each time we start walking down a forbidden path, we trample the weeds that once clogged the way. Gradually it becomes a paved highway of ease which we can even fool ourselves into thinking is God's direction for us!

I am convinced that many people forsake their calling—God's will for their lives—when they allow their minds to think what they ought not to have been thinking. They toy with the thought, "This is too difficult for me." Gradually negativity consumes them. The lives of those suffering without Jesus lose significance. They abandon God's highest for their lives and give in to their ruling emotions.

A great danger is to walk into God's calling with the thought, "If I don't like it, I can always quit." This person will. He has already programmed himself for defeat and escape before he has begun.

Besides dumping emotions into the "too-difficult" cauldron is the tendency to swim in the boiling mud of "happiness thinking." Many Christians allow their wayward thoughts to determine that God wants them "happy." But God cares more about the perfection of our characters than our momentary happiness. Consider the words of Paul in 2 Corinthians 7:4, "I am overflowing with joy in all our affliction." Paul was toughing it out. This was not an easy time. Was he happy? Was he grinning every moment? Was he having fun? I doubt it. But he had joy—overflowing joy. James 1:2 exhorts us, "Consider it pure joy, my brothers, whenever you face trials of many kinds" (NIV). It doesn't say, "Run from the pain and be happy!" It says to consider the trials as pure joy. Nowhere in Scripture did God say we'd be happy all the time. In fact, God tells us we are going to cry (Ps. 30:5, Ps. 126:5). But in the tears, in the sorrow, in the pain, God always speaks of joy. He desires to build into our lives lasting joy and contentment that will endure through any unhappy circumstance.

A fixation on happiness causes people to be impatient with God and to lose faith. Because of faulty "happiness" thinking they believe God is not capable of pulling them through heartache, difficulty, or trauma. They think that since they aren't happy, God couldn't possibly mean for them to continue on. They bail out. Their spiritual lives are stifled. They sacrifice deep joy and contentment on the flimsy altar of temporary happiness. Don't give up. Determine to walk on through. Maintain your commitment. Be patient. At the other side is more than all you are seeking.

The Bible says, "For you, O God, tested us; you refined us like silver. You brought us into prison and laid burdens on our backs. You

let men ride over our heads; we went through fire and water, but you brought us to a place of abundance" (Ps. 66:10-12 NIV).

Besides confusing contentment and joy with happiness, we also continually churn the sea of hurt in our minds into destructive tidal waves. Jesus came to be our Savior to freely forgive our sin. But we forget that He also came to heal our hurts (Ps. 147:3).

Jesus was wounded that we might be healed, not only of sin, not only of disease but also of hurt (I Pet. 2:24).

Jesus longs to fix the brokenness of our spirits. Our selfishness, negative characteristics, anger, and spiritual immaturity work against us to inflict great pain in our lives. But sometimes the pain is not our fault. It can be the heart-piercing result of the adventures of living and loving. Through Christ, no matter what the cause, the hurt does not have to remain.

What a valuable lesson to live here on the mission field. You can't arrive on the mission field with emotional baggage. Once the cultural stresses, language difficulties, impossibilities of simply living and eating, health troubles, ministry demands, family adjustments, and homesickness hit, extra emotional baggage will destroy you.

But what about your side of the ocean? Your life is not whole if your heart is full of holes. Do not live captive to old hurts. Tell each individual one to Jesus. Release them to Him. Ask for His healing. Choose to be done with it.

When I find life here on the mission field so heavy that I can't bear to live it, I stop and listen to the thoughts of my heart. There I discover the pain of dealing with Beninese drivers who shake their fists at me after they nearly cause fatal accidents in their foolhardy, ram-rodding of their vehicles down the road. I discover the pain of having my language skills insulted, the pain of constant interruptions, and the pain over young church leaders that have fallen into immorality. I may uncover aggravation over the fact that nothing in this country is ever easy—from the pressure-less water, electricity black-outs, the crackling phone, to beggar-swamped shopping.

Nothing works like it should. Nothing is easily accomplished. Many days just living is a challenge. The stresses tear at relationships. All these things for me become one thing—pain. The only way to healing is to discuss it with the Healer and to give it to Him. You and I can't live life without pain. But you don't need to let it destroy

you. Do not live captive to today's hurts. If you have a list of grievances jabbing around in your mind, deal with it.

Whether at home or in a distant country, be free in Jesus.

Satan's attack begins in our minds. Learn to recognize his subtle
tactics. Resist him (James 4:7). "Be of sober spirit, be on the alert.
Your adversary, the devil, prowls about like a roaring lion, seeking
someone to devour. But resist him, firm in your faith, knowing that
the same experiences of suffering are being accomplished by your
brethren who are in the world" (1 Pet. 5:8-9).

If I hadn't known how to deal with Satan's attack on that sunny
day, I'd no longer be telling the people of Benin about Jesus. The
impact Christ has made in Benin through our lives would not have
occurred. When we do not resist Satan's alluring, deceptive thoughts,
we join ourselves to his way of thinking. Our thoughts determine the
course of our lives. Guard your thoughts. Fight to force thoughts con-
tradictory to Scripture into submission to Christ. The mind cannot
become a playground for enticing, seemingly harmless ideas contrary
to Christ. It must remain the first line of battle.

Put on the helmet of Salvation.

Remember, spiritual warfare begins in the mind.

*Let the words of my mouth and the meditation of my heart
(thoughts of my mind) be acceptable in Thy sight, O Lord, my rock
and my Redeemer (Ps. 19:14).*

---

[1]John MacArthur, Jr., *The MacArthur New Testament Commentary on
Ephesians* (Chicago: Moody Press, 1986), 360.

NINETEEN

Perfect Your Swordsmanship

God's command to "open their eyes" is a command demanding action. These words do not specify solely defensive measures but offensive warfare tactics which result in enemy confrontation. Of our opposing army Ephesians 6:12 states, "For we are not fighting against people made of flesh and blood, but against persons without bodies—the evil rulers of the unseen world, those mighty satanic beings; and great evil princes of darkness who rule this world and against huge numbers of wicked spirits in the spirit world" (Living Letter).

The battle is not spoken of as a single event but as a continual engagement—"we are fighting." Furthermore, God clearly expects our presence on the battlefield, not just to defend previously gained positions but also to attack to destroy the stronghold of the enemy. 2 Corinthians 10:3-4 tells us, "For though we walk in the flesh, we do not war according to the flesh, for the weapons of our warfare are not of the flesh, but divinely powerful for the destruction of fortresses."

A fortress is the place where the enemy holds up or regroups or the place from which he reigns. A fortress can not be overcome on the defensive. A fortress can only be overthrown on the attack.

The exhortation in Ephesians 6 continues with these words, "(take) the sword of the spirit which is the word of God" (verse 17).

After prayerfully donning the spiritual armor, I physically open my hand to receive the sword of the Spirit. Its purpose is twofold. With it we defend. With it we attack. Before a soldier goes into battle with his sword, he must prove it. He must practice with it. He must memorize its weight, its balance. As he grips the hilt, it must become an extension of his own arm. He cannot successfully combat the enemy until he knows his sword and has become one with it. Neither can we.

We must have God's Word reverberating through our spirits. We must live in it so it will live in us. Our thoughts and our actions must extend from the understanding God has given us of His Word. Through the Word we must be growing in the knowledge of God's character. We must know Christ's authority, His power, and our relationship to Him concerning these issues, before we can victoriously confront the enemy. Knowing the Word dispels fear when we are faced with a satanic attack. If you are not sure of the Sword, you will not raise it confidently. Know the Word.

On the blank pages of my Bible I inscribed spiritual warfare verses that have impacted my life. These guide the way I think, speak, and pray concerning spiritual warfare. Workbook Bible studies are great. Christian books are fascinating. Preachers preach awesome messages. Godly parents and friends are phenomenal sources of spiritual truths. All these are excellent guides. But your faith cannot be based on what anyone says. You must exercise your beliefs based on what you have studied in Scripture. If your faith is not there, then it really is not there. And you will someday be rudely awakened to this fact by coming up faith-shorted in a time of difficulty.

The greatest testing ground for my faith has been the mission field. I find myself questioning,"Why do I believe what I believe? Is it Truth or just Americanized Christian religion?" I must know the scriptural basis for what I believe. I must embrace these completely as mine, so I can teach from an unshakable foundation.

I come into contact with Africans who participate in questionable church groups and cults, people in evangelical or Catholic churches, and new Christians. What I share with them is always the same. If you can't scripturally confirm the message preached, reject it, even if it was a missionary who preached it! Our absolute authority must be the Word. We must follow It, not humankind.

One church group in Benin is called Celestial Christianity. Supposedly the angel Gabriel descended from heaven and revealed to its founder a "better way." I feel for the angel Gabriel. He is always blamed for these things! This particular group has an interesting concept of worshiping Jesus, which is blended with performing sacrifices and using voodoo curses on their irritating acquaintances, families, and friends. Obviously they have not read the "love your neighbor" part of the Bible yet! They saunter around in pristine white robes, chef-styled hats, and bare feet. They cast off their shoes in the belief that all the ground they walk upon is "holy." I can't think of any ground less holy than Benin's. Holy to me does not mean having to watch your step while walking through the bush, avoiding wet foliage, and realizing that awful smell emerging from your shoes was not caused by a stray dog.

Another church group calls itself the Renaissance Church. When we first arrived in Benin, this group taught that vomiting and diarrhea were the evidence of the fullness of the Holy Spirit. We've experienced our share of those maladies since our arrival, but we never believed it had anything to do with the Holy Spirit! A more recent teaching nearly caused riots: a godly man will seek out his neighbor's wife. Obviously these folks *did* read the part about loving your neighbor! Why do people believe such twisted things? Because someone they trusted instructed them. Either they haven't been taught to examine the Scriptures for themselves, or they can't.

Our Baptist church in the village of Tanta began out of the ashes of a cult. This group had disbanded its cult gathering after members began realizing, on their own, that what the visiting church leaders were teaching them was not in the Bible. A year later they invited Jeff to their village. One of their men, Justin, trembled with excitement as he read through the Baptist Beliefs with his open Bible. He repeatedly turned to people sitting with him saying, "Look, right here, do you know what the Bible says?" He had been longing to know Christ—to know the Truth—but had been given lies instead.

We must brandish the Word as Christ used the Word. Jesus used Scripture to fight satanic confrontation. Consider the account in Matthew 4 of Jesus' temptation. Every time Satan tempted Jesus, He wielded the Sword against him. So must we.

We also see from Scripture that Jesus rebuked Satan (Matt. 4:10-11), demons, and sickness. A desperate man brought to Jesus his son with a severe problem. A demon caused the child to have freakish seizures. These resulted in vicious burns from falling into cooking fires or near-death experiences from being thrown into pools of water to drown. Jesus "rebuked the demon." The boy was instantaneously healed (Matt. 17:14-21). When Simon Peter's mother-in-law was suffering from a high fever, Jesus "rebuked the fever, and it left her" (Luke 4:38-39).

To rebuke means "to check; repress."[1] To repress means "to suppress; quell."[2] In confrontations with the enemy Jesus exercised His divine right to squelch Satan's activity. The authority Christ exercised on earth, we—based on our position in Him—also have the right to exercise. We, in Jesus' name, have the right to suppress Satan's activity. We are unworthy sinners, who, in Christ's authority, have all power over the enemy (Luke 10:19-20).

Jesus said, "Whatever you shall bind on earth shall be bound in heaven, and whatever you shall loose on earth shall have been loosed in heaven" (Matt. 16:19). Through Christ whatever forces we bind in the physical world are bound in the spiritual. Whoever we set free from satanic bondage in the physical world will be free in the spiritual. We have the authority in Christ to bind our enemy (Matt. 12:28-29), to speak against the powers which blind people, to render them powerless in Jesus name, to wield the sword of the Spirit, and to open blind eyes.

Before we left the States Jeff and I started praying over Benin in the name of Jesus, in His authority, to bind and rebuke Satan's power over the people. We pray according to 2 Corinthians 4:4 that the people's eyes will be opened to see the Truth of Jesus. We pray with the words of Isaiah 61:1 in mind that Jesus will rip the chains of Satan's captivity off the people. We pray, in keeping with Ezekiel 11:19-20, that Jesus will give the people receptive hearts so they will respond to Christ. We continue to pray in this way over people groups, individuals, villages, and voodoo cults.

During one of our Stateside adventures, while at a world missions conference at Bell Shoals Baptist Church in Tampa, Florida (2001), Jeff and I were privileged to hear Dr. Larry Reesor passionately speak of the lost of the world. In his hands he held a ream of paper. Each page was filled with names of people groups scattered across the earth—more than a billion people—who have yet to encounter the Word of Christ, who are bound for hell. As each page slipped from his hands onto the floor, a deep grief gripped me. A torrent of tears cascaded down my cheeks for the individuals those names represented. In those moments my spirit touched the very heart of God. His heart grieves for those in bondage and abounds with a passionate desire for the lost to enter into a relationship with Him. Would that I had a thousand lives to give to tell people around the globe about Jesus! Yet, even a thousand lives would not be enough. I am here in Benin. I cannot go to the whole world. Would you go in my place?

After the conference I searched the Internet and found Wycliffe's Joshua Project 2000[3], which listed the names of the unreached people groups of the world. I may not be able to go to each one, but I pray over each group by name and request that Christ send someone to them to tell them of His love. You and I are locked in time and space. We cannot go everywhere, but we can affect the world for Christ through warfare prayer from wherever we are.

The words we use are not important. The Person in whose authority we stand is the important part. We must knowingly, decisively enter into the battle. We must take the Sword, draw a line on the battlefield, and say, "In the name of Jesus, no more. No further. You are finished here."

We strolled in the dimness down the rough dirt hallways and across the sparsely furnished chambers. My hand casually scraped the scraggy, brass colored, earthen walls. It was a king's palace but as unlike the majestic palaces of European kings as mud is of sparkling water from a pure mountain stream. The Beninese guide halted and spoke softly, reverently, before the door to a special room—the Black Room. If the king had committed a huge blunder or had lost a war, he would walk in that door and out again. Three days later he would die. We moved on. Once again the guide's voice dropped in humble respect as he stood before the king's personal idol, sitting in the dust in a specially carved niche in a wall. It was a shapeless mound blackened through sacrificial blood libations poured liberally on its head. The honor given this slime-covered mound of dirt repulsed me.

Having grown accustomed to seeing Benin's multitude of idols, I thought no more of the incident. One night, I was suddenly awakened from a sound sleep by a sharp sense that someone was trying to curse us. I saw in my mind's eye a bulky, grasping hand extending itself from that nasty, alien-looking idol to attack us. In Jesus' name I took authority over it, rebuked it, bound its power, and demanded that it leave us alone. It left. Instantly I was at peace. I re-squished up my pillow into a comfortable contortion and went calmly back to sleep.

Our home rests along the edge of a shady footpath, about a kilometer from one of the only paved roads that run up-country. We live in a small valley, surrounded by graceful palms, orange trees with thorny limbs, and mango trees laden with wild mangos and poisonous snakes. Outside our compound walls fertile fields are hand-tilled with short-handled hoes. The gentle sounds of cultivation and the choruses of hundreds of birds hang on the sweet air.

Often, though, the tranquility is shattered by the screech of brakes and discordant screams of crunching metal. Constant, incredible accidents occurred on the descent of the paved road. The trucks that travel the road are excessively overloaded, are in disrepair, and travel at ridiculous speeds. Yet, nothing can account for the frequency and bizarre character of those accidents.

We had just arrived home, exhausted, from a three-hour drive from the country of Togo and the tedious work of two border crossings. Jeff wasn't just exhausted; he was sick. Noticing that we were lacking even the bare essentials of onions and tomatoes, I left Jeff comfortably stretched out across our waterbed, hopped in the car, and headed toward our village market.

At the end of our path I encountered a macabre scene. While plunging downhill, a tractor-trailer had lost control. One lone house, under construction, stands near the bottom of the descent. The builder had returned to his hometown to search for more workers. While he was gone, his kid brother had arrived for a visit. Finding no one there, he was standing leisurely by the site when the truck suddenly careened out of control and crashed into him.

I drove up immediately after the accident had occurred. Everyone was looking, but no one was helping. I raced back down our little road to rouse Jeff. Jumping out of bed, he bolted back down our bumpy pathway and didn't return for hours. No competent hospitals are in the bush where we live. In fact, the competency of the hospitals on the coast can be questioned easily. Even if the doctors are educated, they lack materials and trustworthy analysis methods.

Jeff had instantly become the makeshift ambulance driver. People at the scene had loaded the victim into the back of our vehicle. A policeman rode shotgun as Jeff drove as quickly as possible to the hospital in Cotonou, an hour away. Unfortunately, the young man died before they arrived. Because Jeff had brought the man in, he was obligated to pay the morgue fees so they would care for the body. Helping anyone here is costly.

This accident, added to many, many others, was more than strange. I asked why the people thought so many accidents occurred on that stretch of road. I was told an incredible story. Years ago a huge idol dedicated to the python god stood on that general space. The road crew had smashed it to bits and rolled the black top over the shattered pieces of clay. The idol had been destroyed. The evil remained.

When a group of prayerwalkers came, we prayed over this area as we drove from one site to another. Later, from our terrace, I began to pray for the Lord's intervention. I bound Satan's empowerment of the Dan (dahn), the serpent god, over that stretch of road. I broke, in Jesus' name, Satan's authority and requested that the Lord stop the accidents. I don't know everything concerning spiritual warfare. All I know is that we have an awesomely powerful God who has won the battle with Satan. I desire to stand in His victory and free others to do so, too.

Since the prayer coverage, a few tires have blown out. A fender-bender occurred on the opposite hill. A pickup truck catapulted off the road halfway up and plunged into the deep cement ditch along the edge because the truck bed was overloaded with cows! The cows just stood there, tied to the wreck with ropes around their necks, all skinny and forlorn looking, waiting for rescue. That was an amusing sight. Another truck's axle broke. But the frequency and intensity of the accidents ceased.

After our second furlough I arrived home to Benin to multiple bouts of malaria. I could not shake its grasp. Month after month malaria kept its sting of fatigue and fever on me. One day, while I took up spiritual arms in prayer, these words were spoken strongly to my spirit, "If you will stop rebuking me, you'll stop being sick."

With renewed vigor I continued to engage myself in the battle! Shortly after that, during a Bible study, one of our African brothers, Paul, prayed diligently over me. He asked God to restore my health. I hadn't said a word about how I felt. Honestly, I had been too ashamed to share that I once again wasn't feeling well. From that moment, years ago, God healed me of malaria. I haven't had it since.

We don't have to yell for the creatures of darkness to hear the authority of Christ being spoken through us. Shouting indicates a presumption that we have something to add to what Christ has already done. That is pride. We encounter Beninese brothers who snap their fingers or march with energy back and forth, thinking to force Satan to listen to their commands. These are dangerous practices. We have nothing in ourselves to bring to enemy encounters. If we add something to Christ's name, we are immediately usurping His authority, rather than acting in it.

We don't have to be physically next to the enemy's fortress to do battle. We don't need to be in the presence of one who is bound. We simply must believe with the centurion that Christ is the supreme authority of the universe. His authority must be explicitly obeyed. Whether you are living in America or at the end of an overgrown dirt path in Africa, you can take authority over the power holding a people or a person in bondage and set them free. This is not only our privilege but also our obligation.

Jeff and I may be called to Benin, but we all are called to open blind eyes. The people of the world will remain lost in Satan's dark domain unless you join in the battle, confront the enemy, and break his power in Christ Jesus.

Hold fast your armor. Perfect your swordsmanship. Join us in the battle. A gap exists in the line without you. Their eyes cannot be opened unless the fight is fought from your position. You may not know it, but you hold a strategic place on the front lines. Your comrades in arms are counting on you.

Hurry, take your place on the battlefield.

He trains my hands for battle; my arms can bend a bow of bronze. You give me your shield of victory, and your right hand sustains me; you stoop down to make me great. You armed me with strength for battle; you made my adversaries bow at my feet (Ps. 18:34-35, 39 NIV).

---

[1]William Morris, editor, *The American Heritage Dictionary of the English Language* (Boston: Houghton Mifflin Co., 1981), 1087.

[2]Ibid., 1104

[3]Wycliffe Joshua project 2000, Web address: *www.ad2000.org/re90106.htm*

TWENTY

The Source

The soft crackle of their feet slapping against the grasses of the overgrown path filled their senses as they ran after the trucks that gradually jostled out of their reach. The sweat poured off their glistening bodies. The odor of the freshly hand-tilled fields and body heat mingled with the passion of the moment. Even after three kilometers their cries continued to chase the retreating vehicles.

"Please don't leave us."

"Please don't forget us."

"Please, come back and tell us more about Jesus."

They were in a race but one unlike any we have ever seen. They ran after the ones who could help them obtain the true Prize—forgiveness of sin, peace, and an eternity in heaven with Jesus Christ.

As the vehicles disappeared into the thick brush, these runners' pleas continued to pierce the hearts of the young Christian men and women tightly crammed into the truck beds. Tears flowed, unchecked, down their cheeks as they heard the cries.

"Please, we want more of Jesus."

Dougia, a village lost in a valley deep in the tangled bush, is a voodoo stronghold. White flags held aloft on tall, naked poles give evidence to recent sacrifices to the serpent god. Unusually enormous and numerous clay mounds stand as evil sentinels beside each red-walled compound. Smaller idols, as pieces of metal, or broken shards of pottery stuck haphazardly in a circular fashion in the dirt rest under protective shelters with rusting tin roofs. Life-sized, painted statues in human form are set up along footpaths and in the sacred forest. These mar the lush countryside. The villagers knew no other life than the one handed them by their ancestors—until Dutton Bonnell arrived.[1]

Early in 1974 Dutton, one of the first Baptist missionaries to Benin, braved the arduous trail that led to the village of Dougia and shared Christ with the people. Some turned to Jesus, a small church was born, and a simple cement-block building was constructed.

His love for the people wasn't limited to their spiritual needs. The physical difficulties and excessive poverty of the village burdened him. A nearby river, which flooded fields during rainy season and transformed footpaths into impassable rushing streams, cut through unsanitary, contaminated land.

Regardless, the village women hiked long distances through the spindly, rich vegetation, to dip their metal basins into the river's murky depths. They extracted water for drinking, cooking, and washing. They had no other source.

Dutton brought the solution. Men were hired. With short-handled hoes and battered buckets they began to force their way into the unyielding earth next to the church. Slowly, as bucket-full by bucket-full was hoisted to the surface by a fraying rope, a well emerged. Pure water was discovered many meters underground. So it was that the church, which brought the water of Life, also brought life-giving water to the compounds of thirsty people.

The well water was abundant. But the spiritual well was seized by violent hands and sealed shut.

November 30, 1974. President Matthieu Kerekou renounced the country's ties with democratic societies and proclaimed a new constitution would be established on Marxist-Leninist principles.[2]

A year later The Revolutionary Council, in an aggressive act, ripped down the cross from the church and declared the building a school.[3] The village elder, the one responsible for giving the church its land, was threatened with death if the Christians continued to worship there. Contact with Dougia was severed.[4]

The band of Christians became discouraged. Deadly consequences forced them to stop singing together. They stopped praying together. The spiritual well dried up. Years passed. The government abandoned the church. It stood empty. Forsaken.

In 1990, after the fall of communism across Europe and in Benin, SBC missionary Asa Greear, along with Christian brothers, visited Dougia and the former church building. Cobwebs crowded the corners. Foul-smelling bats nested in the roof, but the building was intact. They threw open the doors. Fifty people poured in to attend the first worship service in 14 years. Twenty became faithful.

Then 1991 arrived. As Jeff worked with the youth scattered across the southern region of Benin, he cast a vision of purpose. The youth could become an army of church planters. They benefited by joining together to study God's Word for retreats and conferences, but how much greater if they, at the same time, took what they were learning out to those who had not yet heard! Grow and go. The vision was caught.

Twenty young people from Cotonou's Vodje (voh-jay) church, after hearing the plight of Dougia, prayerfully decided to go. Roberte was among them. Their pastor, Venance Kouton, the compelling encourager behind the adventure, committed to stay in Dougia for an entire month.

The youth met early one Friday morning, rented several trucks, gathered up food, a generator, film equipment, and their sleeping mats. They stuffed themselves and their gear into the beds of the ramshackle pick-ups and headed out. Sixty kilometers of hole-infested pavement sizzled under the tires. They tightly held on. Forty kilometers of washboard dirt road set up jarring vibrations from hubcap to tarp canopy. They clung to the sides for support and sang in vibrato.

Then they bumped off the road and stopped. An impenetrable wall blocked the trucks' way. The dense undergrowth had overtaken the rugged path that led to Dougia. Not deterred, the young men pulled out machetes and hacked back the protruding limbs and thorny bushes. Cautiously, a few steps at a time, they carved out a three-kilometer path through which the following trucks plowed. And they arrived in Dougia.

They were fatigued by the journey and the intense workout, but they didn't quit. They'd arrived for a purpose. From compound to compound they walked, gathering the family groups under shady mango trees and sharing with them the New Birth. And they fell in love. The people of Dougia became intimately precious to them.

As the sun slipped beyond the growing shadows of the earth, they set up the generator, stretched the ends of a sheet taut between two tree limbs for a screen, and waited. But they didn't wait long. Out of the sun-forged compounds, the people poured. Curiosity and the fascination about a film in their village brought them out in droves.

Under a brilliantly starlit sky, 10 of the curious surrendered their lives to the Lord of power and salvation.

Saturday the youth rose early and met with the new believers and the old. They opened their Bibles and shared the promises of God. Tremors of excitement ran through the lives of those who'd allowed the joy of knowing Jesus to become still. Together the new, the old, and the youth walked the ancient paths, past the eyeless idols, past the sacred forest of enemy gods, and told the thirsty people about the True Source, the Lord Jesus Christ.

The intense heat of the day gave way to cooler, refreshing breezes that gently rustled the palm branches and announced the arrival of night. The youth worked to prepare the meeting ground. They asked God to prepare their hearts. They longed for the villagers of Dougia to know Jesus. Using drama these Christians portrayed to the people the reality of Jesus Christ. Pastor Venance testified about his former dedication to evil voodoo gods and the freedom he'd found in Jesus. In the gathered crowd, choices were made and voodoo abandoned.

Early Sunday morning as the sun swept across the trees and fields and dark shadows fled, the youth rose as one and went to the cement-block church. They prayed and waited. First one, then two together, then others streamed from their clay homes until the church was packed. The old men, the staunch voodoo worshipers, the women, the young men, and the children streamed in and wrestled for a place to stand. A multitude hung in the windows and encircled the four walls of the church. Nearly to a person, the entire village was present. They were thirsty for Life. When the opportunity was given, more than 100 people confessed their need of the Savior.

As the afternoon deepened, the youth sadly gathered their gear, rolled up their mats, stuffed it all into the dusty, waiting trucks, and climbed in.

All the while the believers watched, helped, and lamented.

As the trucks slowly eased down the newly cut path, they chased after the youth through the scratchy weeds, grasped their hands, and pleaded,

"Please don't leave us alone."

"Please don't forget us."

"Please, we want more of Jesus."

And on they ran and cried, until they could run and cry no more.

The village of Dougia wasn't abandoned. Shortly after, Evariste, another of Vodje's youth, and Jeff visited Dougia and taught the Christians. Evariste gave weeks of his life to live with the people of Dougia—to train, teach, and evangelize them.[5] Time and time again he returned, for he loved them and became attached to them. And the believers drew water from the well to quench his thirst.

May our hearts cry out as they cried:

"Please, I want more of Jesus."

As the deer pants for streams of water, so my soul pants for you, O God. My soul thirsts for God, for the living God (Ps. 42:1-2 NIV).

---

[1]Dutton and Marilyn Bonnell were Southern Baptist missionaries to Benin from 1971-1987.

[2]Marilyn Bonnell, *Yesterday, Today, Then and Now*: Benin Baptist Mission 1970-1995 (Self-published, 1975), 140.

[3]Ibid., 148.

[4]Ibid., 131.

[5]The church in Dougia has remained strong since the youths' visit. It now has 80 participating adults and has mothered two churches.

TWENTY ONE

Surrendering to Suffering

Little did I know the deep, passionate love God would pour on our lives for the people of Benin. This love is completely of God, remains steadfast, and surmounts any difficulty that cascades unexpectedly on us. Never could I have guessed the incredible depths of joy we would experience in seeing people turn from their spiritual poverty to embrace Jesus Christ. Nothing surpasses the thrill of leading Kwassi to Christ and then to see him zealously go tell others of Jesus. When Jeff and I witnessed the baptism of 15 people in one of his three preaching points, tears of overwhelming gratitude flooded my eyes.

Little did I know that in this adventure God, time and time again, would also take me beyond what I felt I could endure. Depleted of strength, depleted of will, depleted of ability, I'd weep with the Apostle Paul the words, "We were burdened excessively, beyond our strength, so that we despaired even of life; indeed, we had the sentence of death within ourselves" (2 Cor. 1:8-9).

Yet, these words don't sound like the great apostle Paul I've heard preached all my life. In fact, I've never heard anyone preach on these verses. Paul was so depleted of emotional, physical, and perhaps even spiritual strength due to the overwhelming weight of responsibility he carried, he didn't feel he could keep trudging on. He was desperate and despairing of life—not because of sickness but from a complete abandonment to the Call God had placed on his life.

From the personal glimpses Scripture reveals of Paul's life, he clearly endured incredible physical and emotional pain. In chapter two we looked briefly at his hunger, his cold, his viper encounter, his thirst, his sleeplessness, his shipwrecks. Besides these he also suffered severely from whippings and beatings with vicious clubs (2 Cor. 11:23-27). At one point his own countrymen heaved heavy, jagged rocks at him to smash his body into a bloodied mass. Presumed dead, he was dragged angrily across the rough ground, his head bashing against the stones, sticks, and debris littering the countryside. Surely the dogs followed, scratching and licking the glistening, red trail woven by his blood. Horribly bruised, gashed, and filthy, he was abandoned to the hungry scavengers of the sky and field. The Christians encircled his battered body. Without a doubt they were praying for this awesome man of faith. God breathed strength into his broken body. Paul stood up. Surely every move he made was a determined effort against engulfing waves of pain, as he returned to the very city of people who had just stoned him (Acts 14:19-20).

Paul suffered the harsh indignities of imprisonments (2 Cor. 11:23). Heavily chained day and night, the iron links rubbed his wrists and ankles raw and caused his limbs to ache while prohibiting any free movements. His bed was the clammy dirt floor. Moisture, which gathered on the low, rock ceiling, dripped on his face as he struggled to sleep. His midnight companions were the roaches and rats that crawled over his restlessly sleeping form.

On top of this he endured the discomfort of an unending, probably physical, problem (2 Cor. 12:7). Paul may have lived every day of his life in pain. Emotionally Paul was tried on every side. He was so violently hated that 40 Jewish men pledged together to a hunger strike until they succeeded in killing Paul. The ending of his life was worth theirs (Acts 23:12-21). Everywhere Paul traveled, people attempted to kill him. He lived each moment of his reborn life with this alarming reality (2 Cor. 11:26-27). When being lowered in a basket over the city wall (Acts 9:23-29) or escaping at midnight on horseback (Acts 23:23-24) or on foot from angry mobs and crazed murderers (Acts 17:5-10), death was always in pursuit. No wonder he was sometimes sleepless.

Added to all this misery, Paul was forsaken by those to whom he had ministered, forsaken by his friends. Listen to his pain-filled words: "All who are in Asia turned away from me" (2 Tim. 1:15). "Make every effort to come to me soon; for Demas, having loved this present world, has deserted me" (2 Tim. 4:9-10). "At my first defense no one supported me, but all deserted me" (2 Tim. 4:16).

Paul knew, intensely, the searing, heart-branding scars of abandonment.

At every turn he was mocked by false teachers who tried to undermine the faith of his new converts (see Galatians). He lived under the constant pressure of deep concern over the young churches, as a father jealously standing guard over his newborn struggling to breathe (2 Cor. 11:28-29). He feared for his children in Christ (2 Cor. 11:2-3) and depleted himself completely, willing to die as a sacrifice for them in order to deepen their faith (1 Thess. 2:8, Phil. 2:17). Every growing pain the churches felt, every cry of the infant Christians, ate into Paul's spirit and drove him to prayer.

Of his own life and the lives of the other apostles he wrote,

"To this present hour we are both hungry and thirsty,
and are poorly clothed,
and are roughly treated,
and are homeless;
and we toil, working with our own hands;
when we are reviled, we bless;
when we are persecuted, we endure;
when we are slandered, we try to conciliate;
we have become as the scum of the world,
the dregs of all things, even until now" (1 Cor. 4:11-13).

Paul willingly surrendered his life to suffering for the One who had suffered excruciatingly for him.

But Paul does not leave us standing and gaping open-mouthed at the enormity of his trials and deadly weariness. He finishes 2 Corinthians 1:9 with these words, "We had the sentence of death within ourselves *in order that we should not trust in ourselves*, but in God."

Paul knew the way of escape. The key is self, or rather the eradication of self. God compels us beyond our limits to where we throw ourselves in emptiness upon our limitless God. There, in our desperate, despairing state, we discover His sustaining power.

When Paul said, "I can do all things through Him who strengthens me" (Phil. 4:13), he was proclaiming ability to endure the extremes of life (Phil. 4:11-12). Before we are strengthened, we must know our utter weakness. Only the weak can be made strong. Only the empty can be made full. Only in desperation do we know the end of ourselves and our ability and experience God's.

When we are depending upon self, we are not depending upon God.

Paul knew. All these unimaginable experiences caused him to abandon self and learn absolute trust in God.

During our first term I was harshly confronted with the cruelties of life evident in this impoverished society. In 1991 the average life expectancy in Benin was 45 years for a man and 50 for a woman. The average income was only $400 a year. The national hospital was unsanitary and lacked supplies. IV bottles hung from tree branches. Blood stains marred the walls. Ants and cockroaches crawled across the filthy floors. Many women and babies died in childbirth.

Two men that we knew lost children to illness. Emmanuel, our house worker, had a serious bout of typhoid and almost died, just after our arrival in the country. People constantly arrived at our gate begging for assistance, money for food, money for medicines, money for medical procedures. Everyone seemed to be constantly sick. On the streets fingerless lepers and polio victims, without money for crutches, pleaded for gifts. Christians were sometimes persecuted and churches burned.

Late one night we awakened to insistent pounding on our gate. A boy, doing somersaults while the adults held a Bible study at a near-by preaching point, had been instantly killed when, inexplicably, he landed on a rock hidden in the weeds and broke his neck. The Christians prayed over the boy's body for hours. Finally they were reconciled to the fact that it was not the Lord's will to raise him up. Now several of them stood hammering on our metal gate at midnight. They sought to transport his body to his mother's village, 30 miles away. No taxis were available at that late hour.

Wearily Jeff crawled out of bed and went to where the boy lay. He watched as they embalmed the lifeless form by pouring kerosene down the throat. Jeff watched the rigor mortis set in and grieved as all the boy's earthly possessions were gathered up into one small cardboard box. Jeff drove on dangerous dark roads, during the blackest part of the night, to deliver that young man, dead, into his mother's arms.

Life felt harsh.

Even our children were challenged by the unmasking of life's realities. During that time an African friend gave birth. As 10-year-old Ryan held the newborn baby girl in his arms, he looked up at me with sorrowful, pain-filled eyes and asked "Will she die, too?"

Missionaries weren't exempted from suffering and tragedy.

Richard and Carmela Bartels, Chandra and little Victoria, along with many other missionaries, had met at the American Recreational Center for an evening of fellowship and laughter. Women grouped around the shimmering pool, talking and sharing while earnestly watching the children swim. The men were inside, catching a ball game. Jeff was out of the country, attending a youth training camp in Nigeria. As evening approached I felt urgently compelled to get home. I quickly gathered up Ryan, Kevin, and Kari and headed out. We were barely in the door when the phone rang.

In those minutes of travel between the Center and home, Kari's best friend, two-year-old Victoria, had drowned. Surrounded by all that life, all that godly laughter, all that joy, she somehow slipped into the water, unseen, and was gone. Richard, realizing Victoria had suddenly disappeared from his side, stepped outside and saw her small form at the bottom in the pool. Throwing himself into the water, he brought her limp body to the surface. No attempt to revive her succeeded.

Maybe in America, the land of technology and advanced medicine, she would have been breathing again, but not in our Africa. The familiar but strange voice coming over the line told me Victoria's perfect, sweet face didn't look frightened. No anguished struggle was written in her features. Only peace.

I hung up, stunned, and fell to my knees as tears wracked my body. In convulsions of sorrow I struggled. It was impossible for her to have died that way, with all those missionary moms looking on.

The grief overwhelmed me, angered me. Carmela and Richard were precious friends and part of our close-knit missionary family. Their loss was ours to share. "What did You do?" my heart screamed out at God, "blind the eyes of her guardian angel? Have him turn away while she drowned?" No words were spoken in answer to my angry tirade, but immediately an image flooded into my mind of Victoria's guardian angel standing in the pool, with arms open wide, to take Victoria to her real home.

Richard and Carmela told of gathering up Victoria's little body for the drive to the morgue. When they stopped before the doors, Richard stepped out and took Victoria for the last time from her mother's arms. Then he turned and placed her in the waiting arms of an elderly African man, with gray hair and eyes deeply etched with tenderness and compassion borne of pain. It was to them like looking into the eyes of the Lord Jesus and surrendering their baby to Him.

Richard picked up Victoria's body from the morgue for the funeral. He dressed her and laid her carefully in the simple, hand-hewn, African casket on their bed. Our mission family gathered around, shared, wept, and prayed together. Kari stood close and asked to kiss her little friend good-bye. She, not understanding, wanted to go with Victoria, in that box, to heaven.

Moments later we joined a huge crowd in the yard. Christ was preached. The victory of His resurrection was proclaimed. Did a multitude receive Christ that day? No. I only know of one child whose spiritual search began that day: Kevin, our second son.

Richard and Carmela didn't quit. They picked up their cross, worshiped Jesus for His sustaining grace, and continued to tell men, women, boys, and girls about our magnificent Savior. They were willing to be poured out as a sacrificial offering that Benin might know Christ.

In our family Jeff had broken bones that weren't properly cared for due to the inefficient medical care. I watched while Jeff, suffering from a kidney stone, had his IV run dry. I was convinced he was going to die before my eyes. Malaria was a problem. Then hepatitis attacked. Jeff spent six weeks in bed turning yellow and being wretchedly ill. His attack was soon followed by the illness taking its turn siphoning the strength out of Kari, Ryan, and Kevin. Ryan turned such a florescent yellow that I would gasp when he walked up behind me while I was fixing my hair in the mirror. The contrast of skin color was shocking.

After our first term we returned Stateside. We were tired, weary, wrung out, drained, and sobered. I had begun to realize that a calling to follow Christ was a calling to suffering. I had easily received the word about the joy to be found in Jesus, but I'd missed the lessons on weeping, the fact that "Weeping may last for the night, but a shout of joy comes in the morning" (Ps. 30:5).

Scripture is filled with words on suffering: "Suffer hardship with me as a good soldier of Jesus Christ" (2 Tim. 2:3). If I am a good soldier in His army, I will suffer.

"Join with me in suffering for the gospel according to the power of God" (2 Tim. 1:8). Consider this. God's power draws us into suffering. Somehow, I believe we have overlooked this truth. We just want His power to get us out of suffering! God's goal for us is to learn to endure, to live victoriously through suffering, through difficulty, through terribly unpleasant circumstances, for Him. Like Paul.

"Consider it all joy, my brethren," James 1:2-4 says, "when you encounter various trials, knowing that the testing of your faith produces endurance and let endurance have its perfect result, that you may be perfect and complete, lacking in nothing." Faith is perfected, not in escape, but in endurance.

Further, Philippians 1:29 states, "For to you it has been granted for Christ's sake, not only to believe in Him, but also to suffer for His sake." We are privileged to suffer in Christ and for Christ. It is a privilege we most often flee from instead of embracing.

"Therefore since Christ has suffered in the flesh, arm yourselves also with the same purpose, because he who has suffered in the flesh has ceased from sin, so as to live the rest of the time in the flesh no longer for the lusts of men, but for the will of God" (I Pet. 4:1-2). Here we are commanded to take up suffering as a weapon, to arm ourselves with it. Suffering is part of our spiritual armor. Our suffering is vitally important to God in the spiritual battle. Suffering makes us more useful and powerful in His hand.

At the end of that first term, God was calling me to surrender to suffering. I knew to what suffering I could be surrendering. I reasoned: *Satan uses suffering to destroy. Christ uses it to mold a life, to build character and faith.* I wanted to run and hide from suffering. It hurts. But to run from it was to deny Christ and throw myself onto the one who would destroy me. I couldn't deny my Savior, so I slipped to my knees and wept in surrender to whatever pain He would bring into my life, so that Jesus would be seen in me. I surrendered with my eyes wide open. I knew the diseases and struggles that we had lived through in Benin. I knew what awaited us in our return.

The Lord didn't whisper sweet promises to me of health and ease in our coming term. But He promised me His faithfulness.

Does surrendering to suffering, to what God would bring into my life to create godliness in me, to make me the most useful to Him, cause suffering to occur? No. Neither will it keep suffering from happening. Surrender simply puts us on our knees in submission before the fact. In this attitude, in this position, God can readily work.

I once noted in my Bible that death represents afflictions, persecutions, painful situations, distresses, and sicknesses. But life is the character of Jesus lived through our lives. Without death we have no life. If we do not suffer, we do not change. We do not grow into Jesus' life.

Suffering, that we might not trust in ourselves, but in God.

Self is only forced out on its knees.

But we have this treasure in earthen vessels, that the surpassing greatness of the power may be of God and not from ourselves; we are afflicted in every way, but not crushed; perplexed, but not despairing, persecuted, but not forsaken; struck down, but not destroyed; always carrying about in the body the dying of Jesus, that the life of Jesus also may be manifested in our body. For we who live are constantly being delivered over to death for Jesus' sake, that the life of Jesus also may be manifested in our mortal flesh (2 Cor. 4:7-11).

TWENTY TWO

There's One Up!

Growing up on the mission field gives our children a host of different perspectives on life, most of which are good. Admittedly, however, some are a bit odd! Our children have surprised us in their interpretation and reactions to their African environment and in the confusion they have experienced in returning to their American one.

House help. What a misunderstood concept! We don't have a maid. I imagine if we had a maid, my house would be spotless. I'd be sitting in a leather, overstuffed chair enjoying crumpets with my tea while the air-conditioning hummed quietly in the background, muffling all the outside noises that attempted to break in through the tightly closed windows. No, we don't have a maid. What I have is help. I need help. Without someone around to daily clean the entire house of dust blown in through the windows, to sweep out the sand tracked in through the doors, to scrub the bathrooms from the invasive, quickly growing mold, to soak the vegetables in germ-killing bleach solution, to fill the water bottles from the filter, to keep the windows and fans clean, to buy beef off the roadside butcher's table (early, before the flies amass), to haul water from the cistern for the washer for each cycle when the faucet water turns dark brown, and to kill the snakes, I'd never be able to do a thing! Just accomplishing the tasks necessary to live in this environment would consume every minute of my time.

As it is, any shred of knowledge concerning cleaning methodology contained in a house-helper's head is tediously taught by the woman of the house—me. For the villagers house cleanliness is achieved on a need-to-use basis. The center of their floors are well swept, but until the corner needs to be used, why sweep it? (Besides the pile of corn stored on that side of the room is in the way.) When a need arises to use the table, they wipe it. It's that simple. The dishes are washed and stored, wet, in a large metal basin with a cloth tossed over the top. They are dried just before use, because if they are dried earlier, they will just get dusty and have to be wiped all over again. Those who have cement homes never wash the walls of their houses. "Why bother?" they ask. "They'll just get dirty again. Besides, we can't afford the soap." Their cleaning utensils consist of a rag and a collection of long bristles tied together with a scrap of string. The latter is their aerobicizer-broom, which can only be used by very, very short people or those planning on having future back problems. Their dirt compound, of all things, receives the greatest attention. It is swept daily, to perfection, with that handle-less broom. Their reasoning does make sense. The only thing they do in their homes is sleep, and that only during the rainy season. Everything else is done in their real house—the great outdoors.

So you can understand why, even with intensive training, my house-help washes fuzzy, light-colored towels with dark rugs and doesn't know that a leather purse should not go in the dryer. They tend to use scratchy steel scrubbers on new Teflon pans and on the shiny lids of plastic garbage cans. After years together I still have to point out the dust-ball-laden spider webs and remind them to remove the inch of crud living on top of the fluorescent lights. To them trimming back the trees means complete eradication of all the beautiful, shade-producing branches, when I just wanted the one dead limb lopped off. No matter how long people work for us, they come up with strange variations to our directives.

One day I asked Emmanuel to make twice-baked potatoes. Arriving in the kitchen later after several hours of teaching Kari, I discovered he had prepared several kilos of potatoes. That was good. He had also boiled a dozen eggs. Not good.

I restated, "Emmanuel, I said twice-baked potatoes, not potato salad." He energetically and innocently responded, "Yes, Madame. I will scoop the cooked potato out of its skin. Then I will take the yellow of each egg, mash it with the potato, then place it back in the skins."

Not quite. He was supposed to mix the potato with cheese! Right color, wrong ingredient! He had deviled eggs and the potato recipe turned around! We just can't assume understanding. We must follow up on our directives.

Another time the wondrous odor of burnt sugar wafted its way through every corner of the house. When I arrived in the kitchen to investigate, I discovered Emmanuel up to his elbows in water as he scrubbed the detached bottom of my stove. I guessed the scenario. It was the "Houdinis."

Even if Tupperware is sealed airtight against ant invasions, the amazing Houdinis magically enter. In defense we created our own disappearing-act illusion. We spread the Houdini-infested cereal on a cookie sheet and place it in the oven. Voila! The ants disappear. In theory, they flee. In reality they probably just shrivel into nearly invisible Houdini balls. The "ant-less" cereal is re-dispensed into the Tupperware and later eaten.

I sensed our current problem was of similar origin. "Emmanuel, what happened?" I inquired. "The ants got into the sugar, so I placed the bag in the oven and turned it on."

"Emmanuel, you know you can't put plastic in the oven."

"Sacks aren't plastic," was his honest response. He'd grasped the concept that Tupperware was plastic, but after 11 years of working with us, he couldn't transfer that knowledge to a clear sack! He gets it now, though.

House help is like having a really old child working around you, when you were convinced your three children were enough. Sometimes it all goes well. Sometimes it all goes wrong. You wonder if the help is really a secret plot to drive you insane.

All in all, while I am in Africa, I have house help. At times it does have its humorous consequences.

I worked hard to keep Emmanuel from picking up the children's toys or from completing our youngsters' abandoned jobs. Although he is in our house to help, the children have always had responsibilities to accomplish. Still ideas not quite in accordance with mine niggled their way into our children's heads.

I do not remember what the issue was, but Kari didn't appreciate my negative response.

"I said, 'No, Kari!'"

In an exercise of her four-ishness, Kari stomped her foot and angrily retorted, for the only time in her life, "I hate mothers. I don't need a mom!" Then, stomping dramatically all the way, she fled to the security of her room upstairs.

Her antics didn't create her sought-after offended airs. Instead, her dramatics were quite amusing. Stifling the laughter that threatened to explode from my lips, I thought seriously of how to calmly diffuse the situation.

Quietly, I followed her to her room and found her sitting on her bare mattress, arms folded across her petulant chest. The clean, folded sheets were sitting off to one side, begging someone's attention.

Gently I said, "Well, if you don't need a mom, then you can make your own bed."

Still belligerently angry, she pouted, "You know I can't do that."

"Then you do need a mom," I responded, thinking I'd trapped her.

"No, I don't need a mom," came her hasty retort, "What I need is a maid!"

The wildly designed African cloth has names. During our first term I was thrilled to go to the biggest market in all of Benin, which stretches a mile in each direction and is stocked with amazing amounts of fabric, tin dishes, suitcases, jewelry, cheap baby clothes, mountains of tomatoes, and packages of buggy macaroni.

One can easily become lost in the complex maze of dilapidated, old shanties tightly squeezed against multitudes of bold, pushy sellers.

The singularly strange thing is that all the cloth sellers are situated side by side in one gigantic area. All the jewelry-sellers roost together. Likewise the purse-, shoes-, and dish-sellers cluster by kind. I cannot inconspicuously consider a piece of fabric, for everyone in the entire section now knows I am looking for cloth and begins to clamor aggressively for my attention. It's an experience!

This particular muggy day an African friend, Ginette, and I maneuvered around the mud-puddles and by myriads of cloth until I finally picked out a green-and-off-white-printed piece. After debating the price and paying, I asked the market mama the name of the cloth.

"Leopard," it seemed she said.

"Great!" I thought quite contentedly to myself looking at the green, foot-like blobs imbedded throughout, "Leopard paw prints!

How African!" I promptly took the material to a seamstress and had a typical, broad-shouldered, Benin-style outfit tailored from it.

The first time I wore it, I happened to be in the presence of Ginette, when some other friends came up and started admiring the cloth. Experimenting with my newly acquired African knowledge I promptly told them the name of the fabric and proudly explained, "These spots are leopard paw prints."

"No they're not!" Ginette corrected me. "The seller didn't say 'leopard.' She said 'lepreux.' You know, the fingerless people."

Oh. Those paw prints weren't leopard prints but fingerless leper hands. So much for my French. At least leopard and lepreux are right next to each other in our French dictionary. I was close. The dress is a great conversation piece.

As I've indicated, at every major corner in the city of Cotonou stands an army of beggars. Legless guys come scooting by on tiny-wheeled platforms. With pleading faces these men hold their hands up toward our car window. Crippled people on homemade crutches or those who drag themselves around by their hands offer you an opportunity to ease their suffering with a few coins. And we have lepers, fingerless, toeless, grinning lepers entreating you for a penny or two of mercy. With what they have left of hands, they roll them in a pitiful, universal motion of helpless supplication. We give. Then, afterward, we head for the antibiotic soap.

One day, when Kari and Kevin were quite little, I caught them playing with their fingers bent down half-invisible on each hand. Seeing my curiosity they gleefully ran over to me, proclaiming, "Look, Mom, we're lepers." I groaned. All these sights had worked their way, slowly, insidiously, into our children's lives!

Another time I found myself quite startled by Ryan. I'd refused his request, but he wasn't willing to give up. He bent down a bit, conjured up his most piteous expression, rolled his hands graciously up and out at me, and said, "Pleeease?" just like the beggars. I stared at him incredulously. He hadn't even realized his mimicry! When I pointed it out, he gasped, then laughed. How subtly we are influenced by our environment.

Kevin finds Africa a treasure-house of pets. For years he captured and kept chameleons. We'd often find one perched on his shoulder or resting calmly on his head. When a fly was spotted, he'd grab his mottled green friend and point it as one would a gun. Seconds later its long sticky tongue would shoot out and whack the fly on the head. With a couple of smacks and crunches the tasty snack would disappear, wings, feet, and all.

Bush babies, which look like squirrels but have hands like monkeys, live high in the scraggly fir trees in our yard. One day a nest of babies fell to the ground. While Kevin was tenderly rescuing them to raise, Emmanuel stood close by, declaring how delicious they were to eat. In fact, that is always the conflict. What we consider pets, the Africans call "good eat'n"—the cats, even the rats.

Kevin has kept a number of ball pythons (non-venomous snakes) that we'd found either in our yard or in the fields around our house. Belle, Chip, Jasmine, and Beast are now somewhere living again in the wilds, much to the dismay of the Africans who know us best. We let lunch and future wallets go. Pythons are a mystery to me. Here in the south of Benin they are worshiped. In the north they're eaten. And Kevin befriends them.

These animal adventures have hooked me into activities I'd rather never have experienced. Like helping Kevin force-feed Belle. She wouldn't eat the offerings of baby chicks that he'd walked baking kilometers into the neighboring village to buy. Kevin read that some snakes won't eat in captivity until they are force fed. How did that translate? Kevin killed a mouse and while he was keeping the snake's mouth open with a twig crosswise, I had to cram the dead mouse down its throat with a pair of tweezers until the snake began to swallow. Yuck. That one wasn't listed on the Benin-Mom job description!

We had a delightful experience with a baby-blue diker of the antelope family. On stick legs he'd follow after Kevin, slipping on the living room's tile floors, and nibble at Kevin's calf hairs. Its little hind-end was at a perpetual angle higher than its cute, furry, tiny head. We fell in love with Chewy. But he had been too young when he was separated from his mother and didn't live long. We were so sorry. So was Emmanuel. Chewy would have made a good stew.

Kari was only a year old when we stole her away from the States. Our first return trip, three-and-a-half years later, was quite an adventure! As I dressed for the flight, Kari approached me, grew wide-eyed, and yelled, "Mom, what did you do to your legs? You look like Ginette!" My black pantyhose frightened her. She thought something terrible had happened to my lower extremities! She insisted that I show her the pantyhose from the elastic waistband top, down to my black wiggling toes. Kari had never seen them before. It's much too hot in Benin to even consider wearing anything as close-fitting as pantyhose. They aren't even sold in the country!

In fact, Kari's question raised some other questions. We once had a bright, energetic, volunteer woman doctor working with us in village clinics. In her determination to keep bugs from biting her legs, she wore black pantyhose. After she and the team left, I paused to wonder what the Africans had thought of the half-black, half-white woman!

Kari's questions on our trip home were unending, beginning with the Benin airport's new, first-ever luggage conveyor belt. She'd never witnessed automation! Although we traveled in August, we arrived in Brussels to a 50-degree temperature—extremely cold weather to our Africanized bodies' thermostats. Kari screeched when she hit that first toilet seat. The cold porcelain was a startling shock.

When we washed our hands together, Kari plunged her small fingers under the running faucet, then suddenly pulled them back, crying out at the same time as if she'd been burned. Afraid I'd accidentally turned on the hot, rather than cold, I quickly asked her, "Kari, what's wrong?" With bewilderment she replied, "That's cold!" Our pipes roast in the walls of our house and rarely spit out anything cooler than lukewarm. She'd never encountered frosty faucet water before!

Our first morning in America dawned bright, cool, and beautiful. After a long sleep we were ready to get out and explore. Grateful to be together again, my mother and I caught up on our lives as we strolled along the weather-worn, shaded sidewalks. Kari pushed her brand-new baby doll in a stroller silently behind us. It was calm. The green manicured lawns, stone and ivy, two-story elegant homes contrasted starkly with the predominantly brown color of our surroundings in Benin.

After we walked for several blocks, a late-morning jogger ran past. Kari looked up at the man and proclaimed in amazement, "There's one up!" In her world everyone rose at dawn and stayed out until dark. She hadn't seen anyone working outside; therefore, she figured everyone in America was still in bed!

She discovered that her grandparents' walls were hollow (ours are cement block), which really troubled her; that Sunday School was in English, and that huge snails didn't crawl unsuspectingly on American church benches to be snatched up by hungry women for lunch. In fact, American church pews were padded!

After laboring over several crates of goods to be sent back to Benin and after removing our personal items from the house we'd been graciously lent for furlough in Brinkley, Arkansas, we stuffed our borrowed station wagon full of last-minute things we would use Stateside and began our final journey to say good-bye to our parents.

As we passed the church, we decided to stop, one last time, for a quick soft drink with the pastor, Jim McDaniel, and staff, our cherished friends. As we sat there, already tasting the bitterness of separation and enjoying the preciousness of Christ's love we shared, Kari very pointedly asked,

"How come other people don't pack up all their things and go to other countries?"

Good question.

Growing up internationally deepens, challenges, and "strangifies" our children's lives. They love it. Just ask them. Between Ryan's junior and senior year of high school he spent the summer in the states working as a YMCA counselor at Camp Kern. He wrote:

"I just want you to know that my little sister has just about destroyed my resolve not to be homesick. I doubt she let you read the letter she sent me, but it didn't help in my battle against the emptiness I feel in missing you guys. Well my time is ticking away, and in a short 19 days I will once again rejoin my Benin clan. It's strange, when I am there I refer to America as home, and here I refer to Benin as home. Odd . . ."

Odd, but delightfully rich. Not everyone feels at home on two, abstractly different continents.

The same Lord is Lord of all, abounding in riches for all who call upon Him (Rom. 10:12).

TWENTY THREE

Lightning Bolt

With growling thunder and streaks of white lightning, the menacing winds blew dark, billowing storm clouds over the village of Tchetti (chet-tea). Shrieking, the people scattered for cover. Pierre, a young Christian, gathered his family members into their simple home to escape the oncoming barrage. As hurtling raindrops resonated sharply against their tin roof, Pierre's son curled up on his straw mat against the cement block wall and fell fast asleep.

With a terrifying, horrendous crack a flaming shaft of light burst through the wall above the sleeping child's head. Xevioso, (hey-vee-oh-so) the thunder god, had struck. The booming explosion, combined with the boy's frantic screams, catapulted Pierre into the room. He pulled his trembling son into his arms. Although frightened, the child's life was intact. A smoldering, gaping hole, left by the lightning bolt, sizzled just inches above the boy's head. Exploded debris from the wall, like discharged shrapnel, lay strewn across the floor.

Gripped by a paralyzing fear, the residents of Pierre's compound quickly called for Xevioso's priest. Urgently insisting that Pierre join them, they commenced a ceremony to appease Xevioso's anger, so he wouldn't attempt to claim another life.

Pierre stepped out calmly and boldly among them and said, "No. I will not participate. The all-powerful Lord Jesus is my family's protection." Being new to the faith, he didn't know how to further explain his trust in Christ. When the winds abated and rains stilled, he sought out a phone and called his pastor brother, Venance Kouton, who lived four hours away in the city of Cotonou.

The first Baptist missionaries were invited to Benin by the Yorubas (your-uh-bahs), a people group that had migrated from

Nigeria. The Benin missionary focus for years to follow was the Fon (phone) and Gun (goon) peoples. During our Benin Baptist Mission's study of *Experiencing God* by Henry Blackaby, God began expanding our vision to all the unreached people in Benin.

More than 53 different people groups and languages exist in this country. Not one of these groups is evangelized. At that time 11 groups had not yet even been introduced to Jesus nor experienced the freedom in salvation that He alone gives. As a mission family we took up a burden of prayer for all Benin's people.

We were returning from a family vacation to a game park situated on the savannah of northern Benin, where, on occasion, you may chance to see a majestic lion, a troop of inquisitive baboons, or a trumpeting elephant. Suddenly, our tire went flat. Getting trapped in deep, dry, sand; becoming stuck in bottomless, slimy muck, or suddenly experiencing the wobble of a deflated wheel are everyday driving hazards in Benin. Driving without a healthy spare is like opening a soft-drink bottle with your teeth (a habit our Beninese friends practice). It can be accomplished but at great risk. From the moment Jeff replaced the flat, we began hunting the arid landscape for a repair shop.

Throughout the hot, dry journey, as clouds of copper dust marked our passing, Jeff and I had been confronted with the total absence of churches among the scores of cylinder-shaped mud and thatch villages through which we passed.

The next village was Basila (bah-sil-lah). After parking our vehicle next to a massive stack of bald, rimless tires which marked the rickety shanty of a tire repairman, Jeff stepped from the truck. A man, standing nearby, spoke to him. Abruptly leaving aside all the customary greetings about health and family, he pointedly asked, "To which God do you pray?" Converted from an animist faith to one in Mohammed, he was yet seeking truth. While the coal iron was heating to adhere the patch to the tire, Jeff introduced him to the name of Jesus. A mosque edged the road. Grotesque idols and their tiny, rusting temples encircled the huts. But not one church or Christian group was to be found in this village of Anii people. The awareness of the absence of Christ in these lives weighed heavy on our hearts.

After our vacation, Jeff and Pastor Venance, during their weekly prayer time together, requested that God send someone to share Christ with the people of this region. God quietly responded, "What about you?" Jeff was astonished by the question. We'd already journeyed to Africa and left our beautiful house, our precious family, many of our possessions, our culture and language, and the ease of life in America. He had surrendered all he knew in obedience and was amazed that Christ was still asking for something more—that yet another calling was beyond the Call. After a few moments of deliberation, with the heart of a servant, Jeff answered, "I'll go."

That's when the phone call came.

Several days later Jeff and Venance left for the laborious drive to Tchetti. Hours up-country, at scenic, boulder-shaped, granite hills that protrude from the scraggly bush and scrawny trees, the pavement ended. Further and further from the pavement they slid over the rutted, muddy road until they finally arrived at their destination.

Excitedly, Pierre welcomed them. Before they could wipe the grime of the journey off their faces, he gathered eight people from the compound into his small home so that Jeff and Venance could share the forgiveness and power of Jesus. They explained that Xevioso held no threat for a Christian. After having watched the changes in Pierre's life since he met Jesus, and after listening intently to the words of the pastor and friend, four out of the eight gave their lives to Christ.

Several weeks later Jeff returned to Tchetti with Evariste and other men to conduct a two-night evangelistic campaign. As each day slipped into obscurity, 400 people abandoned their cooking pots, homes, and evening activities to view films projected onto one of our bed sheets and to listen to a life-changing message. Twenty-five people knelt in acknowledgment that Jesus was Lord and began to attend a weekly Bible study Pierre led.

From there the Word rapidly spread. Although Pierre had no theological education and hadn't even had the opportunity to be baptized, he began enthusiastically sharing Jesus with others. Countless villages were without Christ. Pierre needed direction. Kneeling, he prayed for God to guide him. Each time he prayed, God impressed on him a village name. A few days later, a delegation from that very village would visit Pierre and extend a personal invitation to him to come tell them about Jesus.

In the tiny village of Atakpame (ah-tahk-pahm-may), Prosper, a voodoo priest, bowed his head and surrendered his life to Jesus after listening intently to Pierre's message. He had never known peace. He was tormented by the very gods he served. Through Christ he severed forever the bondage and for the first time slept peacefully.

Purposefully, he gathered all the voodoo paraphernalia that clung to the walls and floors of his home, grabbed a can of kerosene, and walked hardened, village trails toward the bush. Villagers stopped in their tracks in horrified realization of what Prosper intended.

Fearfully they began to follow and plead, "Don't do it! Don't do it! Prosper, you'll die!"

But he continued to firmly place one sandaled foot before the other. Where the trees, overburdened with heavy leaves, formed a natural boundary, he threw down his old, useless gods, doused them in kerosene, and set them aflame. The impassioned crowd shrieked as a crackling explosion burst from the blazing images.

"Prosper, they are angry," they screamed. "See, that's evidence of their power. You are going to die!"

Prosper responded, "If I die, it is not due to the power of voodoo gods but to the Lord Jesus Christ who is calling me home. I'm following Jesus." Months later Prosper remarked to Jeff, "I'm not dead! I don't fear anything anymore. I'm at peace with God."

Across the hills and valleys new groups sprang up. They built wall-less, thatched structures. Using freshly cut tree limbs stuck between forked branches for benches, the believers gathered in deep hunger to hear the words of Christ. The discomfort of their seats was greatly outweighed by the thirst of their hearts. In their exuberance they began writing praise songs to Jesus in their language, Ife (ee-fay). They joyfully walked many difficult kilometers through winding, forest paths to other villages to share with them the Good News. Yet, no one had taught them about evangelism!

When Jeff forged through the paths to visit, the people sheepishly mentioned the songs they'd written and the people they'd told about Christ. They innocently asked, "Is that OK?" Would that everyone who found Christ responded with such incredible zeal!

When Al, a missionary evangelist to Cotonou, traveled to Tchetti with a team of Beninese Christian men, he returned absolutely awed. As day ended, on a Friday evening, he arrived in the distant village of Atakapame. The 40 who normally attended Pierre's Bible study, along with 40 others, eagerly waited under the thatch roof. To the light of a lone lantern, they studied God's Word.

Afterward, the village elders, dedicated voodoo worshipers, convoked Al and Pierre to a meeting. Uneasily, they presented themselves, wondering what lay in the hearts of these men. Al and Pierre were astounded as the elders met with them and begged them, "Come again and tell us more about your God." Incredibly, they graciously offered the new Christians land for a church.

Saturday evening, as the cover of darkness enveloped the skinny trail, they turned onto a dry creek bed riddled with irregular, deep ruts cut by swiftly flowing water during rainy season. The foliage hung tightly over the jarring path and vigorously scraped across the windows of the vehicle as they jostled by.

As they arrived at Bongo-fe (bon-go-fay), a village no one yet had visited with the message of Jesus, the unusual sight of headlights glaring into the black night gathered the entire village. Vehicles rarely traveled their way. When the villagers glimpsed the light-skinned man, they requested a forum to hear about his beliefs. When Al finished preaching, the head elder asked him, "May the whole village accept your Jesus?"

Sunday, as the bright morning turned into a burning, cloudless day, God had another surprise waiting. In Outele (Oh-tel-lee), where Pierre conducted his third Bible study, 80 people patiently waited while they sat on incredibly uncomfortable, branch benches under a temporary structure they'd constructed. After the service the village elders eagerly sought out Al and Pierre. They led them a short way through the bush to a jungle-snarled piece of land that men energetically cleared with steady swipes of their machetes. It was a gift for a permanent church building.

In just four months four churches were planted among the Ife. The awakening continues. Hundreds upon hundreds have heard God's Word and surrendered their lives to the Lord Jesus.

Don't get frantic when a lightning bolt jolts the ground beneath your feet. God is calling you to action.

God has a plan!

The people who walk in darkness will see a great light; Those who live in a dark land, the light will shine on them (Isa. 9:2).

TWENTY FOUR

Invitation

Jeff was exhausted.

It all began as we crammed the minutest spaces available in suitcases with every imaginable and unimaginable item. It was an attempt to take all the wonders of America home to mall-less Benin at the end of our first furlough.

During this flurry of activity we called, one last time, back to Benin, to see how things were going.

"Oh, Jeff," said our colleague, Bobby Couts, from a distant end of the crackling line, "We're so glad you called. We've just been talking about you. Can you take the business manager's job?"

I heard and was horrified. Alan Kahalawai, our last career business manager, left the field because of severe illness. In response, Phil Oakley, one of our church planters, left his ministry and temporarily managed the position. Now his wife, Beth, needed to escape the mosquitoes and malaria of swampy Cotonou, or leave the country! Jeff was the only choice left for the job. They desperately needed someone immediately. Jeff, without a selfish consideration said, "Sure. I'll do it." I about died.

We'd labored in France and gained our required French. We'd thrown ourselves into intensive, difficult Fon learning and attained the required proficiency level. Language acquisition had consumed most of our first term.

We were ready to get back to Benin and fully into our youth work. Things weren't going the way I'd planned.

From the moment we signed on the dotted line for missionary service, someone always reminded us, "As a missionary you must be flexible!" Facing this new situation, I didn't feel like being flexible.

During the entire flight back I gritted my teeth. The business manager's position was the hub of the mission. He held the missionaries' salary bag. He juggled visas and residence cards. He performed as mission liaison to obstinate government offices. He reserved flights and secured tickets. He managed the numerous housing difficulties, plumbing problems, peeling paint, and leaky roofs. He directed the missionary guesthouse, bought its supplies, and supervised its cleaning. He coordinated the endless repairs on the road-weary vehicles. He slaved over the accounting books. He solved all the problems. And somewhere on the side he mish-ed (my short word for doing the work of a missionary).

Jeff hadn't hesitated on the phone to say, "Let us pray about this." He failed to pose any questions such as, "Can we investigate other options, first, rather than me taking over the position?" My servant-hearted husband had simply replied, "Yes." I was mad. I was steaming mad. I was mad at my colleagues for not finding another solution. I was mad at God. I didn't want Jeff to be the business manager.

Back in Benin, I discovered the storage boxes, now dusty and mildewed, in which we'd carefully packed our lives before furlough. I cleaned, set everything in place, and dove into school with the children. I worked hard at making Jeff miserable, because I was miserable. He was gone all the time and was stressed when he was home. If the mission office was locked, someone would look for him. If the electricity blacked out at the guesthouse, no matter what obnoxious time the clock screamed, he'd crawl out of bed to check it out. Every weekend he threw himself into youth work and church planting to maintain a balance between his office work and his passion for growing people in Christ. Every day I grew more hostile in spirit.

Finally, Jeff looked at me and said, "Get over it. This is the way it is and is going to be." He wasn't being mean. He was being right.

Tough words.

But they forced me to face my anger at God. I finally spouted at Him, "Was this just a big mistake, or was Jeff being the business manager Your plan?" Then I ducked, afraid of the answer.

It wasn't long in coming. In my daily Bible reading I stumbled and fell, broken, across these words, "The Lord of hosts has sworn saying, 'Surely, just as I have intended so it has happened, and just as I have planned so it will stand'" (Isa. 14:24).

That hurt. I got right with the Lord, right with my husband, and right with my mission family. All my rightness didn't make Jeff's job any easier, though!

Jeff became physically, mentally, and emotionally exhausted. But he hung in there.

In the middle of Jeff's second year in the office, the Lord sent us relief. A career business manager arrived in Benin. As he prepared to enter into his appointed position, Jeff began to seek God's direction. He'd realized that the young men he'd trained to carry on the youth work for the nation were capable of doing just that. This was the ultimate goal—for Jeff to work himself out of a job. Benin didn't need a full-time youth pastor anymore. Interestingly, if God hadn't limited Jeff's time with the youth by trapping him in the business office, he wouldn't have arrived so quickly at this realization.

Furthermore, one of Jeff's key youth leaders, Valentin, had returned from Campus Crusade for Christ training and had established a ministry at the university. Jeff needn't double Valentin's efforts. The time to move on had arrived. A blazing fire had been set in our hearts for all the people groups of Benin. So many of them had never yet heard about Jesus. It was time that they did! Our search for a people group began.

Jeff and Renee Hale lived an hour north of the coast in the village of Allada (al-lah-dah). Jeff served as music minister to Benin's Baptist churches. He taught them to truly, indigenously, worship the Lord in their languages. They would use their drums and dance in their services. Centrally located, he traveled north or south as his ministry demanded. Additionally, the villages around Allada were responsive to the Word. Jeff had already fathered four churches among these Ayizo (eye-ee-zoe) people. Their continuing needs as babies in Christ along with the burden of countless others desiring to hear, coupled with the crush of his music ministry, had Jeff snowed under a massive, weighty ministry avalanche—in Africa!

My Jeff sensed God moving his heart toward the Ayizo.

I wanted to move to a village near Tchetti, Savaloo (sah-vah-lou). Steve and Shawn Allen, evangelical missionary friends of ours, had called the Flintstonian landscape of Savaloo home. There, where the earth uncannily spit up mountainous boulders and flung them across the flat terrain, women spend their days sitting under squat, dilapidated shanties under the sweltering sun, pounding unyielding, granite rocks into sharp-edged gravel. Handmade gravel. I can never imagine a more explicit image of hell. Circumstances forced our friends to leave, heavy-heartedly, just as village after village in the surrounding area had begun to beg them to come and tell them about Jesus. Instead of being able to respond, they painfully purchased plane tickets back to the States. I wept for the people.

Jeff and I needed a solidified front. Jeff conducted a survey among the Ayizo villages to evaluate their spiritual receptivity. The day Jeff left, the children and I earnestly prayed that if God wanted us to serve Him among the Ayizo, He would issue Jeff an invitation.

A young man, Cyriaque, accompanied Jeff. Cyriaque once held a great job as a lab technician in Cotonou until he heard the words of Jesus, "Go into all the world and preach the Gospel" (Mark 16:15). In response he literally sold everything he owned and traveled the Ayizo villages to tell them about Jesus. When Jeff teamed up with him, he hadn't started any churches, but his message of Christ had made a lasting impression on the lives of many.

Together they visited eight villages. In each they received a warm welcome. Brown, glistening bodies gathered from fields and all corners of each amber-tinted clay lodging to eagerly listen to their words. In one village, Dodji Bata (doe-gee bah-tah), the people assembled under the leafy protection of an enormous baobab tree to escape the torrid heat. Jeff opened to Psalm 1 and exhorted them to walk on God's path. A shriveled, white-haired man, hunched with age, a homemade pipe perched between his rotting teeth, pointed directly, unwaveringly at Jeff and questioned, "How can we know how to walk on God's path unless you come back and teach us?"

Immediately, we started searching for a home in Allada, the central Ayizo village.

The Lord issued an invitation. Another calling within our Call had been mandated.

We simply responded. The results would be eternal.

What is God inviting you to do?

Then I heard the voice of the Lord, saying, "Whom shall I send, and who will go for Us?" Then I said, "Here am I. Send me!" (Isa. 6:8).

TWENTY FIVE

Inheritance

Thin, reed mats for beds were strewn across the cement floor of the dormitories. Showers were self-fabricated by heaving up water from the deep well and pouring it into work-worn buckets before transferring it to a tin can to be dribbled over a sweaty head.

Toilets were available on campus, but flushing instructions were meticulously given. The villagers were only familiar with the bush and the rare outhouse. They'd never seen toilets before! Where the water swirled to afterward was a matter of great curiosity, discussion, and concern.

Before Jeff could choose a village in which to begin work, God had a plan. The Benin Baptist Youth Committee had chosen to host a youth camp at an agricultural school right in the heart of the Ayizo people. They designed the week to train the youth as soldiers of Christ. They would learn to witness, with the goal of starting a church in the pineapple-growing village of Sekou (say-ku).

After intensive Bible studies in the airless assembly hall, the youth walked dirt roadways and narrow paths, under the glare of an oppressively hot sun, to witness, compound by compound, to the people. The villagers responded eagerly to their message. One night 250 people ventured to the school grounds to stand and view the Jesus film. The campers, aware of their responsibility, scattered among the visitors.

As the film drew to a close, Jeff was deeply moved as the youth broke off into groups with men and women and personally shared Christ with each. Afterward several requested that a church be started at Sekou.

Another invitation had been issued.

The camp ended on Saturday. Sunday morning Jeff returned to Sekou with a truck full of Christian young men from Cotonou. Twenty-five people from the village were present to learn more about following Jesus.

Every Sunday following, until we found a home in Allada, we roused our children early, ate a hasty breakfast, and headed for the hour's drive up-country to Sekou.

Turning off the pavement we followed the meandering, one-lane road to the village school. Palm branches, scraped smooth and tied together with fine wire, made up the walls. Skinny, unfinished teak trees created the main frame of the structures and held aloft the rusting tin roofs. As we entered one, thick dust stirred into swirling clouds in response to the movement of our sandaled feet across the fine sand floor. Armed with toilet paper we carried in the car, our children joined us in the process of wiping the morning grime off the tabled benches. Then, leaving one or more of our family to welcome those who would arrive in our absence, we walked the shady village paths to greet each person who lived there.

Sometimes a cool breeze would rustle the sea of green leaves around us into waving shades of living color. Other times the trees, laden with brown, airborne dirt, stood motionless and ugly as they awaited the cleansing rains. We received wet handshakes from women drawing water from the well. Children raced to our sides and accompanied us. They clung to our hands each step of the way, as if we were their day's treasure. Carefully picking our way through the spiky leaves of pineapple plants, we'd weave our way into fields to greet men already energetically racing the rising sun and flourishing weeds. We prayed for the sick. We urged each to attend the meeting that they might know peace, joy, and courage through Jesus Christ. Many promised. Few came.

The very first service always draws a curious crowd. Seeds are planted. Relationship causes them to come and stay.

Those who walked past the idol houses on the school grounds, past the Legba and the Zangbeto's sacred house, to attend, earnestly listened to the stories. Jeff taught them six basic characteristics of God—characteristics vastly unlike those of their unpredictable, undisciplined gods. Starting before creation, Jeff, or one of our Christian men, explained stories from the Old Testament. These stories revealed who God is, people's sin, and their need of a Savior. After the lesson my responsibility was to help the people re-enact what they'd just heard. Eagerly they'd step forward to take roles as Cain and Abel, those who built the Tower of Babel, or as Moses and the people of Israel crossing the Red Sea. Their cultural adaptations caused the stories to become vividly real, for their lifestyle identifies with that of Christ's so much more closely than do yours and mine. We taught them, but they revealed to me insights into the Bible I'd never seen with my American eyes.

After the acting adventure, Jeff would ask what characteristics of God they had gleaned from the story. One by one the people would speak up and explain, "God is all-knowing. He knew what the people were doing." "God hates sin. The people were disobeying." "God has all power. He confused the languages of the people." Little by little, in this way, they came to understand the love and authority of the real God, His passion for people, His purity, and His hatred of sin.

Months passed. As we started teaching the stories of Jesus, excitement flowed across those gathered.

"Pastor," they enthusiastically said to Jeff one day, "we believe everything you've been teaching us. We want to start praying together. When can we start?"

We hadn't yet taught them about the death and resurrection of Jesus Christ! Like Apollos they already believed with all their hearts the message, although it was incomplete. Before they established prayer meetings, they had to know the rest of the story. They needed to turn their lives over to Jesus Christ as their Savior and Lord. We quickly threw out our preplanned program and jumped to the end.

Several days later we met on Etienne's compound. Pigs, chickens, and children grunted, squawked, and shrieked around the cooking fires and around the homemade palm-wine still in the yard. An unsteady, wooden table was placed in the middle of the few benches Etienne scrounged together. Night fell. A sightless night like one that can only be known in an African village. Someone brought a flickering lantern that cast a yellow glow on the inner circle of faces gathered there. The walls of the huts reflected the light and cast strange shadows across the numerous people standing in a cloak of darkness to secretly listen and observe. Christ was preached. No one moved. All waited attentively for the Word. The challenge was issued, "If you will pledge your life to serve Jesus, and Him only, then stand up." Eleven men courageously stood before watching friends and relatives and committed their lives to Christ. Etienne, not knowing the Old Testament Scripture, boldly proclaimed, "From this day on, my wives, my children, and I will serve the Lord." A church was born.

Several days later Jeff and I visited Etienne to see how his new faith in Christ was going. After walking only two days with Jesus, Etienne stated, "Wow, Jesus! I love Him intensely!" These new believers didn't yet know how to pray, nor read the Bible, nor how to confess their sins daily. But they had Jesus. Jesus was enough!

Three years passed. As the sunlight filtered in through the ragged, palm-limb walls and sparkled like glitter off a multitude of floating dirt particles, I stood among the worshipers in the Sekou church. Praise songs, drumming, and dance flowed aggressively, joyously before the Lord. As I joined, my mind drifted back to the beginning days, when, at times, not one person attended. I rejoiced as I reflected over the five who first became faithful, then the 11 who surrendered to Jesus. Overwhelmed, I looked around the room bursting with people. I worshiped the Lord for His salvation and awesome goodness.

Suddenly, a vivid image filled my mind, of Jeff and me, no longer standing with the backs of our legs scraping against wood benches but standing in heaven surrounded by a sea of brown faces. My singing ceased. My eyes overflowed with tears. Quickly I looked down to regain my composure. But when I raised my head, once again all I could see was a multitude of Africans worshiping with us before the Lord in heaven. My spirit knew that each precious person in the throng of worshipers was somehow linked to us, because we'd simply been obedient to go. And I wept. What tremendous encouragement God gave us in those moments: a future vision to hold onto in face of obstacles. God had promised that our work would have eternal value. I long for that great day when we will stand with our brothers and sisters in Christ before our Father! No greater reward, no greater purpose for living exists!

Lord, grant us the Ayizo as an inheritance (Ps. 2:8).

After these things I looked, and behold, a great multitude, which no one could count, from every nation and all tribes and peoples and tongues, standing before the throne and before the Lamb (Rev. 7:9).

TWENTY SIX

Cola Nuts

Yves, his legs trembling to support his thin frame, stumbled once again on the short walk from school to his compound. For weeks he hadn't been feeling well. Now his feet were as heavy as the cement blocks used in building the new schoolrooms.

"That building," he reflected, his thoughts swirling in a hazy fog, "was built by the government. But the villagers, devoted to their voodoo worship, attribute the construction to a blessing brought through the preaching of Jesus in the deteriorating, palm-branch schoolhouse. Odd that they can see one truth but not the other," he pondered.

Although clouds flitted across the sun, Yves couldn't account for the sudden chills that tore up and down his body in violent quakes. Hearing the shouts and cheers of his friends, he painfully turned his neck to face the dirt soccer field, with the net-less, wood goals. A game was in progress. He watched, longing to join his friends as they nimbly kicked the wadded, paper ball with their bare feet. But he was far too weak. He ached all over. He had to go rest.

A rise in the path caught his foot and nearly sent him sprawling at the base of the Legba idol resting next to the Zangbeto house. Suddenly, his feverish mind was transported back to his childhood— to following his father to the Oro coven, the sacrificial goat tugging resistantly behind him on a tether. The smells, sounds, and wrestling with the other boys as they waited for their fathers to return from the sacred temple after the sacrifice rushed upon him.

He could hear the bawling goat and the freakish Oro whirling noise and could taste the roasted meat. It was always about blood. Blood and alcohol. His pounding headache throbbed with the haunting beat of the Oro drums he was compelled to play. Even though others meekly followed the worship of their fathers, Yves despised it all. He knew it wasn't right. He knew it wouldn't release him from the emptiness clutching his heart.

He didn't know what could, but he secretly studied his cousin, Francois. Francois was one of the first to go listen to the stories told in the dilapidated schoolroom. The missionaries and evangelist usually visited during the day, but once they visited late in the evening. Yves, with his senses heightened through the sickness that ravaged his body, felt again the cool slap of the breeze on his face that night as he crept through the rough corridors left between the village huts.

He silently eased closer until he could see the lantern's glow dimly illuminating the faces of those gathered around a table in Etienne's compound. He hid in the shadows and listened. Another chill shook his body as he recalled each detail. He heard them tell the story of the death of the God-man, Jesus. The image of blood again sprang back into his spinning mind, but it wasn't the blood of squawking chickens or bellowing goats. It was the blood of Jesus on the cross. Jesus, a dead man who returned to life by Holy power.

The night unfolded through the eyes of his memory, up to the moment when Francois stood and said, "I will follow Jesus." Even though Francois was the eldest son and his father a prominent figure in the community, Francois respectfully refused to continue to participate in his mother's worship of the serpent god and his father's Oro worship. Instead of being afraid, Francois seemed changed, at peace.

Yves could see his roof peeking over the distant compound wall. He shielded his eyes from stabbing sunlight, which made the convulsions worse. He lurched toward the shade, but it made ice race through his veins. He longed to sink onto the dirt where he was and just sleep, but he pushed forward with his last ounce of strength. He had to get home. Home—that was the feeling.

When Francois asked Yves to join the group of Christians, just to listen, his father had refused to let him. Yves' pleas to his father, combined with the prayers he'd prayed to Francois' God to change his father's mind, echoed back and forth in his fever-churned brain. His father had miraculously relented and permitted him to go to the new church with Francois. The growing group made him feel at home. Their love had drawn him to Jesus.

He felt his body stiffening. Shards of pain shocked through his feet to head with every step. He had to concentrate, to focus on something outside the excruciating pain.

The sensation of slipping under water returned firmly to his mind. The memory of being wet and cold sent shivers up and down his sick body—baptism. He had stood with the others, some of the first in his village to believe, and waited his turn. As he stepped into the portable baptistry that the women had filled from the icy depths of the well, he looked up into Pastor Jeff's clear, blue eyes for encouragement. He'd never been underwater before. Jeff laid a calming hand on Yves' shoulder, then lifted his other hand toward heaven. He spoke in the name of the Trinity and gently eased Yves under and up out of the water. Death to life.

Yves vividly recalled the multitude of curious young and old from the village who gawked incredulously at him. Among them were his friends who laughed and mocked. He longed for them to know the peace that Jesus had brought his life. Life. He'd never been so sick before. He felt his life ebbing away. But it didn't matter anymore. He knew Jesus.

Jesus. With thoughts jumping at him from every direction, this one was worthy of clinging to. Grasping at that singular thought, he pitched forward into his compound and collapsed onto his thin mat.

In my mind, I've imagined that what happened next went something like this:

"Yves!" his mother cried, and ran, weeping, to his suffering form. All the herbal potions she had administered to him had been for naught. "It's sorcery," she rasped through her tears to the hunched grandma who hobbled into the dimly lit room. Without a word the ancient women turned away. Crucial minutes ticked by as she prepared the remedy. She ordered one of the children to catch a pigeon, while she precisely cut a cola nut into the prescribed pieces.

The children ran about the compound until they cornered one by the lime tree. Blocking its escape, they caught it by its sharp talons. They brought it squirming and flapping to grandma. With a decisive slash of the razor blade, the squirming ended. A bowl, clutched in one of her long-fingered, shaking hands, caught the blood. With knowledge born in darkness, sacrifices, and voodoo worship since her birth, she carried the blood, the cola nut, and black, hot pepper into Yves' room. She gingerly knelt next to his still form. She held the secret to breaking the sorcerer's curse. Yves would live. She stirred the cola pieces into the warm pigeon blood, rolled them in the pepper, then bent low over Yves' face.

Muttering incantations, she wedged a piece of cola nut between his stiffening lips. Yves' eyes flew open. He tried to move his arms to push her away, but they were paralyzed to his side. He thought the name, "Jesus", and spewed the foul nut from his mouth. Again the old woman crammed the cola nut between his clenched teeth. Vehemently, Yves ejected it.

Once more she twisted the nut into his mouth. With all the force he could muster, he spat the offensive nut far from him, where it fell into the dirt. The disgusted voodoo mama whispered venomously into his ear, "That's your decision, then. You die with the god you've chosen."

Words meant to cut Yves' resolve visibly relaxed him. He had made his decision. At 15 years of age, he had won his final battle.

Yves died. The new Christians mourned but also rejoiced in Yves' witness and courage in Christ. To the last moment of his life, he had been determined that if he died, he would die in Christ.

LuciLLE Burns

Alice married Eric, Etienne's younger brother and a zealous disciple of the Oros. With the zeal of youth Alice enthusiastically joined her new compound's life. She strolled to the well with Etienne's wives and niece, Agate, laughing and teasing. Mindless of the scratchy branches and thorny shrubs that tore at her arms and legs, she gathered wood from the teak forests to cook Eric's meals. With a heavy basin of large, fragrant pineapples to sell, she hiked the miles that separated their hut from the market; then she bartered for goods they needed before returning home with the throng of village women who congested the road.

Alice was content. Her mother-in-law didn't beat her. No one yelled at her much. In fact, Eric's family was unusually kind. The women quickly became sisters, sharing secrets and dreams. When Etienne's wife, Pelagie (pel-a-gee), invited her to church, she quickly acquiesced. The gatherings proved a delightful break in her weekly routine. Every Sunday she rushed through her chores to afford the hours away from home. The lively singing, the praise dancing, and mind-boggling teachings at the Sekou church intrigued her. Alice had never heard such stories before. The words read from the Bible made her full, yet hungry for more.

Jeff told Eric about Jesus. Etienne witnessed to him. His Christian cousins spoke to him. But he refused to listen. Irritated with all the talk about Christ, he laid the final blow. He forbade his young wife to attend services. Brokenhearted, Alice stayed home while the others made their way to the dusty, palm-sided church.

Within a year of their marriage Alice gave birth to a beautiful baby boy. Five months later the baby became seriously ill. With love, following a Sunday morning service, the entire church trooped over to Eric and Alice's. We held that precious baby in our arms and prayed. Wondrously, he was completely healed by the power of the Lord.

Eric, touched by God's hand, relinquished his former interdiction and allowed Alice to come to church. He, though, refused to have anything further to do with Jesus.

Then, suddenly, Eric fell dreadfully sick. Holding Eric upright on the back of an old motorcycle, behind the driver, Etienne transported him to a nearby clinic. But with the limited medical skills and supplies available, his condition grew rapidly worse.

Frantic for his brother's life, Etienne hastily tramped the miles that separated his village from the paved road. He stood there, hailing bush taxi after bush taxi that zipped by, in a desperate attempt to find one empty and willing to transport his brother's suffering body to a hospital.

Finally a taxi stopped. Rushing over bone-rattling roads, they picked up Eric, already unconscious. Hastily, they made their way over a long road riddled with washboard bumps that led to a hospital situated far from the main road in a grove of tall trees.

Etienne, still holding up his brother's limp form, nearly crumbled under his weight in despair when he heard the words, "We can't help you. We're full." After steeling himself against the disappointment, with renewed determination, Etienne and the taxi driver set off again, this time barreling down toward Cotonou, 45 minutes south. Arriving, they urgently carried Eric inside the dirty, hand-stained, clinic walls. Gingerly they laid him on a table. The doctor examined Eric, looked sadly at Etienne, and said, "I can do nothing." Not willing to accept those ominous words, Etienne once again climbed into the dusty, airless confines of the taxi. As his motionless brother leaned heavily against him, he commanded the taxi driver back north another 40-minute drive to the bush hospital in Allada. The roads were chillingly dark. The oncoming truck lights blared into Etienne's blurry eyes. Midnight had long since fled. The luminous, waning moon was dipping into the dusky horizon as they whipped into the hospital's overgrown compound.

Pleadingly, Etienne shouted, "Someone, come help me with my brother!" They came. But, once again they repeated the fateful words, "We can do nothing."

With a heart of lead and extreme fatigue hounding every movement, Etienne ordered the taxi man to carry them home, to Sekou. The sun whispered the promise of another cloudless, blazingly hot day, as they carefully laid Eric on a comfortless, straw mat on the clay floor of his home. Alice, Etienne, his wives, and friends watched as Eric's shallow breathing slowed and stopped.

It was over.

But the grief had just begun, the grieving for one who died without Hope. As victorious as Yves' death was in Christ, Eric's death was shrouded in the horror of the eternal torment he'd just entered.

Alice, with tears cascading down her cheeks, bound both of her feet in rags, the feel of which she would never forget. The rags announced her widowhood. They proclaimed that her dead husband's body slept within the confines of her house. They cried out for pity and would be shed only when her husband's disease-tormented body was lowered into the ground in the dead of the night. She clutched her baby to her chest and privately wept for the man she had known for less than two years.

The village women gathered around her. With tears brimming in their own eyes, they admonished her not to cry. Tears are not accepted in their culture. They are fought. They are denied. They must be stopped.

Before Jeff and I woke that Saturday morning, Agate, ready to share her dreadful news, was already waiting for us on our terrace.

"Was there anything more we could have done to secure Eric for Jesus?", we pondered. We hurt. How could any of our people die, Christ-less, without our feeling deep remorse?

In the afternoon we visited with Etienne's family. We sat silently with them on old wooden benches set up against the hut's cool mud walls in the warm shade. Then, led by Etienne, whose eyes were unrecognizable with grief, we walked to another part of the compound and to a different door. There we took off our shoes and, barefooted, walked in to view Eric's body. His body rested on his sleeping mat against the hard, dirt floor, in a small, windowless room. They'd hung new cloth from the rafters to hide the barren walls. By Eric's lifeless side sat a tin bowl to collect contributions to help defray the funeral expenses. Then Etienne guided us across a small plot of land next to his house, to where they'd buried his daughter several years before, and his mother, who'd recently died. Now they were digging a hole for Eric's body. We handed a few coins to the grave diggers, out of respect for their work, the final work that would be performed for Eric.

We read Scripture to our Christian friends, prayed, then parted to return for the funeral that night.

In those brief hours the compound had been transformed. Thousands of brilliant stars stared down on the scene from a moonless, ebony canopy. A generator, speakers, microphone, and lights blared sound and light into the night. The fluorescent bulbs, strangely out of place in this electric-less habitation, cast long shadows over the faces of the villagers milling about. As we wandered into the mass of people waiting for the appearance of the rough-hewn, wood coffin, we were greeted and offered water, which we raised warily to our lips in a pretense of drinking.

Spotted by Etienne, we were ushered into the sultry, funerary room, which was crammed tight with perspiring people. Etienne had brought us into the inner circle where only trusted friends and relatives set foot, to watch the tearing of the cloth. One by one meters of colorful cloth were handed to the family's representative, who always presided over funerals. He announced to Eric's spirit, whose body was now laid in the coffin, "This cloth is from your wife and newborn son." Then he ripped the 12 meters down to six. With half he covered Eric. The other half he presented to Eric's wife and child to wear in respect and memory of their dead. Repeatedly, he called out the names of those giving cloth and tore the fabric. It was as if his tearing symbolized Eric being torn from life and his separation from them in death.

We never saw Eric's face. The face cloth originally placed over his sightless eyes to shield them from the eyes of the living had been removed when he was wrapped in a shroud. A trusted family member was given guardianship of the face cloth, so that no one could steal it to use in sorcery against the family.

The ripping done, we retrieved our discarded shoes and continued into the cooler air of the night.

An Oro man, distinguished by the band of palm leaves worn about his waist, placed basil at the funerary door and poured a solution over it. This offering was to chase evil spirits away. Later he would go to each door of the compound to repeat the process. Unknowingly, the very things they practice to ward off evil invite evil to come.

The rest of the Oros arrived, singing and pounding on a wide, reed-like tube, to claim their own. Several marched into Eric's death room and raised the casket. They carried Eric's coffin feet-first through the doorway. Then they forcefully retreated once more into the room. Three times the act was repeated. All the while they chanted to Eric's spirit that this was no longer his home. His feet were never to set foot here again. His place was with the dead.

At a quick pace, with their chants proceeding and following the dead, the Oros hastened toward the yawning grave.

Agate shrieked. Flailing her arms she began to run hopelessly about, completely undone. The sight of her beloved uncle being carried away to his grave by the godless Oros, instead of her brothers in Christ, was a vision her sensitive spirit couldn't bear. Faithful to the Oros in life, Eric was placed in the merciless earth by hands and words that honored Satan.

The village men encircled the grave. The women, a few paces off, being careful not to trip on the sticks and wild shrubs of the untilled land, sang in competition with the Oros' loud clamor. Mats were brought and set on the casket, now resting in the grave. Those who would stamp down each layer of soil with their feet stood close at hand and waited.

A feeble lantern lit up the grave and the living closest to it. Its light played off the underside of the huge, banana-tree leaves hanging deathly still over the grave in the breezeless midnight.

Suddenly all grew quiet as Etienne intervened. He respectfully requested their funeral master to permit a word to be spoken by Remy, their pastor. "For," he explained, "the brothers of Eric believe in Jesus."

Surprisingly, he relented.

Remy stepped forward from the deep shadows.

The Oros, caught unaware, began yelling to disrupt the crowd. As they moved off the scene, we could hear their secret, whirling growls filling the night. Then they were gone.

Remy spoke to the crowd about the uncertainty of life but the certainty of Jesus. He prayed that God would comfort the people and bring them to the Truth.

The Christians said, "Amen." Hesitantly, the silent crowd wandered back to Etienne's family compound.

The smoky haze from the cooking fires clogged the stars from view. With their long-handled, wooden spoons, women, close relatives, and friends stirred the boiling contents. The grieving, sleep-deprived family not only had to prepare for the ceremony, pay to have a coffin quickly made, and hire a generator and grave diggers, they also had to host the multitude by feeding the people a worthy meal. Etienne had spent every cent he possessed in an effort to save a life that was lost. Now in Eric's death Etienne begged and borrowed to afford to place his brother's stiff body in the ground.

Tears stung our eyes as the Oros carted Eric off in death. A great sadness settled on our hearts. Eric had chosen wrongly. We will never know if one last word of Jesus to Eric would have counted. When we arrive in heaven, maybe the Lord will spare us the grief of knowing.

The death of Yves rings in our memories with sorrow and joy. We will see him again. He has entered into eternal, knock-your-socks-off, outrageous, joy. Yves chose well.

Have you made your choice? Have you decided for Jesus? Any other choice is a choice against Him.

Does your faith have the courage to resist, or are you still chewing on the cola nuts crammed into your mouth by this world?

I eagerly expect and hope that I will in no way be ashamed, but will have sufficient courage so that now as always Christ will be exalted in my body, whether by life or by death (Phil. 1:20 NIV).

TWENTY SEVEN

What Power Do You Have?

As a child I loved Tarzan movies, but I never thought Jeff and I would be in Africa living one!

After hours of cautiously maneuvering our vehicle along deeply rutted trails, Jeff parked by the village of Akpomey (ahck-poe-may). Akpomey is beyond the edge of nowhere. The village's bamboo huts, set on wooden stilts, are tucked against a silent river that viciously floods during rainy season but dries to a trickle when rains cease.

The river is the center of the village's existence. Drinking water is drawn daily from its swirling murkiness. Clothes are scrubbed and bodies are bathed along the verdant bank.

Jeff and his team greeted the inquisitive group who immediately gathered around the white man and strangers. At nightfall the team would show the Jesus film. Excitement passed from person to person as the word spread. A film was an unheard-of event in their village.

Early the next afternoon Jeff and a team of Christian brothers set off on foot from Akpomey for a more remote village. Sweating profusely in the heavy heat from balancing a generator, projector, and film equipment on their heads, they trekked along the well-worn footpath through the shoulder-tall weeds down to the muddy edge of the swollen river. Men with large, dugout canoes ferried them across to an area slashed free of tangled undergrowth. Locked in this inaccessible corner was another of the four churches planted due to the faithfulness of one man—Paul.

In the fall of 1997, while Americans feasted their eyes on trees bursting with brilliant golds and reds and Benin sweltered under a relentless sun, Paul, a Christian from the port city of Cotonou, was informed by the government that he was to be a schoolteacher in

Akpomey. He whistled in dismay at the news. Akpomey, even by Benin's standards, was a hardship post—a distant, impoverished village, without electricity, without wells, without markets, without motorcycle taxis. Akpomey was a post no teacher wanted. Paul went.

Immediately upon his arrival he was confronted by men representing the Zangbetos and Oros. They didn't ask; they demanded that he join them in their satanic rituals. Paul boldly refused. "I am a follower of the Lord Jesus Christ," he confidently stated. "I will not join you." Consumed with anger they shook their long fingers at him and retorted, "Every teacher who comes either joins us or flees the village in terror." Paul once again strongly replied, "I will not join you." With menacing threats, they left.

As a heavy blanket of darkness enveloped the village, Paul lay down to sleep. Abruptly, he startled awake by a deep-pitched,

whirring noise, announcing the dreaded presence of the Oros. Hostile clanging, yelling, and drum-pounding revealed that numerous voodoo worshipers had surrounded his thin-walled hut. Paul rolled off his mat and onto his knees. There, he sought comfort from his Father. While a spiritual battle raged outside, peace flooded his heart. Although besieged by messengers of evil, he crawled back onto his rough mat and swiftly fell asleep.

Before the sun's rays could rise above the earth, men crept down the creaking ladders of their homes and moved as one to Paul's. Short, loud claps, signifying that guests had come, caused Paul to step out among them. The group confronted Paul with defiant urgency.

"What power do you have?" they demanded.

Puzzled by this odd greeting, Paul replied, "I have no power."

"No," they said, "You do have power. What power do you have? Last night we came to pronounce curses against you, yet not one of us was able to utter your name. Something prohibited us. We could do nothing against you. What power do you have?"

Understanding, Paul responded, "I have no power but Jesus Christ."

Three days later the men apprehensively approached Paul once again. Standing rigidly around him they assaulted him with the same pressing question, "What power do you have?"

"I have no power," Paul answered.

"You have power. Last night the chief priest of the Oros died. We know it had something to do with you. You must have some power."

Paul, realizing the awesome hand of God in these events, quietly said, "I have no power other than Jesus Christ."

"Tell us more about this Jesus," the men said. A meeting of the village elders convened. Land was given for a church building.

Paul taught school and witnessed. Some believed. A small band of Christians formed and prepared to construct a church on their land but not without first uncovering some truths. The land had been given as a test of Christ's power. Deeply hidden under the leaf-burdened limbs and low-hanging palm fronds were fierce idols. Their unholy power had obliterated any previous building attempts. Each had strangely ended in disaster.

One builder fell critically ill. A partially finished building myste-riously burned. Another's solidly formed walls suddenly collapsed without evidence of human intervention. The land challenged the Christian's beliefs and the authority of Jesus.

Taking courage in the power of the Lord, the Christians, with short-handled hoes, destroyed the idols and scattered their dust over the land. The amulets, buried to give power to the idolatrous images, were retrieved and burned before Jesus Christ. With machetes the Christians cleared the land in joy and with firm confidence set the poles for the church structure. The village watched. One aged voodoo worshiper conspired with his daughters. At the bewitching hour of midnight, while the village sought sleep and the spirits prowled in the night's deepening gloom, the threesome slipped through the frightening, dark paths to the Christian's land. The idols hadn't stopped the work, but the unmentionable objects, held fearfully in their trembling hands, would. With clandestine movements they noiselessly buried sorcery, certain to destroy the progress of the Christians.

Days later, leaning on his worn cane, the old man shook with unbelieving shock as, in evidence of Jesus' power, he witnessed the Christians worshiping together under their thatch-roofed church, a church built on Christ on land on which no one could build! Even the sorcery had failed. His daughters were bewildered and intensely curious. Soon they, too, joined the Christians. Their father, the voodoo faithful, and adepts watched in speechless awe.

Testimony of Paul's incredible faithfulness to his powerful God spread. Other villages invited him to share with them the loving, forgiving, life-changing message of Jesus Christ.

With Akpomey's unsanitary conditions, sickness is unavoidable. Travel from there to anywhere is next to impossible. Yet, Paul not only taught the children during the school year, he stayed during his needed summer break to train young Christians in their new faith.

Two years later Paul was offered a new teaching position.

In a country where nothing happens quickly, the village quickly petitioned the government, saying, "Paul is the only teacher that ever came and stayed. He loves our children and us. We want him back." The very people who had determined to frighten him into fleeing their village begged government officials for his return!

Paul considered. His fiancée strongly refused to follow him to such a destitute location. Life in Akpomey is two steps beyond undesirable. Paul chose. He returned to Akpomey. He decided to sacrificially serve, to go where no one else would go, that others might know Christ, rather than marry.[1]

Paul's power is Jesus Christ. What power do you have?

You shall receive power when the Holy Spirit has come upon you; and you shall be My witnesses both in Jerusalem, and in all Judea and Samaria, and even to the remotest part of the earth (Acts 1:8).

---

[1]In 2000 Paul's fiancée, a godly woman, relinquished herself completely to Jesus Christ and married Paul. They now have a baby boy.

TWENTY EIGHT

Taking Every Foot

Bone weary from driving the dusty, tire-slashing roads, of trying to intelligently answer the barrage of curious questions the prayer-walking team tossed my way, and from translating into the local language words the team publicly spoke, I said to the Beninese brothers who accompanied us, "OK. We'll stop this one last time. But we will only greet the mayor and leave. We've got to get back."

Dark, boiling clouds threateningly danced over the swaying palms with a promise of an imminent cloudburst. We were already late for our rendezvous with Jeff, our Ayizo teammates, Bill and Margie Belli, and the medical team at the makeshift medical clinic's site several villages away. And I was dead tired. I wasn't sure I could think another coherent thought in English, much less verbalize another word in Fon.

The African Christians had earnestly pleaded their case. "We told the mayor we would be coming today. We must make an appearance." I understood. Their honor was at stake, as was our reputation for future ministry in the area. So, without an ounce of energy left, I agreed.

I parked our four-wheel-drive vehicle beside the exotic, untamed vegetation which grew in profusion across the dirt path from the mayor's house. With heavy feet we heaved ourselves down from the once-white vehicle and trudged across the deep, dark sand.

As a grimy-faced group, we rounded the corner of the mayor's dwelling. His home appeared no different from the hundreds of mud domiciles we'd already tramped by that day. But, I'm certain we were an unusual sight. Our vehicle's air-conditioning had croaked out its last breath of cool air days before. Now our bodies were relentlessly subjected to the heat. The resulting, unavoidable drenching of sweat glued the billowing grit kicked up by our tires and tossed through our open windows to every exposed portion of our bodies. The addition of the incredible humidity disallowed the opportunity of simply brushing off the offensive filthy powder. One touch transformed it into tattoos of brown, serpentine streaks. Our eyes shined from beneath our Benin facials like those of cartoon characters. Our clothes, having been clean and well-pressed early that morning, were now wrinkled, damp, and dirt-encrusted—distant shadows of their former state. Our feet cried out for someone to reinstate the ancient art of foot-washing. No one heard them. If they did, the horror of touching our clay-caked toes would cause them to flee!

The magnificent, brown skin of our African brothers fared well by comparison. Their tightly kinked black hair still stood perfectly in place, while our hair drooped unfashionably in the muggy oven of late afternoon.

After a prayer for strength, a smile, held in reserve somewhere deep in my being, leaped to my face. I held out my right hand to the mayor, clasped the one he offered, and bowed slightly as I greeted him. A simple wooden chair, styled with a semi-reclining back and legs low to the ground, held his slight frame. His lounge rested to the side of the lopsided doorway to his electricity-less, dirt-floored home. He patiently sat there, with a semicircle of empty benches positioned to his left and right, in the clearing of his compound. He'd been expectantly waiting for us.

"And how is your wife, your children, and your work?" the greetings went on. Each of the volunteers, having learned from experience and now without my prompting, shook the mayor's hand in turn, dusted off a spot on a bench, accepted the bowl of water offered them by one of his wives, and lifted it to their lips, pretending to drink.

The greetings done, I looked up at the rain-sogged clouds and spoke, "Mayor, we are so very pleased that you invited us here this afternoon, but we cannot stay. It is late. We were due back to meet with the others an hour ago. It's about to rain. We beg you to allow us to go," I politely requested.

He said, "No." I'd never been told "no" to a request to leave before. But he didn't just stop there. "I know what you have been doing," he stated. "I know about the medical clinics. I know how you have been evangelizing the villages around this one. You must evangelize us, too!"

A surge of amazed shock bolted through my heart. I'd never, in all my years of walking with Jesus, been commanded to share His message before! Furthermore, this command came from a non-Christian man. A voodoo worshiper.

We didn't leave.

Within 10 minutes, 60 eager faces gathered before us, completing and overburdening the circle. Some stood on their bare, leathery toes to grab a better glimpse of us over heads blocking their view.

With the fervent prayers of the team being lifted behind me—for me, and for those who'd come—I told the people about Jesus.

They listened. We offered them Christ's gift of salvation.

Hands were publicly raised and prayers spoken aloud in confession of sin and in their personal need of a Savior. Could we evaluate the depth of those commitments? No. Regardless, when a person opens his life to Jesus, Jesus responds. He takes seriously any step toward Himself!

God commanded Abraham to perform a physical act, "Arise, walk about the land and through its length and breadth." Then He promised Abraham an incredible thing. He said, "for I will give it to you" (Gen. 13:17). As Abraham walked across the land in faith, each footfall claimed the soil it fell on, according to the promise.

The Lord also spoke the same words to Joshua and the people of Israel. "Every place on which the sole of your foot treads, I have given it to you, just as I spoke to Moses" (Josh. 1:3). Joshua's feet and the feet of the Israelites had to be present on the soil of the land for it to become theirs.

We believe God's promises to Abraham, Joshua, and the Israelites are ours for today. The physical land we walk on and the places we put our feet in the name of Christ will be given to us spiritually. Our feet walk in authority. Awesomely, God has granted us Foot Power!

Therefore, we invite prayerwalkers—powerwalkers—to visit Benin and to walk the villages of the Ayizo. As their sandals slap across dusty compounds, they grasp how to pray more knowledgeably, specifically. In the name of Jesus they gain the land for Christ through the presence of their feet on the soil. Is it any wonder God says, "How lovely on the mountains are the feet of him who brings good news, who announces peace and brings good news of happiness, who announces salvation" (Isa. 52:7)?

We have difficulty looking good out here. But God regards our filthy, soil-stained feet and calls them beautiful.

Prayerwalking teams compose a vital part of our strategy to win the Ayizo. They arrive singly or in conjunction with medical teams. Early each morning we load up the equipment, recheck our iced-filtered water and sandwich supply, and turn to the Lord. Grounded in prayer and with the spirit of adventure, the team ventures out. Jeff seeks either villages bound in voodoo worship, in which no evangelical influence exists, for the clinics and prayerwalking, or we go to encourage a work recently started.

Our daily travel requires navigating nearly impassable roads or plowing down bush-burdened footpaths. Four-wheel drive isn't an option. It's a necessity. One time the rock-strewn path I was driving instantly mutated into a slimy, dark bog. With Mark Thompkins, an avid off-roader by my side giving me careful shifting instruction, we slid and sloshed along until reinstated on solid ground. I fail to understand America's fascination with off-roading as a sport. We daily off-road on the road out here! A machete, kept by our truck door, is sometimes our only solution to extracting our sinking vehicle from oozing, slippery mud. With it, ever-present palm branches are whacked down and levered down under the tires for traction.

The prayer team begins with a gargantuan task: helping set up the clinic. The clinic may be in a windowless hut with rats running the rafters and chickens and chicks scooting around our feet; a filthy, cement-block school, or tiny, bamboo church (walls optional). Mindful of their task, they pray fervently for the patients as Christ is preached, sicknesses are diagnosed, and medicines are distributed. As the clinic team ministers to the overwhelming physical needs of the people, the prayerwalkers cover in prayer the surrounding villages. Everywhere we travel, they stay focused on prayer, whether they bounce along in the car or walk through the villages surrounded by a mob of smiling, big-eyed, affectionate children. In compound after compound we request permission to pray. Rarely does a person refuse. Each Ayizo is seeking any blessing he or she can procure from any god. The volunteers, in English, call on the Lord to set the villagers free from Satan's power so that they might surrender to Christ. In the local language, the Beninese Christians who accompany us pray that God will heal their sick, give them a great harvest, bless their lives, and reveal to them the True God.

In the beginning we intended to simply pray when we prayer-walked. But that idea was quickly abandoned. As we enter villages, the people leave their huts, their work of preparing foods, weaving baskets, or caring for the sick, and come to us, sometimes in crowds of 30 to 40. They wait expectantly before us for a word. And we tell them about Jesus. They gather in the drizzling rain; squeeze into cramped, smoky, cooking shelters, and even climb up into trees in gripping spiritual hunger to listen to the Word that has the power to transform their lives. We share Christ and pray in small marketplaces crowded with sellers and buyers. We speak of Christ's unparalleled love. We pray before men in colorful, embroidered, ceremonial African dress, in the middle of secretive meetings and before the members of Ayizo kings' households.

After each presentation, we ask, "Would you like to have your sins forgiven? Would you like to know this Jesus?" Each time people respond by saying, "We accept your words." Then, unashamedly they pray loudly, courageously, in front of family and friends, and open their lives to Christ.

One village, in particular, will stay in my mind forever. I was just explaining to them the words they could say to turn their lives over to Jesus. I hadn't said, "Pray these words." I hadn't encouraged them to repeat after me. I hadn't yet given them one instruction. Suddenly, as a group they started to repeat the words I was speaking. They were too eager for Jesus to wait until I finished.

At times I have trembled, wondering if people were only praying because of our unusual presence. But once, as the volunteers and I asked people if they wanted to pray, one woman looked straight at me and boldly said, "No!" Her refusal grieved my heart. Yet, that one experience revealed to me that the Ayizo have no cultural problem accepting nor refusing publicly Christ's gift.

Before the plane could lift off Cotonou's runway to carry a medical and prayerwalking team from Westside Baptist Church, Gainesville, Florida, back to the States, a village leader sought one of our Ayizo evangelists with these words, "We knew that when the people came to pray for us that something Good had come into our village. We knew they were children of God. Would you please come and teach us about Him?"

During Westside's stay we had prayerwitnessed in numerous villages, including the village of Togo. As we found in the other villages, its reliance on voodoo sacrifices for health, for abundant crops, for life itself was evident in the presence of multiple, sinister idols, charms on sticks, and woven archways over the village entrance. The tan, mud walls of the homes blended with the grassless, well-swept, ground on which we walked. Togo was unremarkable. It looked like all the other villages we'd visited. As we passed by empty homes, their wooden windows and doors shut tight against any invasion of their privacy, we prayed for those who lived there. As we walked by voodoo idols, we would pray in Jesus' name that their power would be broken. We hadn't sensed an outpouring of God's power and presence flowing out from us. Mostly, we'd felt the extreme heat of the sun on our backs and the exhaustion of our bodies.

After the team members were well-settled back into their American routines, I sat on our terrace and listened as Pierre, an Ayizo evangelist, spoke. The people of Togo had excitedly shared with him that after the prayerwalking team visited, all those who had been sick in their village had been healed! The sicknesses usually prevalent in the village were no longer present. Greater still, the villagers weren't attributing this phenomenon to their idols of mud and rusting iron; they were glorifying the God of the prayerwalkers and attributing this blessing of health to the prayers we'd prayed in the name of Jesus! Pierre spoke unemotionally with me, as if God's working in this way was simply a normal occurrence of faith, while I, the American missionary, was completely overwhelmed!

The Gainesville teams ministered in mid-July 1999. During the first week of August, a cholera epidemic swept across the Ayizo, killing scores of people.[1] As soon as Jeff and I were aware of the crisis, we raced up the hill from our home to the Allada bush hospital, the central hospital for the Ayizo people. Its old, decrepit structure was bursting beyond capacity. A makeshift ward had been set up in the unruly, tall grass of the courtyard. Patients were strewn about, lying on mats on the ground. A few beds had been dragged out into the open and were in various stages of being set up. People milled aimlessly about in distress, while nurses and aides rushed about in an attempt to alleviate suffering. We were ushered straight into the administrator's office in time to hear his frantic plea on the phone, "No. We need help now! We only have enough medication to treat 80. More than 100 are already here. Please, you must act now, or people will die by nightfall." He flung down the receiver with an anxious clatter and looked at us. "Red tape," he said. "They can't help until tomorrow. Tomorrow will be too late."

"What supplies do you need?" Jeff asked. A list was quickly scribbled. Jeff took off immediately for Cotonou to purchase the needed medicines using IMB crisis-relief funds. Later that afternoon we returned to the hospital, our vehicle crammed full of IV solutions and medicine. The administrator wasn't there. He'd gone out to hunt for the contaminated water source, the epidemic epicenter. We settled onto the wooden benches outside his office to wait. With heavy hearts we watched the frenzied courtyard activity. Suddenly a piercing wail consumed the air and shattered our hearts. Any mother on earth, in any culture, in any language, would have recognized that soul-wrenching moan. In dismay I turned. She stood, over the still form of her child, hands clenched across her breast. Cholera had won.

Grief flooded my heart. God had given us the Ayizo to win to Himself. Here they were dying, without Christ, before our very eyes.

But the medicine was given. Three hundred lives were saved to possibly yet turn to Jesus before it was too late.

The people in the villages around Togo, as well as Togo, drew their water from a muddy swamp. The surrounding villages experienced the horrible sting of cholera. Yet, not one person from Togo contracted the deadly disease! Again, the villagers of Togo praised God for the prayers offered for them by the team—prayers they knew kept the cholera away! What a tremendous witness of God's power!

When God called us to the Ayizo, He impassioned our hearts with these words, "Behold, you will call a nation you do not know, and a nation that knows you not will run to you, because of the Lord your God" (Isa. 55:5).

After all these events I knelt before the Lord and wept for allowing us the unequaled privilege of seeing Him work in such incredible ways. We had experienced exactly what the Lord had promised—people running to us, to find out about our Savior—Jesus. We've seen the beginning of the Ayizo's return from enemy land and are walking the villages in prayer, our feet firm and toes digging down on the promise.

Where are your feet taking you? What ground are you claiming with them, through prayer, for Christ? Have you consciously, while prayerfully walking the land, taken your home, your neighborhood, your state back from the possessive hand of the enemy?

I challenge you to step out of the comfort and security of America. Be willing to pay the price to go physically into the vast countries of the world. Walk through their lands with feet empowered by God's promise. Call on Jesus to break their bondage in Satan. Pray over the people knowledgeably, based on what you've seen and experienced. Take back every foot, two feet at a time. Then God will give us the land, the peoples, for Jesus!

Remember God's exhortation to Joshua and his feet:

Have I not commanded you? Be strong and courageous! Do not tremble or be dismayed, for the Lord your God is with you wherever you go (Josh. 1:9).

---

[1]A total of 577 cases of cholera were noted. It was reported that 176 people died.

TWENTY NINE

Antpaste

In the past six years we've transformed into electronic missionaries! We may be living near people who still hammer shards of steel into knives on a rock while they hunch in the dirt next to their bellow-driven fire. Hunters, with homemade flintlocks and crossbows, may creep soundlessly through the trees and fields around our home, not for sport but to feed their hungry families. The Ayizo women may draw water from a well, search for firewood over which to cook their meals, and may never have seen ice. But we've entered the rapid-paced new millennium.

Our telephone lines are haphazardly strung on lifeless sticks set crookedly in the ground. Our phone system is an old cast-off one that France bequested to Benin many years ago. Regardless, we send and receive email—often with great difficulty. Snail-mail letters rarely arrive anymore. (Even when they did arrive, some took anywhere from months to five years to get here.) Email has overtaken the printed word. We have email correspondents and Ayizo email prayer partners. We possess a web page *(http://dwmweb.com/ayizo)* and all the responsibilities of keeping our information current and up to America's information-starved society's standards. We definitely live, at the same time, in two vastly different worlds!

The instantaneous electrical transference of information from this continent across the vast ocean to America has resulted in a tremendous phenomenon. In the past, a letter with an urgent prayer request would arrive in the hands of dedicated prayer partners after the crisis had passed. Today, generally, when God gives us patience, grace, and the cyber monster doesn't eat our crippled, weak, Benin emails somewhere in the troposphere, our prayer partners receive and pray over our urgent needs. So, why are the Ayizo surrendering to Christ? E-prayer!

Our ministry spans two continents. We have an information ministry that builds relationships, endears people to the Ayizo, and even has resulted in correspondents coming to the field as volunteers. At the same time we are ministering to our Ayizo people desperately locked somewhere between the age of Christ and satellite phones.

All this creates intrigue about our life in Benin. The most common question cybered over invisible wires is, "What is a typical day for you?" Immediately I laugh and try to imagine that myself. Every day is fraught with unscheduled surprises and glitches that take control away from careful planning.

First of all I am a child of the living God, who has called me to this present, unique task. Secondly, as a wife, I am Jeff's companion, helper, ministry support, and confidant. Then, I am a mom: a Homeschooling mom. When God gifted us with Ryan, Kevin, and Kari, He also made us responsible for growing them in godly character. Long before we left the States, we believed that Homeschooling would be our best avenue for this development. The time I have invested in our children, whether it has been enjoyable or momentarily unbearable, has been rich and has already begun to return to us one-hundredfold! Bible study, prayer, Scripture memory, mathematics, English, reading, art, and the like consume a good portion of my days, along with an overabundance of interruptions!

Interruptions can be sellers pounding at the gate, church leaders searching for Jeff, African friends traveling in the vicinity, thirsty hunters hiking home, beggars, a young Ayizo Christian suffering persecution, or a rare phone call from villagers who think shouting accelerates understanding and hastens the message over the line. That is my most challenging ministry—the ministry of interruptions!

In between grading papers, managing the household maintenance, and keeping Jeff in chocolate-chip cookies, I do what you do. I pray and practice keeping the prayer channel continuously open. I witness to my neighbors. I travel to Ayizo villages to train the women in Christian character. And I teach Fon literacy.

It happened unexpectedly. As Jeff and I were developing our "End Vision"—what characteristics we believed the Lord wanted the Ayizo churches to own before we left them to proceed to another unreached people group, it became obvious. For the Ayizo to be firmly ground-ed in Christ, they had to read God's Word, daily, for themselves. Most of the Ayizo can't read. Ayizo isn't yet a written language. But every Ayizo understands a sister language—Fon. Fon has a New Testament.

God impassioned me. Never having had any training in literacy I sought His inspiration. God impressed me to teach Fon reading in the same manner I had taught our children to read. As I worked with a small group at our Sekou (say-koo) church, a method gradually emerged. With Bill Belli's encouragement the method became a widely used Fon literacy book. Now I instruct potential teachers how to teach literacy as a ministry to illiterate Christians and voodoo wor-shipers. In the pages of Fon phonetics a person not only will learn to read but will find the Savior. What joy Christ pours on me when I see a man or woman, who never sat in a classroom, reading Scripture, quietly or before a congregation! When God takes the untrained, the unknowledgeable—like me—and pours within them His Spirit, the results are amazing. All He needs is our willingness to step out in Him. He'll do the rest.

But no day or week is typical. Each has a life of its own. Some leave us gasping for breath. Others flow by on a current of excited energy. Then there are those that just are.

We live in a shady valley off a seldom-traveled dirt trail, not far from the two-lane, paved roadway to the north. The amount of traffic traveling this hilly stretch, in this underdeveloped country, can be amazing. No weight limits are enforced. Cars burdened with a tipping mountain of benches, bikes, baskets, and black, plastic, gas contain-ers, wobble along. Windshield-less trucks nearly implode with exces-sive cargo that rises above the weight-flattened wheels. Bulking bags of homemade charcoal, firewood, baskets of tomatoes and pineap-ples, clay pots, unshucked corn, and cotton bales, stuffed into over-flowing truck beds, come barreling down the road. When we glimpse the bouncing heads of daring passengers clinging to the baggage summit and the bawling goats fighting for steady footing on the shift-ing surface, we cringe. We involuntarily duck when a voluminous, tilting vehicle careens toward us on a curve. We pray when we see trucks' broken remains scattered across the pavement.

Not only do overloaded vehicles interfere with Benin's national life-expectancy averages, they also interfere with our telephone.

Our telephone wire, before it makes its way over the well and across the fields to our home, crosses the road. One week yet another truck ripped down the line and bent the pole. The workmen at the Allada water station, who work diligently to supply us lovely, brown, iron-filled water, rushed out and retrieved the broken wire from potential theft. The frequency with which this happens can become discouraging. We alert the phone company and wait weeks until it gets around to the repair. Sometimes the company's truck is indefinitely at the mechanic's. Sometimes the ladder is broken. Sometimes Jeff, using our vehicle, picks up the workmen from the local company office, drives them down to our road, and watches while they fiddle with the repairs. Each time he urges, "Put our line up higher on the pole. It'll save you time and money from continually coming to reattach it." The idea hasn't yet struck a receptive heart.

Email can't happen over a severed line, even if those emails desperately need to be sent!

Then we had to abandon our intended schedule to cart the family down to Cotonou. A strange rash had sprouted on Ryan's face, necessitating a visit to the dermatologist. It turned out to be fungus. Jeff had a fungus, too—but in his ear! Gleefully, I discovered that the French word for fungus re-translates into English as "mushrooms." Jeff had ear-shrooms!

Later that week I attempted to listen to one of my father's taped sermons. I placed the cassette in Kari's newly repaired tape player and plugged it in. Oddly, it did nothing. Suddenly I smelled wires burning. A mouse, lizard, roach, or maybe all three species at a fellowship dinner had eaten into the cord, thus dooming it to death by frying. I didn't listen to the tape. It's not like I have a neighbor from whom I can borrow a cassette player! I was disappointed. I had been looking forward to some spiritual refreshment.

Afterward, the children wanted to watch a video—but the VCR decided to eat the tape and not rewind. We have miniature snakes that look like worms, intestinal parasites, and grand night crawlers. But the VCR? Perhaps it had a tapeworm.

Electricity. This week and all weeks are the same. I think someone must be sitting on a bike attached to a generator somewhere out in the wilds. All day long he pedals with furious intensity. At night his energy wanes. As his fatigued feet pedal more slowly, the lights grow dimmer and dimmer until just a flicker remains. Then, suddenly, with a burst of renewed energy, he flips those pedals with vigor. For a few minutes the lights burn brightly. The CD player bellows enchanting music. Then, abruptly, the electricity plunges again. We have brown water. Why not brown light?

Then we have ants. Our house is infested with multiple varieties of the fiends. We have day ants and night ants. We have Houdinis, the kamikazes, cleaner ants, and army ants. The kamikazes have me baffled. If I boil water, they'll be there. They hot-foot it across the stove and dive into my teapot, not one at a time, but by the thousands. It must be a sacrificial rite or a demented Jacuzzi craze! One morning the temperature cooled off enough to crank up my dribbling coffee maker. I pulled out the filter only to discover an incredible nest of kamikazes. Hurrying, as hundreds stormed eagerly up my arm, I dumped the mess into the garbage can, washed out the filter, and proceeded to make a delicious steaming hot pot of—ants. How disgusting! The little pests had made a nest in the mechanism. In search of what? I'll never know. Three pots later I finally achieved ant-free water.

The cleaner ants are big, fat, long, black ants that prowl the floor at night. If you step on them, sometimes they'll squish blue. I've never figured that out one, either. But, they are God's vacuum cleaners. Since a vacuum is an unheard-of Benin extravagance, we don't have one. So, we appreciate their effort. Leave a dead roach on the floor at night, and voila, it's gone by morning.

Army ants seasonally storm our house. They are a fascinating study. Nights during hunting season they charge out of their underground nests by the millions. The soldier ants rigidly stand guard on either side of the marching column with their pinchers held menacingly aloft. Or, they form a solid, hovering chain over the nest entrance. I discovered that if I stuck a stick into their chain, they would aggressively cling to each other as an unyielding ant-rope that I could pull and twist until they decided to attack the holder of the stick. They're great bugs!

One midnight I walked into the school room, flicked on the undulating light, and noticed that a previously white wall was now a moving mass of black. Nonchalantly I called to Jeff, "Jeff, I think we have a problem." Unfortunately, our two-foot tall, anti-bug spray can was empty. So I grabbed the Lysol. It didn't faze them, but Off did! We stomped, smashed, and sprayed the little creatures into submission. Then Jeff checked outside for the source. Millions of army ants covered our compound. For an hour we engaged in a fierce battle to defy their siege on our house. This is an important rule to ant-combat: keep stomping! One hesitation in movement will result in a stream of hunters running up a leg—an uncomfortable situation at best. One made it all the way up to my neck and dug in. Army ants don't flick off. They must be yanked from the skin and always take a hunk of flesh with them. We grabbed an old mustard bottle, filled it with kerosene, squirted it across their little heads, and tossed in a match. Roasted ants are not a delicacy I crave, but it was the only way to turn the tide of the conflict.

Finally, after extended warfare, we won back our home. Intrigued as to what was hidden under the former pulsating, concentrated mound of black ants near our schoolroom window, I cautiously picked my way across the yard. Flashlight in hand I discovered the remains of a tarantula. The ants had been eating it.

I knew that tarantulas existed in northern Benin. But how fascinating to discover that they were in my yard! We have army ants, tarantulas, and poisonous snakes. Neat.

One night, when Kevin and Ryan were still pups, they left two chameleons in a cage outside. The next morning, heeding Kevin's frantic cries, I raced to Kevin's disappointed side. All that was left in the cage were skinless, chameleon skulls. Army ants. No matter how long we live here, we always find surprises lurking around the corner!

Normal is feeling ants walk across your arms, to jump up in the middle of the night to fight the biting kamikazis off the waterbed, or to put your cake plate pedestal on a dish of water to prevent them from interrupting a birthday celebration.

One evening I set a luscious, mouth-watering piece of chocolate-chip pie on my dresser and jumped in the shower for a quick rinse. Returning, I glanced toward the video Jeff had just started, instead of looking at my plate. Taking the wedge of pie in my hand, I bit off a healthy, hungry bite.

Suddenly the sensation of hundreds of running feet tickled across my face. In anger, I chewed anyway. They couldn't have my

American chocolate chips! They deserved to die. You know Africa is getting to you when you consider that ants get their "just desserts" when they wind up being eaten!

The most consistently, aggravating ants that infest my life are the tiny ants that love hiding out in the bristles of my toothbrush. Day to day, week to week, I have to check it, then whack the 20 or so anties off before applying toothpaste. When I forget, I end up spitting out bunches of little dead bodies. Antpaste isn't my favorite form of cavity prevention.

In a week we'd been de-telephoned, electrically de-electrified, mushroomed, kamikazied, and antpasted. Just typical days for Benin.

What is a day like in Benin? Like nothing you've ever experienced before. It may be heartbreaking or filled with moment-to-moment, Three-Stooges comedy routines. One certainty remains: with the joy of Jesus in your heart, a childlike sense of wonder, humor, and triple dosing of creativity to carry you through, it is a life gloriously stuffed beyond full!

Rejoice always; pray without ceasing; in everything give thanks; for this is God's will for you in Christ Jesus (I Thess. 5:16-18).

THIRTY

Stand Firm

My legs trembled with nervousness. Jeff, unruffled, stood calmly by my side on the platform before the thousand people who had packed the auditorium.[1] As I looked across the sea of faces, tears of gratitude for each person present, for each person committed to pray for missionaries and their people, battled with the tension of our spotlighted position.

"Last December, a few weeks before Christmas, during the Week of Prayer for International Missions[2], did you pray?" Hands flitted into the air from every location. Earnestly glancing from left to right to capture the eyes of those with upraised hands, we continued but could barely speak for the emotion that barred our voices, "We want personally to say, 'Thank you for saving our lives.' "

Christmas. We love the Christmas season. From the stroke of midnight on Thanksgiving through New Year's Day, our house is a riot of Christmas colors and smells. We exchange our African oil paintings and watercolors for treasured Christmas scenes. We spread boughs of pine over the bookcases and doorways. We hang beautiful green wreaths, replace white emergency candles with red, and decorate every coffee table with sleighs, rocking horses, music boxes, manger scenes, and precious treasures the children have made over the years.

Kevin grabs the red stocking cap off Kari's Christmas teddy bear for the head of our 3-foot, wooden, African old-man statue who stands quietly by Jeff's desk. Then he gives the statue a neckscarf made from a Christmas table runner. We can't make a snowman, but we have Christmas woodsman! Exotic Christmas candles perfume the air with cinnamon and orange spice, while the aroma of baking gingerbread greedily fills all the corners and cupboards of our home.

We've even fashioned a multitude of glittering white snowflakes to hang from the branches of the trees in our front yard! Then we have bows—red bows. We tie them around candlesticks. We tie them on the Christmas tree, terrace pillars, on chairs, on our six-foot giraffe, on Kari's vast stuffed animal collection, and even on Kevin's brass, African animals that line the bookshelf in his room. Our home is transformed from simple living quarters to an elegant Christmas shop. It is obsessive but beautiful. In Benin, if I want beautiful, I have to create it.

Very few things in Benin remind us of Christmas. Granted, in the past few years the city of Cotonou has begun to string a few, limp lights here and there. We've even glimpsed a very dark-skinned, skinny Santa encouraging people into a store. But the attitude of the Beninese toward Christmas measures far, far below the holiday spirit of Americans. Even the educated Beninese consider Christmas a minor holiday only for children. If they have the means, they may present them with a tiny trinket as a way of remembrance, but nothing more.

The villagers don't know Christmas exists. Their big celebration happens on New Year's Day. If a way is found to buy a piece of cloth to give to a special person, it will be bought, given, and valued as a reminder of the giver as long as the cloth holds color. Every person will travel back to the family village, by foot, by taxi, by dugout canoe, or by indescribably cramped, side-winding buses.

One New Year's Eve Jeff and I were horrified to see people crowding in unreasonable measures onto the human-sardine-packed train. People were spilling out the windows and doorways. Nonetheless, more people shoved in, throwing their luggage up into the cabin, over and onto the heads of the wedged bodies. As the train started to rumble along the track, stragglers caught the metal hand rails on the sides of the narrow landing step and clung on for dear life. And it was their lives they were tossing to the roar of the clanking, metal wheels. Comfort in travel means nothing here. Getting there does.

Being home for New Year's Day is paramount to the Beninese. Even the most impoverished houses will host a special feast. Everyone dresses in his or her best African booboos and bombas and kneels, one by one, before the elders of the family to receive a blessing for the New Year. On that day, each person across the country is caught up in a spirit of thankfulness, not in anticipation of the New Year, but for the joy of having lived the last year, for so many of their friends and relatives hadn't.

Though we have lived here for 12 years and have adapted to many new cultural ideas, Christmas still remains our holiday focus.

Malls, brimming with sparkling decorations and saturated with crystal carols that proclaim the coming celebration and Christ's birth, are completely absent from Benin. However, one West African phenomenon floods our hearts with anticipation—one unusual element has linked itself indelibly to the holidays. For us the Harmattan heralds the coming of Christmas as does snow in Maine. Yet, absolutely no similarity exists between the two. In fact, I cannot think of any two things more abstractly different!

The Harmattan—seasonal, heavy dust carried by high winds from the Sahara Desert—dumps itself on Benin toward the beginning of December every year. It resembles fog but is fine dirt swirling through the air like water droplets. When it is thick, it covers the sun, which hangs in the sky like a hazy, gray moon in a science-fiction movie. It cools the temperatures and lessens the incredible humidity. It blankets the trees, flowers, tables, tile floors, the counter tops, the chairs, the beds, the pictures, and everything, including the Christmas ornaments. It rests in the air like stale smoke wisping about the hallway.

We sweep it away. We wipe it away. But, magically, within minutes it is back. We even set the table with the plates upside down to keep them dustless for the coming meal! Yet, I cannot decide which is worse—a heavy or mild Harmattan. A mild Harmattan brings its own horrors. It does not lessen the heat. It does not diminish the humidity. Rather, it relishes it and clings to each water molecule hidden in the weighty air. Humidity is airborne water. The fog is airborne dirt. Water plus dirt equals mud! Air mud. You walk through it. You breathe it. You wear it. Sweat no longer drips off your arms in clear, salty, rivulets but rolls off in brown, mucky clusters. Two consolations are to be found in the Harmattan. First of all, it acts as a continual mud pack, so I will never wrinkle! Second, it announces the approach of Christmas!

Our Thanksgiving was a bit different in 2000. Jeff was gone. He traveled Stateside in mid-November for arthroscopic surgery on his shoulder. Something in his muscles and tendons had snapped. He could no longer toss a basketball nor put on a shirt without great pain. Jeff, the athlete, could have lived with the problem of the shirt but not with the problem of the basketball.

Even without Jeff's presence, Ryan, Kevin, Kari, and I continued with the tradition of inviting all our Peace Corps and local missionary friends to a festive Thanksgiving celebration with stuffed chickens and African, white, sweet potatoes, which we diligently dyed orange. While we opened cans of priceless cranberry sauce and pumpkin, which we had carefully transported across the ocean for the holiday, Jeff, along with his parents, back in he States feasted on American turkey.

He was gone for three long weeks. We decorated the house, lit the aromatic, apple-spice candles, and decked everything in its Christmas finery—everything except the Christmas tree. We wanted to share that experience with Jeff. It looked like Christmas. It smelled like Christmas. It was to be our last month-long Christmas with Ryan home, for college beckoned. We planned to do it all. We had breads, cookies, and a gingerbread house to bake.

We were excited at the prospect, even though we knew that making formed cookies was usually a disaster in the heat, for the nearly frozen dough always turns to mush by the time we wedge it from spatula to cookie sheet. The true challenge is not to sweat on the cookie dough. No matter how we create it, the candy, stained-glass windows in our gingerbread houses always melt to goo after several days. At least they melt rather than being eaten by the ants!

The ants. I place the intricately decorated icing-and-candy gingerbread masterpiece on a pedestal cake plate which is then placed on a plate of water. The water slowed down most of the ants, until the Houdinis starting constructing bridges with the extra cookie dough. We hung icing-coated cookies on our Christmas trees in the States but immediately learned that Benin ants are fearless, eager hunters that can uncover the slightest, sticky scent hidden among artificial green branches.

Since we couldn't place the tree in a bucket of water for fear of electrocution, the ants won round one. We also discovered the humidity here causes the cookies to slide off their red ribbons and "ker-plunk" onto the floor. Broken cookies, melting icing, and voracious-ly hungry ants. Not a pretty sight. The humidity won round two. Cookie-less tree or not, we were going to have a grand month, filled with all the Christmas activities our family enjoyed. Christmas is our favorite time of the year.

We were anticipating Jeff's arrival on Sunday, December 3, with all the joy of Christmas elves, until Saturday night. "Mom!" Kari cried distressingly, as she bolted for the bathroom and became vio-lently ill.

The lethargy she'd experienced all day boiled into a sudden high fever and upside-down stomach. I settled her back in bed with con-cern and prayed. My spirit stayed watchful all night.

The Harmattan hung hazy and cool on the early morning air. Rare shivers skipped along my bare arms. Seventy degrees was nearly intolerably chilly. I relished the sensation. The sun-shadowing dust clouds' diminished temperatures were a refreshing break from its nor-mal energy-extorting, tropical glare.

I watched as Ryan revved up Jeff's motorcycle. After Kevin, seat-ed behind him, situated his helmet, Ryan gunned the engine and sped across our spacious, dirt yard to the gate. After it clanged heavily shut, I listened to the steady beat of the cylinders as they zipped along our foot-beaten, wooded path. Ryan was scheduled to preach in Sekou. Kari needed me at home.

While I relaxed on our wide terrace and enjoyed a quiet moment with the Lord surrounded by a peaceful blanket of stillness the Harmattan ushered in and around the motionless trees, Ryan and Kevin joined the loud, energetic singing of the people who gathered for worship.

After prayer, Ryan walked confidently forward. Opening to Ephesians 6 he began to enthusiastically preach a compelling mes-sage on aspects of spiritual warfare. His words pierced the hearts of the listeners. They were words they would never forget, "Therefore put on the full armor of God, so that when (not if) the day of evil comes, you may be able to stand your ground" (verse 13, NIV).

"Do not be afraid," Ryan continued, "but be forewarned that those who engage themselves in battle, who are effective on the field of combat, the enemy will likewise attack. Be ready. Trouble may come to your family. You may become sick. You may be robbed. But, don't give up the battle. Stand firm."

After a quick lunch we traveled the hour's distance to Cotonou. Kevin and Ryan walked the potholed road to the American Recreation Center, while I rushed Kari to a local French clinic. The doctor gently examined Kari but couldn't diagnose her problem. He sent us on our way after inconclusive blood work. Kari perked up but not enough to go to the airport. Alone, I stood in the sweltering heat and press of bodies and watched for a glimpse of Jeff's handsome face. He walked through the customs gate, looking eagerly for me, with his tender arm held against him in a sling. I pushed my way anxiously to his side and gratefully welcomed him home. Yet, we did not go home. We stayed, instead, at the mission guesthouse. The long, treacherous, dark drive back to Allada at night was an unwelcome adventure. I needed groceries only available in Cotonou. Jeff was exhausted.

Monday morning, while Jeff tried to re-accustom his body to the extremes of a six-hour time change, I battled the lawless traffic and pushy street vendors to earn the privilege of entering a few grocery stores.

After 1 p.m., laden with bulging plastic bags, I walked into the guesthouse. "Mom," Kevin said as he urgently met me at the door, "Kari is much worse." I dropped the bags and ran to her room. Even without the confirmation of a thermometer, I knew from her beet-red face that she had a fever of more than 105. Jeff and I rushed her to the clinic. Malaria. She needed a quinine IV.

Jeff scrounged around outside for something with which to board up the empty air-conditioner hole in an effort to keep the voracious mosquitoes out of the clinic room in which Kari was confined. Mission accomplished, Jeff walked wearily in, prayed with us, and drove home to Allada with the boys. I stayed with Kari in the clinic. After three weeks of being on different continents, we were once again separated.

In Benin you do not leave a person alone in a medical institution. The nurses are not vigilant. IV's run dry. Medications are missed or mistakenly given. A caregiver is expected to stay with the infirm at every moment. That was me. After two sleepless nights Kari's condition improved.

Late Wednesday afternoon, December 6, Kevin's 15th birthday, Kari was released. Jeff raced us home, dodging overburdened trucks and taxis driving backwards on the wrong side of the road; passing the pineapple fields of Sekou, and finally pulling into our welcoming yard.

Scrambling into the kitchen I threw together a quick supper and a cake from a mix Jeff fortunately had stashed in his luggage. We were utterly fatigued yet happy to finally be together as a family. We wished Kevin "Happy Birthday" and promised him a grand celebration on Saturday, since circumstances had caused us to miss the day.

Jeff handed Kevin one gift. As Kevin reached into the layers of wrapping, a lopsided grin leapt to his face. Deodorant. His favorite deodorant that he had requested from the States. Kevin was content. It doesn't take much to please an MK.

The week had been tough. Kari was still recovering. Jeff was fried with jet lag and the added stress of Kari's illness. I was exhausted.

Thursday we plunged into the joy of setting up the Christmas tree. Christmas CD's were singing. The candles were glowing. The twinkle lights were twinkling. Christmas had arrived.

Friday night our laughter split the quiet night as we hung tight as a family and enjoyed a hilarious video Jeff had taped while in America. Laughter lingered in our home as we hugged good-night and headed to our rooms. Laughter that was to be violently shattered.

We didn't know it then, but they'd been watching us all day. In our wildest imaginings we never thought it would happen. It happens to other people in other countries, but not to us—not here and not now.

In the serenity of our bedroom, Jeff rested comfortably against the pillows, waiting for me. Suddenly our door burst open. "Mom, Dad, there are guys with guns out there!" Kevin and Kari frantically shouted. The icy fingers of shock squeezed my heart. Jeff bolted from the bed, grabbed his shorts, and flew to the phone in the dining room. He heard unnerving sounds of voices yelling and confused commotion outside. He drew the receiver to his ear but immediately tossed it down in frustration. The line was dead. Cut.

Quickly reaching down I drew on a discarded pair of short overalls to cover my skimpy nightwear. I knew I only had seconds. The clothing wasn't enough, but it was all I could do. My thoughts were whirling. I yanked my engagement ring off my finger and flung it under our bed. More scared than I have ever been, I cried out, "Jesus, in your name, I bind Satan." Before I could speak another word, the security of our home was explosively shattered. With a resounding bang and clatter our back door was brutally broken down. It was the most horrible sound I've ever heard in my life. In seconds a hostile man in military fatigues and wielding an authoritative shotgun in his hands stood glaring at me from our bedroom's doorway. "Move out!" he hollered at me.

"But my daughter," I anxiously blurted in my concern for Kari's welfare. Unyieldingly he once again forcefully commanded, "Move!" No question remained as to the penalty for rebellion. Quivering head to foot from the emotions that surged through me, I stepped into the hall. Entering into my room, he reached over to Kari, paralyzed from fear, and pulled Jeff's physical therapy pole from her hands. She'd been intending to fight the man with it. Without further word she followed my slowly retreating steps.

We were marched down the hall, past our living room, and were forced to kneel on our sharp-tiled, dining-room floor. Jeff, Ryan, and Kevin had preceded us. We looked at each other with searching, questioning eyes. One man hoisted his rifle to his shoulder, pulled out a hand-held radio, and spoke, "Everything is progressing. We are here."

Immediately one of the six armed men said, "You, Pastor, come with us." Jeff stood and, without a backward glance, stepped out of the room.

My heart lurched heavily within me. Only one robber was masked. That could only mean one thing. We were destined to be shot. My spirit cried out after my precious husband. I waited in dread for the sound of the hammer being cocked and the crack of a gun's report. I was certain I would never see him alive again. On our knees, with terrorizing rifles continually aimed our direction, I contemplated how getting a bullet in my back would feel.

Jesus. Of one mind we loudly cried out to our Lord. Our voices, from our kneeling positions, were raised in dreadful earnestness borne of fear. Angered by our prayers one cruel man strode up to Kari as she poured out her heart to Jesus. He raised his hand, hit her violently across the back of the head, nearly knocking her to the floor, and yelled, "Stop praying!" Beside her, startled by this cruel act and helpless to protect her from the wrath of these godless men, I slipped my arm around her trembling shoulders to comfort her. With scathing hostility the same vile man lifted his powerful hand, struck me viciously across the face, and hollered, "Leave her alone!"

Ryan, enraged at seeing his sister and mother abused, rose defiantly to our defense. Another venomous man beat him down with a blackjack blow to his head. The momentum forced Ryan's chin to smack harshly against the tile.

"Lie still," the man hissed maliciously to Ryan, "or we will do something terrible to you."

We continued to pray in our spirits.

After Ryan's manifestation, they commanded us to lie down. The ridges of the cool tiles scraped against our exposed skin. We quickly became cold. Literally shaking from head to foot, my heart beat wildly as I slowly eased my elbow up until I made contact with Kari's arm. I longed to give her courage.

With every pounding pulse we pleaded with the Lord to make these men go away.

While the drama was being played out in the dining room, the head thief turned to Jeff and roughly demanded, "Where are the keys to the vehicles?"

Jeff led him to our bedroom, scrounged up the keys, and quietly handed them to him.

"Now, Pastor, where is the money?"

Jeff retrieved the key to our cast-iron safe, went to the schoolroom where it was hidden in a supply cabinet, and opened it for them. He did everything he could to keep from arousing further antagonism. If he was to die, let it be so. Meanwhile, he would bring levelheadedness to diffuse any potential life-threatening violence.

Voices. A brief sense of relief flooded through me as Jeff stepped back into the dining room. He wasn't dead yet. He joined us in a prone position, his face down, resting on his arms. They grabbed Ryan and insisted he come with them. They took Kevin out, then me. They ordered us to show them where we stored cameras, kept our CD's, CD players, and jewelry.

Alone in our bedroom with one of the men I blanched at the thought of what might happen, but not another hand was lifted against me. One by one they took us out. One by one they returned us to the dining room floor.

The dogs barked liked incensed, rabid wolves, but our distant neighbors didn't hear. No one came. No one helped us.

The minutes dragged by like the cumbersome, slow action of a terrorizing nightmare. Under their glaring stares, nothing was spared, down to our treasured wedding bands that we were forced to wrest from our fingers.

We kept our faces mashed against the chilling tile for 1 1/2 hours while the men ransacked our house. Then an authoritative command split through the brittle tension in the room. "Pastor, follow me!"

We sensed things were drawing to an end, but to what end? "Oh God, spare Jeff's life," I pleaded.

Minutes later they ordered me, "Stand up and come."

I stood, walked as a sightless zombie across our festively decorated living room, back down the unlit hall, and was directed to Kari's room. Jeff was already there. I longed to fling myself into his arms but sensed the great danger of any unnecessary movement.

He looked at me and calmly spoke, "It's OK. They are just going to lock us in here."

Ryan, Kari, and Kevin entered. Kari huddled on her bed, pulling a blanket up over her quaking body. The men stared at Jeff and rasped, "We're going to kill your guard." Then they locked the door.

A young, Christian man was substituting as a night guard for that month. William carried no gun, only a club. He was there to discourage people from petty theft. No one imagined he'd encounter a SWAT unit of armed men who would, in a combat maneuver, scale our compound wall from all directions and surround our home. It just didn't happen in Benin.

We positioned ourselves on the floor for fear they would shoot us as captive prey through Kari's large window. We prayed fervently for the Lord to save William's life. As we prayed, we heard them rummaging through the house with careless, heavy hands. We cringed as things crashed to the floor and splintered into thousands of pieces. The sounds of gathering and dumping were vivid, harsh noises. Finally we heard a truck engine rumble and pull away.

Silence.

We waited. Were they just outside watching us, to see what we would do? Had they gone?

Minutes passed like hours. Suddenly, to our horror, the doorknob rattled. It rattled again. Someone was trying to open the door. Fear streaked again through my body. Kari gasped. Was it one of the men intending to kill us?

Jeff motioned for absolute silence. As we watched, the throbbing tension mounting each second, the door abruptly burst open. William threw himself into the room with a face as white as ours. Soundlessly, he slammed the door shut.

"What happened, William?" Jeff gently prodded. He tried to calm the man's ragged breathing.

"They tied me up and shoved me into your bathroom," William explained, his hoarse voice just a terrorized whisper. "One robber, with his gun in his hand, said, 'Let's shoot him!' The other responded, 'No. Let's just let him go.' And they let me live. When I thought they were gone, I wrestled from the ropes and set out to find you. But I had trouble unlocking the door."

We praised God for his safety and huddled together until we were sure we didn't hear another sound except the roar of blood in our ears and the frantic beating of our hearts.

Believing it was relatively safe, Jeff hauled William to his feet. They ventured into the house. With trepidation, we fled, afraid of who might be lurking behind the shapeless, black trees.

We didn't sleep that night. With all the beds already occupied with the sudden influx of our family into their small home, Bill Belli, heartsick over the trauma we'd endured, placed a mattress on his office floor for Jeff and me. We lay there through the few remaining night hours, reliving the events we had just experienced. Absolutely shocked, we clung to each other. News of the attack spread rapidly. Long before the light of day began to filter through the Harmattan, African friends gathered on Bill and Margie's front porch to be there for us—to pray and to offer comfort. The Beninese understand grief.

Our house was a horrid mess. Every cupboard, every drawer stood open, their contents spilling in an angry riot across the floor. Only the Christmas tree stood quietly unmolested in its corner. Many precious, irreplaceable possessions had been tossed vehemently into the truck and sported away.

Kevin, greatly angered, spouted, "They've even taken my new deodorant!" Worse than the clothing, our mementos and information contained on our computers—they had stolen away our very home, a home I dearly cherished, even though the rain poured in through the living room skylight, chasing us onto the porch in search of dry space.

Because our home was situated in the bush, we could never return, for the robbers might. We were easy prey. The graceful palm trees, orange trees, bougainvillaea, hibiscus, kingfishers, humming-birds, expansive terrace, the quiet of our home and lives, had all, in a few hours of time, been ripped away. Kevin wouldn't be having his birthday celebration.

Within days, Dr. David Fort, who counsels IMB missionaries in crisis, arrived to help us sort through the trauma and to walk through the heavy fog that had settled in our minds. He gently guided us in sifting through the pieces, the rubble, and the emotions. He adroitly caused us to open all the hidden places of our hearts to each other and to the Lord, so that nothing about the robbery could later consume our lives.

Yet, an incredible problem faced us. Christmas. Everything we'd dreamed of for the month had been malevolently destroyed. Suddenly, nearly destitute and homeless, we resolved that our best chance for recapturing the shambles of our holiday was to go home to America. We had no place to put up our Christmas tree. No place of privacy to celebrate the gift of our lives. Our families in the States needed to place their arms around us. We needed their embrace.

We should not be alive. One thing and one thing alone saved our lives. Early in 2000, while we celebrated Christ's resurrection, a notice had arrived in the mail. Would we be willing to be featured in a national brochure for special prayer among the Southern Baptist churches during the Week of Prayer for International Missions the first week in December?

Jeff and I had turned to each other, speechless. Only seven mis-sionaries of 3,000 career missionaries would be highlighted—one for each day of the week. And we, who lived on the backside of nowhere, unheard of, unknown, were being chosen?

The most horrible experience of our lives happened during that week in December. And we should be dead. But we are living and continuing to share Christ with the Ayizo because of God's plan. For you see, we were featured on day five—Friday—during the Week of Prayer. The very day hostile men broke into our home, threatened our lives, and held us hostage at gunpoint, thousands and thousands of godly men and women were praying for us!

Did you pray? If you did, our entire family knows of no way to adequately say, "Thank you."

A man assaulted sweet, 11-year-old Kari. A man attacked me. Another brutally struck Ryan. We were stunned, but the aggressive acts weren't painful. The tender places didn't swell. Bruises in a multitude of dark, fearsome colors should have spread across our faces. But they didn't. Jesus stepped in and took our blows for us.

They returned. While we were celebrating Christmas in America, new gun-sporting guards, hidden in the branches of our snake-infested trees, watched them pull up to our isolated gate at the lonely hour of 2 a.m. The truck's license plate was covered with black cloth. Four men boldly climbed from the truck and sauntered up to the gate. They had come to finish the job. They paused at the new guard-service sticker posted on the door. Hidden in the leafy shadows, the guards tightened their grip on their guns and held them, unwaveringly, on the men. After reading the notice, the intruders spoke not a word but got back in the truck and drove away.

One of our close, African friends started an investigation to discover who had perpetrated this malicious act against us and received a threatening written message in response. "Stop trying to find out who we are, or we will kill you." Friends were to uncover that the criminals had scouts out, searching for us.

After Christmas we returned to Benin. The thought of abandoning our calling to the Ayizo never crossed our minds. Rather, we are now more deeply committed to it, even if it costs us our lives.

Through our suffering the Ayizo Christians' faith was strengthened. Through our pain God convicted them to regard themselves as missionaries. Many embraced this calling and consecrated themselves to the task, no matter what the cost.

The months following the robbery were the most difficult months of our lives as we tried to find and establish a new home, piece together the devastation, and prepare Ryan to leave for college. But God brought His hand of healing to our hearts—and following it a depth of joy and contentment we never knew existed. Our zeal for reaching people for Christ was strong before the robbery; now it is consuming. God has deepened our lives with a passion for our people that we never thought possible. On the other side of faithfulness is an immeasurable richness in intimacy with Christ. Don't give up! Don't give in! No matter what, be faithful!

We were protected because of prayer. Our ability to confidently return was because of prayer. Our steadfastness to remain is because of prayer.

Do you take seriously the charge to pray for missionaries around the world who are battling fatigue, sickness, hostility, and unknown dangers out of a compelling passion to share Christ with those who have never heard?

Your prayers are their power to stand firm.

Therefore, take up the full armor of God, that you may be able to resist in the evil day, and having done everything, to stand firm (Eph. 6:13).

---

[1]At LifeWay's Glorieta Conference Center (Southern Baptist), Glorieta, NM, August 2001.

[2]Southern Baptists' yearly special prayer emphasis during the month of December.

THIRTY ONE

Come, Walk the Adventure!

The drizzling rain soaked our clothes until they clung to us like sticky, stiff skin. My cloth wrap adhered itself in tangled spirals to my mud-splattered legs. With each step I fought against their restraining grasp.

Jeff and I had vigorously started our walk into the area of the Ci people, but the hike quickly became an incredible endurance struggle. From the moment we left the truck, low, gray clouds flung a fine mist over us. Water droplets slipped off the drenched leaves of the thin trees and slid down the long grasses of the dense flora on either side of the path. Our two guides, barefoot and slight, had grabbed up the heavy cans of fuel needed for the generator and had stomped off at an energetic pace.

My backpack straps were already shoulder-digging when we caught up to the guides at the murky, old river. As we stood in the muck under the branches of ageless, towering trees that spent their days stealing liquid life from the river, Jeff asked me, "Do you just want to walk across?"

I hesitated. If the digital camera hadn't been tucked snugly in my backpack, I would have waded right in. But a sudden drop-off would be a terrible camera disaster. Sopping wet tennis shoes didn't seem like a delightful hiking option, either. We had a long way to go.

"No, let's not this time," I responded. Understanding, one of the men plunged headlong into the water to search downstream for transportation.

Minutes later he reappeared, pushing the remnants of a dugout canoe ahead of him. It was mostly submerged and appeared only worthy of how it was discovered—abandoned.

I watched incredulously as, with a broken and rusty bit of tin bowl, he began bailing out the muddy water and the fish that were contentedly living off the thick algae slime on the dugout's bottom. Emptying the water turned out to be less of a chore than I'd imagined, for the stern was completely missing. Keeping the water from re-swamping the boat seemed the greater challenge.

Once the fish were tossed overboard, I was beckoned to enter. The men held the crazily tipping canoe from swaying too far one way or the other and decided I should squat in the scummy bow of the boat.

Jeff soon joined me. Our joint weight pushed the bow down and the ominously endless stern up. Water, which increased in depth each moment, sloshed around my feet. I wondered if walking across hadn't been the least hazardous choice. I grasped the spongy, thick, rocking sides to steady myself and prayed, earnestly, that we wouldn't tip over. Our gracious friend acted as propulsion and rudder as he swam us across. When the canoe slid with a gravelly scrunch onto the bank, I thought the worst of the trek lay behind us. I was mistaken.

We stepped out of the slime of the boat onto the muddy slime of the shore. The path on the Ayizo side of the river had resisted the rain. The path on the Ci side of the river soaked it up and oozed it out. Every step we took sank our feet into gloppy, foot-sucking mud. We couldn't walk with our shoes on, for after 10 steps our feet weighed as much as did our backpacks. Inches of caked-on mud, grass, and debris encrusted our shoes within seconds of cleaning them off.

Our barefoot guides took the mud in stride. The only change to their steady march was a loud sucking sound as they wrenched each foot free of its mud prison to take another step. But we couldn't walk with our shoes off. Sticks, insects, and other foot-threatening creatures nestled invisibly in this endless quagmire. Jeff slipped crazily from side to side on his sandals as the mud took over beneath the soles and beneath his feet. On top of being weak from a recent illness each step for Jeff was energy-depleting torture. And the rain continued. The 30-minute walk from the truck to the river had taken 30 minutes. The 30-minute walk from the river to the Ci village turned into a very long hour of difficult sludging.

The voodoo worshipers had threatened to work spells to cause rain so this first baptism among the Ci people and the evangelical film to follow that evening could not take place. As we attempted to walk, we prayed that the rain would cease. We brandished our swords in God's battle while our feet bogged down in the mire. Somewhere along that path, the rain stopped!

With literally heavy, sinking feet, we arrived at the village of Lokoli (low-koal-lee). The pathways around the huts were a pockmarked sea of exasperating, worthless, wet clay. Each foot that passed left its singular indention, like jagged waves in a clutching, gray ocean. Molded into walls, it would crumble to dust under the relentless sun. It irritatingly clung to feet but wouldn't create shelter. Therefore, each hut scattered under the village's swaying palm branches was constructed of bamboo.

In our tardy arrival we discovered that the people had already walked to the river for baptism. Before we could trudge along to join them, they returned, exuberantly. Exuberantly we greeted them. We were saddened to have missed the baptism but thrilled not to have to tackle wading through another hour of mud! Twenty-eight people had been baptized!

Bill Belli, who worked with the Ayizo in this remote corner, encouraged them to reach out to the Ci. One morning, just following sunrise, the Ayizo Christians from the village of Houngo Dame (hungo dah-may) gathered. The babies were hoisted onto their mothers' backs, secured with cloth, and the group set out. The market women, who sell rice and fish for breakfast, had not yet arrived, so the team went on without food. They intended to buy something on the Ci side of the river. But as they started on their strenuous hike, the babies began to wail with hunger. The entire group paused and prayed. Their stomachs were empty, too. "God, grant us and our children Your grace today. Keep us from being hungry." They splashed through the river on foot and threw fistfuls of water over their sweaty heads. They marched with determination over the narrow paths and through the scraggly cornfields until they came to Lokoli. But no food was there. The Ci had nothing to offer. Even their water was liquid brown. The Ayizo were afraid to drink it. All day long they tramped through Ci villages under a blazing sun, not eating, not drinking, but feasting on the joy of sharing Jesus.

The Ci were intrigued by the story of Christ. Several villages invited them to return. The sun was edging toward the rose-and-gold-tinged clouds on the horizon as they bid farewell and plodded home. The cool river refreshed their weary feet as they hurried on. Darkness was falling. Finally against the backdrop of the night they could glimpse tiny, kerosene lamps twinkling among the market booths in the distance. The lights indicated that sellers were sitting along the road in the dust, with platters of food.

Then it happened. The babies began to cry. Hunger began to gnaw at their stomachs. Deep gratitude welled up within them for this mighty act of the Lord. He'd even caused hungry babies to still so those starving for Him could be filled.

Ministry toward the Ci had continued. Now a church had been born.

Under a brilliant, star-studded sky the movie was shown! The whole village stepped carefully over the hardening mud impressions to stand and watch. They'd seen the Jesus film the night before and were anxious to see another. They'd never had films in their village before!

Termites also gathered. Huge swarms often amass after storms. Unfortunately, the generator-run projector created the only light for countless miles. My seat close to the projector allowed me the special privilege of having bugs crawl in my clothing and under the cloth I'd thrown over my head. Termites, I discovered, creep under and lodge themselves well in French braids. Sitting there also afforded me the opportunity to smell their little bodies roasting as they crawled in close to the projector's bulb! Happily, I realized the projector served as a bug-zapper. Under sparkling, star-studded galaxies and termite attacks, the message of Jesus and His awesome power were preached.

One woman, with voodoo welts scarring her body, abounded with joy. She presented to Jeff and me an adorable, seven-day-old baby girl. "She is the reason I will follow Jesus," she explained with a radiant smile reaching across her dark brown face. In June 2001 a Westside Baptist volunteer team braved awesome difficulties to bring medical care to Lokoli. This childless woman had come to see the doctors. They treated her, prayed, and she was cured, she said, "because of Jesus." Since the team members had made themselves available to follow Jesus wherever He led, even if it was to a mud-sogged, impoverished village, this woman now belonged to Christ.

We slept that night in a one-room hut, with a thatch roof stretched over our heads. Over thin reed mats and under our mosquito netting we extended our air mattresses and wordlessly fell asleep.

A pig's soft grunting close to my ear and vivacious crowing of roosters awakened me at dawn. The bustle of activity outside our hut was evidence that no one slept past daybreak. The morning coolness rapidly evaporated under the sun's blinding rays. The ground quickly dried and then cracked in the baking heat. Although the rain had made our travel a wearisome task, we had been grateful for the escape from the sun. Now, it was back.

Fifty people arrived for worship. Several new Christian men stood before the crowd and testified of Christ's power. The men were polygamists. All the babies born to their wives, in spite of their sacrifices of goats and chickens to voodoo gods, and in spite of their giving of money and alcohol to the Bokono, died. But when they surrendered to Jesus, their babies lived! Satan is death. Jesus is life.

Jeff preached. They celebrated their first communion. Then a man brought his voodoo amulets, rings, and sacred objects to be burned. One was an ugly, dirty, gourd bowl. He had been taught to believe that it contained his soul. He guarded it zealously, for if it broke, he would die. He boldly placed it, along with other items, on the ground. Then they doused everything thoroughly with kerosene. As it burst into flames that hungrily leapt six feet into the air, victorious praises were sung to Jesus.

Our backpacks were lighter on the return trip. We'd drunk most of the water we'd carried. Our shoes were relatively clean and weightless. The mud had transformed into a rock-hard, bumpy path. We waved and turned toward home. The sun beat down on us with renewed vigor as Jeff and I casually hiked the winding path. Those carrying the projector, generator, and films on their heads hustled energetically to the river. One tall, serious-faced man caught my attention. It was what he held in his hands. Through the church service, the voodoo burning, and the long trek home he guarded, as a treasure, a book. The Fon literacy book.

Missionaries often minister a lifetime without seeing any return on their life's investment. But God has given Jeff and me the immense treasure of witnessing Jesus Christ unleashing Himself on people groups. In six years we've seen the Ayizo and related work expand from four to 67 churches and preaching points. We believe this is because of our partners who diligently pray, who selflessly give, and who sacrificially place their feet beside our dirty, clay-encrusted feet, so that people may be told.

Much work is yet to be done. Hundreds of thousands among the Ayizo have yet to hear.

It may just take you.

Come, walk the adventure with us.

Ask of Me, and I will surely give the nations as Thine inheritance, and the very ends of the earth as Thy possession (Ps. 2:8).

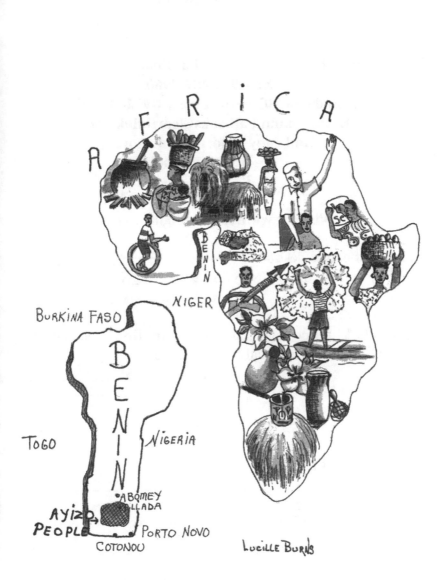

AFRICA

BENIN

NIGER

BURKINA FASO

BENIN

TOGO

NIGERIA

AYIZO PEOPLE

ABOMEY CALLADA

PORTO NOVO

COTONOU

LUCILLE BURNS

How to order more copies of

Beyond Surrender

and obtain a free Hannibal Books catalog
FAX: 1-972-487-7960
Call: 1-800-747-0738 (in Texas, 1-972-487-5710)
Email: hannibalbooks@earthlink.net
Mail copy of form below to:
Hannibal Books
P.O. Box 461592
Garland, Texas 75046
Visit: www.hannibalbooks.com

Number of copies desired _____
Multiply number of copies by $12.95   ___X____$12.95___
Cost of books: $_____

Please add $3 for postage and handling for first book and add
50-cents for each additional book in the order.
Shipping $_____
Texas residents add 8.25 % sales tax $_____

Total order $_____

Mark method of payment:
check enclosed _____
Credit card# _____ exp. date_____
(Visa, MasterCard, Discover, American Express accepted)

Name _____

Address _____

City State, Zip _____

Phone _____ FAX _____

Email _____

These missions books are also available

Rescue by Jean Phillips. American missionaries Jean Phillips and husband Gene lived through some of the most harrowing moments in African history of the last half century. Abducted and threatened with death, Jean and Gene draw on God's lessons of a lifetime.

_____Copies at $12.95=_____

Unmoveable Witness by Marion Corley. An alarming interrogation by Colombia's version of the FBI. A dangerous mishap at a construction site. A frightening theft at his home in Bucaramanga, Colombia. What kept Marion and Evelyn Corley on the mission field for 22 years when others might have returned to Stateside comforts?

_____Copies at $9.95=_____

Awaken the Dawn by Doris B. Wolfe. Christian romance novel set in the jungles of South America involving two missionaries, one a recent widower with two children and the other a young, never-married single woman. He's a pilot. She's a teacher. Dramatic real-life situations test their faith.

_____Copies at $9.95=_____

The Jungle series, also known as the Rani Adventures by Ron Snell. With hilarity, warmth, and spine-tingling suspense, "the Rani Series" trilogy takes readers into the cross-cultural upbringing of Ron Snell, who, with his family, sets aside American comforts to bring the good news of Christ to people in darkness in the Amazon jungles of Peru.

It's a Jungle Out There (Book 1) _____ Copies at $7.95 = _____
Life is a Jungle (Book 2) _____ Copies at $7.95 = _____
Jungle Calls (Book 3) _____ Copies at $7.95 = _____

Add $3.00 shipping for first book, plus 50-cents for each additional book.
Shipping & Handling _____
Texas residents add 8.25% sales tax _____
TOTAL ENCLOSED_____

check ____ or credit card # _____ exp. date_____
(Visa, MasterCard, Discover, American Express accepted)

Name _____

Address _____ Phone _____

City _____ State _____ Zip _____

**For postal address, phone number, fax number, email address
and other ways to order from Hannibal Books, see page 190**